ATTACK ON MARITIME TRADE

By the same author

NAVIES, DETERRENCE AND AMERICAN INDEPENDENCE
NAVAL WARFARE IN THE AGE OF SAIL: THE EVOLUTION OF FIGHTING TACTICS, 1650–1815 (*co-published with Brian Tunstall*)

Attack On Maritime Trade

Nicholas Tracy

Research Associate, Department of History
University of New Brunswick, Fredericton

University of Toronto Press
Toronto and Buffalo

First published in North America in 1991 by
University of Toronto Press
Toronto and Buffalo

ISBN 0–8020–5974–0 (cloth)

Printed in Hong Kong

Canadian Cataloguing in Publication Data
Tracy, Nicholas, 1944–
Attack on maritime trade
Includes bibliographical references and index.
ISBN 0–8020–5974–0 (cloth)
1. Sea control – History. 2. Naval strategy –
History. 3. Commerce – History. 4. Shipping –
History. I. Title.
V163. T73 1991 359′.03′09 C91–094053–3

To Sisyphus, a fellow martyr to hubris, seen by some as a personification of the treacherous sea, and by others as a symbol of the vain struggle of man in the pursuit of knowledge, this book is respectfully dedicated.

Contents

Preface ix
Introduction 1

PART I BEFORE WORLD WAR I 7

1 The Development of Strategic Purposes for Attack on Maritime Trade 10
Reprisal and the Laws of War at Sea 10
Low-Budget Navies – Prize Money and Privateers 17
Bullionism: The Anglo–Spanish Wars 25
Interdiction of Contraband 30
The Shadow of Mercantilism 40
The Spanish–Dutch War 42
The Anglo–Dutch Wars 46
The Anglo–French 100-year Mercantilist Trade War 50
The Problem of Lateral Escalation: The League of Armed Neutrality 65
The Continental System and British Orders-in-Council 70
Free Trade, the Crimean War, and the Declaration of Paris 82
Trade War as a Strategy of Containment 89
The American Civil War 90
The *Jeune Ecole* and the Mahan School 95
Pacific Blockade 97
The Hague Conferences and the Declaration of London 100

PART II THE TWENTIETH CENTURY 117

2 World War I 123
The Blockade of the Central Powers 123
The 1917 U-boat Campaign 139
Assessment of the Utility of the *Entente* Blockade 143

3 The Belligerents' Rights Dispute and the 'New Mercantilism' 153

4 Trade Control and Blockade Between the Wars 175
The Ethiopian Crisis 176
The Spanish Civil War 178
Sanctions Against Japan 181

5 World War II 185
The British Blockade of Germany 185
The Allied Blockade of Japan 190
The German U-boat *Guerre de Course* 192

6 Naval Blockade and Trade War Since 1945 215
Korea 215
Cuba 216
Vietnam 218
Rhodesia 220
Arab–Israeli Incidents 222
Indo–Pakistan War 223
October War 223
The Falkland Islands War 'Total Exclusion Zone' 224
The Gulf War 224
Soviet Attitudes 230

7 General Conclusions 235
The 1990 Kuwait Crisis 244

Bibliography 247
Index 263

Preface

This work began under the auspices of the Chair of Strategic Studies, Dalhousie University, and was inspired by discussions with officers of the British and German armed forces in 1977. During the period 1980–85 teaching duties and other research commitments led to the preliminary study gathering dust. However, further support for the work was made available in 1985 by the Social Science and Humanities Research Council of Canada, which provided a Junior Research Time Fellowship. The work was completed at the National University of Singapore in 1985–86, and at the University of New Brunswick in 1986–90. Work undertaken for the Directorate of History, Canadian Department of National Defence, on merchant shipping as a factor in the outcome of World War II, contributed to this general study. I am grateful for the support of Alec Douglas, its Director, and for the assistance of the Ministry of Defence in London and of the General Council of British Shipping.

Introduction

Until its recent transformation by the United States Navy, the term 'maritime strategy' was generally used to indicate the employment of naval forces to achieve political ends by their impact on international trade. When the American Admiral Alfred Thayer Mahan published his *The Influence of Seapower upon History* in 1889 he demonstrated to the satisfaction of contemporary statesmen that navies employing 'maritime strategy' were the decisive force in world history. The English Admiral, Sir Herbert Richmond, summed up the Mahan theory in 1934, and lent it his support.

> The conclusion to which Mahan was brought by his studies, and in particular by his final studies, of the Napoleonic Wars, as to the part which sea power played in that great struggle . . . was that the economic results which it produced, slow-acting though they may have been, were in the end decisive. Bonaparte had the resources of the continent at his disposal but not the resources of the world. He needed these also.[1]

Three elements were deemed as composing collectively the 'sea power' of a state – shipping, colonies, and a navy. Shipping produced wealth, trained seamen, and provided the foundation of the ship-building business. All these were necessary to enable a nation to sustain a navy, which in turn protected the national merchant marine. Colonies provided the trade goods which sustained the shipping business, and the bases from which the navy operated.

Unfortunately this simple picture of a holy naval trinity intervening decisively in the affairs of man appears less adequate in the light of more recent scholarship, and of recent geo-political developments. It is not necessary to overturn Mahan's and Richmond's theses, although in some important instances they were critically wrong in their facts. Bonaparte, for instance, was not denied the resources of the world. He was amply provided with everything he required provided he paid the price the British demanded. British strategy was a mercantilist one, not a blockade of supplies. Despite important errors Mahan, and especially Richmond, have contributed greatly to our understanding of the function of navies. At best, however, they throw light on a short span of a long history of naval activity.

The capacity of navies to affect world politics through their impact on world trade ought not to be thought of, as Richmond did, as 'the weapon of seapower'. The fundamental war potential of shipping lies in its capacity to transport soldiers. Amphibious operations are the oldest form of naval warfare, and the only form, for instance, of which the great galley fleets of the Mediterranean were capable. Only after the amphibious forces captured key defended harbours could the galleys leave their battle formations and attack trade. In doing so the galleys were recovering their owners expenses, and perhaps earning a revenue, but they were not imposing a critical injury upon the enemy, which could if necessary survive without overseas trade. Modern research has made it clear that Mahanian control of the sea in the sixteenth-century Mediterranean was neither technically possible nor strategically important.[2] What was important was the capacity to strike from the sea against the land, carrying by sea both soldiers and artillery. That was also the dominate function of navies in World War II.

In the post-World War II period the capacity of naval artillery using aircraft and rockets has greatly increased, and nuclear weapons have imposed great limitations on the capacity of navies to mount amphibious operations. Bombardment has become the principal weapon in the naval arsenal. Current Soviet strategic thinking has abandoned the watertight distinctions between naval and military strategy and refers instead to war against the land, and war against the sea.[3]

If trade control is not *the* weapon of seapower, however, it is clearly a function of naval forces and has been so for all of modern history. So consistent, indeed, has been the employment of warships to capture trade ships that the historian is naturally drawn to those few instances when they were not, and asks the question why. That question should be applied generally to the whole issue of 'surprisals and takings at sea'. If so careful an observer as Admiral Richmond was wrong about the function of British trade control in the war against Napoleon it is apparent that the ramifications of 'maritime strategy' need to be elucidated.

Historians are indispensable for the study of strategy, but it is not generally understood what is their role. Strategic planning is based upon 'worst-case scenarios', which supposedly are based primarily upon assessment of an enemy's capabilities. If political systems were perfectly defined it ought to be possible to complete the analytic work with reference only to the physical nature of the enemy forces. Logically there cannot be 'accidents of history'. Practically speaking, however, analysis of international relations has to acknowledge its inability to incorporate in a general theory of state behaviour all the factors which determine events in the real world. No political analysis is ever made without resort to historical models. In no other way can behavioural patterns be predicted. Unless a conscientious effort is made to learn from concrete historical examples, unconscious or uninformed selectivity will greatly degrade the value of the scenario.

Naval history is nothing less than a cross-section of the life of nations. Study of the strategy of trade attack depends upon analysis of many consistent and near-consistent factors which interact under different circumstances. Naval technology, trade conditions and patterns, the constitutions of states, and concepts of international law are broad strands of the rope, and each is composed of numerous variables. Correlations of deductions from real experiences can be used to construct a general picture of the manner in which navies have influenced world history through trade control, and of changes which have occurred in the relationship between naval trade control and international political power. Historical evidence does not replace the analytic work of economists, but economics is no more a precise science than is historiography. The historian may complement the work of the economists by discovering some of the questions which should be asked. By asking them he may provide a measure of the adequacy of economic analysis. Perhaps even more importance should be attached to the ability of careful historical work to dispel some of the false assumptions about historical precedents which have influenced policies.

The precedents to which naval analysts generally direct their attention are the naval campaigns of World Wars I and II. These certainly provide invaluable lessons in the tactics of trade defence, and they also contribute significantly to understanding the utility of economic warfare. The use of naval forces to achieve political results through their impact upon maritime trade, however, is complex. Not all strategic mechanisms were attempted in those wars, and perhaps some that were would be treated with more importance if they were seen as recurring in a larger span of history.

It is of the utmost importance to ensure that the various motives for conducting naval war on shipping are distinguished so that the utility of the strategy can be assessed according to its success in serving those ends. The confusion which exists between mercantilist trade war and economic blockade is paralleled by that which exists between economic warfare and interdiction of logistic supply to the battlefield.

In the total warfare of the twentieth century there is indeed no satisfactory line dividing general economic warfare from interdiction of logistics. Functionally, however, a refusal to acknowledge that a distinction exists has been shown, by the British bombing campaign of 1941–43, to be myopic. The value of denying enemy forces supplies they require for their operations is hardly open to question. The military value of comprehensive attack on merchant shipping is less easily determined. The utility of either strategic purpose, in the final analysis, depends upon practicalities.

Consideration of economic warfare very rapidly passes beyond a study focused exclusively on naval strategy. Nevertheless, naval means of conducting economic warfare are worthy of special attention. They are justifiable on historical grounds, because navies did constitute the principal tools of economic warfare, and they remain justifiable on technical grounds. Even in an age of air power, when whole industrial cities may be destroyed in minutes, the commerce of the sea is an appealing target to the strategist of economic warfare. Indeed the immeasurable consequences of destroying cities adds to the attraction of war against trade. Ships concentrate industrial raw materials and production in an easily identifiable form. Not only are the ships easily distinguished from their background, but by their design it is often possible to identify the particular cargoes carried by each. Furthermore, ships range far from the population centres which must supply their defence. The means of defence, convoy and escort, reduce the efficiency of commercial operation and add to the economic effects of the strategy.

Naval attack on shipping is a strategic system which provides some states with unique advantages. When geography permits, naval forces can execute a relatively narrowly focused act of power, with relatively contained collateral damage. By contrast, control of source of supply, or of markets, requires very large-scale intervention in the international economy. This can only be achieved by a state with massive diplomatic and military power, as well as the economic resources to compensate neutrals for economic dislocation and for violation of national sentiment. Although naval war on trade and logistics is, at best, a strategic system employable by a very few states against a very few others, only a giant such as was the United States in the 1940s and 1950s could hope to achieve major results from acts of economic warfare which did not contain a significant naval element. Even the United States acted in alliance, co-operating with the British Empire which actively employed the naval instrument. Air power against economic resources, if well conducted, can be even more tightly focused than may be naval action outside the enemy state's frontier. The vast collateral damage created by bombing operations appears, since Haiphong 1972, to have greater political implications than does naval blockade.

The historiographic limitations of this text must be defined as clearly as are those of its subject. It is not a narrative compendium of naval history, let alone a *precis* of the laws of naval warfare. It is an essay of strategic analysis which bases its understanding of the strategy of attack on maritime trade upon historical evidence, and employs historical illustrations to substantiate its theses. The primary historical research has been done by several generations of historians. This study abstracts and refers to their initiatives, and places them in context. It is as a dwarf which stands on the shoulders of giants, to which I have added my own primary research for the period 1918–45. The motives for naval operations against trade, the restraints upon belligerent activity, and the results obtained form the subject. It is limited by the predominant interest in naval means of action, and by exclusion of substantial interest in what might be termed the tactical logistic needs of hostile armed forces. There is no satisfactory division between general economic warfare and interdiction of the logistics, but functionally it is necessary for the historian, as it is for the strategist, to observe such distinction as there is. Inevitably there will be some attention paid to control of military logistics, but only to set the proper subject in context, and where it is impossible to disentangle action against logistics from the other strategic reasons for attack on trade.

NOTES

1. Sir Herbert Richmond, *Sea Power in the Modern World*, p. 14.
2. John Francis Guilmartin, *Gunpowder and Galleys*, s.v., 'The Mahanian Fallacy', and John H. Pryor, *Geography, technology, and war. Studies in the maritime history of the Mediterranean, 649–1571*, pp. 176–92.
3. S. G. Gorshkov, *The Sea Power of the State*, p. 213, s.v., 'Fleet against Fleet and Fleet against Shore'.

Part I
Before World War I

The negative motive for attacking trade, that of denying supplies to an enemy, had little application before the nineteenth century. The only important exception was the efforts made to deny Spain its revenues from the mines of Central and South America, but these efforts bore little fruit. As a concept of contraband was created in the sixteenth and seventeenth centuries, naval forces did play a role in denying, or attempting to deny, logistics to military forces. The results depended upon technical and political circumstances, but were not notably successful except when circumstances were particularly suitable.

The predominant motive for attacking trade was the direct profit which could be made by the captor. This is reflected in the laws of war at sea, which are derived from the concept of reprisal. Spoliation of enemy trade could serve a strategic purpose by providing an incentive for investment in privateers, and for recruitment. At a macro scale, it could also lead to the belligerent supplanting its economic rival. The long-term value of trade war lay in its capacity to give to the victor a commanding access to trade goods and markets, to which can be attributed England's rise to economic dominance in the eighteenth century. War itself paid badly, and mercantilist operations tended to transform neutrals into enemies, but the fruits of victory were substantial. The economic power derived from naval strength was convertible into political influence by investment in armies, and by subsidising allies.

The nineteenth century opened with a tendency to reduce the impact of war on trade, and at its end the international community was still developing treaties to restrict belligerent rights. In the Crimean War, Britain experimented with free trade in wartime, a practice which served for Britain a mercantilist purpose because of the strength of its position as an international trader. In 1856 the international community, with the exception of the United States, agreed to the Declaration of Paris which outlawed the use of privateers, and established the immunity of neutral commerce. In the American Civil War, however, the Union government made a major effort to deny to the Confederacy all access to supplies and to trade. Its success was marginal, but the precedent was influential. The industrial revolution appeared to have made states more vulnerable to blockade of supply, and the Jeune Ecole *of the French Navy developed the concept into a central strategic idea. Blockade of supply, driven by a total war psychosis which set aside all the carefully devised treaty restraints on belligerent rights, was to dominate naval strategy in World War I.*

1 The Development of Strategic Purposes for Attack on Maritime Trade

REPRISAL AND THE LAWS OF WAR AT SEA

In the beginning, long before the concept of 'maritime strategy' was formed, there was piracy. Piracy was an endemic condition at sea which has an antiquity at least as old as does trade. Indeed modern scholarship is inclined to treat piracy as part of the general system of exchange.[1] In South East Asia piracy remains an endemic problem, control of which is a major task of navies in that area.[2] It is hardly a matter for surprise, therefore, that the oldest strategic motives for attack on maritime trade are derivatives of the rapacity of pirates, and that trade warfare is conducted in a complex regime of international law reflecting private and public response to the problem of piracy. From the perspective of the twentieth century, the laws of trade warfare appear primarily as restraints upon the considered actions of belligerents. Because of the underlying rapacious motive for attack on trade, however, prize law was at least as important in its function of adjudicating between privateers and naval officers on the one part, and their governors on the other. Prize law ensured that governments were able to exert some measure of control over events at sea, so that the war conducted on trade was compatible with the wider national interests, but the legal regime also prevented governments acquiring absolute control over the activities of their citizens and navies until 1856, when privateering was abolished.

Piracy led to reprisal. The response of traders to the threat of piracy was in the first place to arm themselves in self-defence, and secondly to attempt to recover the value of pirated property. This could be done by application to the courts of law if the injury had been inflicted by a national of the trader's country, and if his name was known. The crowns of Europe have from the middle ages sought to monopolise the right to violence, and hence were increasingly antipathetic to pirates. As often as not, however, the injury had been inflicted by a foreigner. If the foreign courts failed to satisfy the injured trader, his next move was to apply to his own government for a 'letter of marque and reprisal'. In 1295 the first such was issued in England. Initially the prerogative of the Lord Chancellor, they came from 1357 to be issued by the Lord High Admiral in the High Court of Admiralty, although influential gentlemen could still obtain them from the Privy Council in the reign of Elizabeth I.[3] An application for a letter of marque contained a statement of the grievance, and an account of the monetary value to be recovered. Once he had been granted a letter of marque, the trader was entitled to use the armament of his own trade ship, or even to fit out a private warship, for the purpose of waging private war against the nationals of the country which had wronged him.

The right of a king to issue a letter of marque did not absolve him from the need to ensure that his subjects conformed to international norms. A prize court had to adjudicate to ensure that the value of the prize did not exceed the loss to be recovered, and that the prize was indeed of the nationality indicated in the letter of marque. In England, the High Court of Admiralty was made the legal prize tribunal in the late sixteenth century. Perforce, Admiralty prize law was Roman Law, which was itself based on the 'Law Merchant' of the ancient Mediterranean. No purely national enactment could apply to the ships of different nations on the high seas beyond national jurisdiction. As Sir Julius Caesar, Judge of the High Court of Admiralty, wrote in 1592,

> The civill lawes imperiall were best suited for the sea: which for that by long continuance in the most flurishing commonwealth of Rome, they have been many ages since, the most perfect and equal lawes of the world and are generally received throughout al nations about us.[4]

Even now, Roman Law has not been effaced entirely as the underlying law of Christendom. In order to enforce an internationally acceptable law, the national prize courts were held to be outside the control of the crown. In the Reformation period Caesar had difficulty defending the right of the High Court of Admiralty to this extra-national focus, and it has constantly needed restatement. As recently as 1916, the British Judicial Committee of the House of Lords was at pains to maintain the independence of prize courts from the British government. In its summation in the *Zamora* case during World War I, it stated:

> The power of an order-in-council does not extend to prescribing or altering the law to be administered by the court . . . If the court is to decide, judicially, in accordance with what it conceives to be the law of nations, it cannot, even in doubtful cases, take its direction from the crown, which is party to the proceedings.[5]

Private war at sea within the constraints of Roman Law had its parallel in public war. The medieval monarch did not claim the absolute authority of a sovereign, but was content with suzereignty within a recognised body of international law. War could only be regarded as a means of enforcing the law. A king going to war was careful to provide himself with a pretext which was comparable to that of the injured trader who was applying for a letter of marque. Having 'declared war', a king was entitled to exercise 'belligerent rights' over shipping. The nature of belligerent rights might well be contested, but not the fact that a government at war could enjoy them, or that it had to confine itself to them. When in the late seventeenth century Thomas Hobbes put forward a thesis that international relations were outside the rule of law, and existed in a state of nature, he was universally reviled. John Locke reached the same conclusion, but was careful to present his case in deliberately obscure language to avoid prosecution.[6] Only in the nineteenth century did the concept of a lawless international jungle come to have significance.

Attack on trade is a strategy which has not been accommodated easily into the scholastic concept of the just war. For a war to be lawful (*jus ad bellum*) it must not only be fought for a just cause and with good intent by a lawful authority, but it must be fought by means which are likely to achieve victory without disproportionate injury to all parties. Two of the distinctive features of the restraints on the legitimate means of pursuing war (*jus in bello*) are that civilians are not a legitimate target of warlike activity, and that belligerent measures should be able to discriminate in their effects between civilians and enemy military forces. The only way an attack on trade can serve any strategic purpose is if the requirement to discriminate between civilians and military is overlooked. This defect is especially true if the strategy is the negative one of besieging the enemy state, when the innocent population of that state becomes vulnerable to mass destruction through starvation. Strategy on the whole is unconcerned with the legitimacy of the cause for which a war is being fought, but it must take into account the likely reactions of neutrals, who can be expected to be influenced by considerations of legitimacy.

It was not difficult for the lawyers of earlier centuries to overlook the fact that military operations were being directed against civilian seamen, because seamen came from a despised class, and merchant seamen were only distinguished from naval seamen by their employment. Their training until the mid-nineteenth century was identical. In practice more attention was paid to the problem of adjudication between the rival claims of neutrals and privateersmen to the private property seized at sea.[7]

The existence of a codified law of belligerent rights, despite its imperfections, imposed constraints upon strategy. Inevitably, the interests of states led to the recognised laws being changed. This could not be effected by revision of Roman Law because the western half of the Roman Empire was already falling into the hands of 'barbarian' kings at the time of Emperor Justinian's work of codification in the sixth century. In the eleventh century Roman law began again to be studied, and applied to international relations, but the only means available for modification of the law were treaties between states, and the precedents established in courts by their decisions. An early example of the modification of belligerent rights at sea by treaty occurred in 1403 when a draft treaty was drawn up between England and Flanders neutralising Flemish shipping in the wars England was fighting with France and Scotland.[8] It served as a directive to English courts to order compensation paid to Flemings whose ships or goods had been spoiled. The publication in 1494 of the famous Provençal *Consulato del Mare* describing the rights and duties of belligerents at sea provided a statement of legal norms upon which the law of prize subsequently depended. The restrictions upon belligerent rights expressed in the *Consulato del Mare*, however, could never be absolute when national courts were subject to national political pressure. The law of war at sea continued to be modified by the decisions made by prize courts, which established in that way what is known as 'The Course of Admiralty'.

The *ad hoc* development of the laws of war, as they applied to operations against trade, and the conflicting objectives expressed in them, prevented the legal regime acquiring complete coherence, or clarity. Hugo Grotius was commissioned by the Dutch East India Company to prepare a brief on prize law, the twelfth chapter of which was published in 1609 under the title *Mare Librum*. In it he defended the free use of the sea by neutral commerce, and hence the right of such ships to take prizes. In response, John Selwen published *Mare*

Clausum, in which he defended a concept of sovereign jurisdiction at sea which would be incompatible with the right to reprisal. Neither England in the North Sea, however, nor Portugal in the East Indies, was able to enforce the concept. In 1625, Grotius published *De Jure Belli ac Pacis*, but his description of belligerent rights was too convoluted to put an end to wild variation in court interpretations of law.[9]

Over the years it became English practice to avoid explicit definition of the law. This was done to give the greatest latitude to the privateers and naval blockade forces. Naturally neutrals objected, but the Union government adopted the same practice in the American Civil War. The British blockade of Germany in World War I depended upon avoidance of legal definitions, and avoidance of the Prize Court. When cases did come to court during that war, the *Zamora* precedent notwithstanding, British prize courts never failed to enforce British municipal legislation.[10] No violation of international law was occasioned because the British government had been careful in phrasing British statute law that it should not be in conflict, and because resort to the Prize Court was avoided except when the British thought they had a good case, and wished to demonstrate a respect for the law.[11]

The lawlessness exhibited in the conduct of naval operations against trade in the final years of World War I was a consequence of political pressures upon belligerent governments. It appears, paradoxically, that they felt less obligation to conform to the existing rules of war because of the efforts which had been made in the preceding century to clarify and modify the archaean subtleties of Roman Law by treaties, such as the Declaration of Paris of 1856 which outlawed the letter of marque, and the Declaration of London of 1911 which clarified the definition of contraband. Treaties proved to be a weaker restraint than had been the old concept of a pervasive law which everyone violated but nobody disputed.

There could be no return to the full mystique of Roman Law, but in the wake of World War I the foundations were laid for a new international regime which echoed the concept of the unity of Christendom, substituting it with that of the common humanity of man. In 1919 the League of Nations was established. In 1928 the Briand–Kellog pact re-established the idea that aggressive war was illegal. The Charter of the United Nations has extended that idea under article 2.4, but the concept of mutual accountability continues to be undermined by the still-pervasive concept of the sovereignty of states.

As with the old Roman Law, the new law of nations is vulnerable to abuse and interpretation. There is tension between the objective of eliminating war, and that of making it less destructive. If war cannot be eliminated, no state wants a legal regime to come into existence which imposes inequitable restraint upon its capacity to use military force to protect its interests. This tension leads to paradox. One of the foremost authorities on the laws of war at sea, R. W. Tucker, argues that states *de facto* at war are entitled to belligerent rights against shipping even if the war itself is illegal.[12] Despite the problems of interpretation, however, states do continue to be constrained by law. As D. P. O'Connell writes: 'International Law may be considered by some to be a simulacrum of law but it is a phenomenon notwithstanding'.[13]

The limitations imposed on belligerents by the laws of war were respected because the belligerents considered themselves to be civilised men who respected the laws of nations, but also because reprisal was a concept to which all parties could resort. Instances of self-imposed restraint by belligerent states out of respect for the concept of the just war are hard to find, although British blockade practice at the beginning of World War II did to some extent reflect that idea. Generally, the more important consideration was that a state which violated the established rule of law could expect his enemy to do so as well. The pervasiveness of reprisal results from its being a strategic concept which comes into importance whenever technological conditions tip the balance in favour of offensive means of warfare. However, reprisal by the enemy is a weak tool of international law. It tends, as it was in World War I, to be used as a justification for overthrowing inconvenient restraints. More threatening was the prospect of neutrals which had been injured by naval operations against their trade resorting to reprisal. The danger of lateral escalation by the alienation of neutrals is a very potent force.

Besides the pressure on court interpretation of prize law produced by the strategic needs of belligerent states, the courts were exposed to pressure from those engaged in the war at sea, amongst whom there might be numbered the person of the sovereign. In the sixteenth century the regulation of privateering by the English High Court of Admiralty was frustrated by the capacity of powerful men to demand preferential treatment, and by the intervention of the Lord Admiral, who was entitled to 10 per cent of the value of all lawful prizes as well as many other 'droits'.[14] The revenue maintained the Admiralty jurisdiction, and provided amply for the comfort of the Lord Admiral. During the reign of Queen Elizabeth I, the crown might have a further interest in the privateering operation as a shareholder.

Seventeenth- and eighteenth-century changes in English legislation governing the distribution of prize money, undertaken to stimulate investment in privateers and reflecting a growing acceptance on the part of the crown that the captors could not be expected to share their prizes with a government which had not contributed to the expenses, increased the pressures on the courts. The English 'Prize Act' of 1649 required all prizes to be condemned in the High Court of Admiralty, the value of the prize to be deposited in the 'Prize Fund', and one half of it paid eventually to the Treasurer of the Admiralty to support seamen's charities.[15] In 1661 a distinction was established between 'Droits of the Crown', and 'Droits of Admiralty'. The latter were ships surrendered in English harbours, or wrecked, and the Lord Admiral was entitled to the full value. Droits of the Crown were divided between the captor and the crown until 1692, when the crown waived its share.[16] In 1708 Queen Anne's government enacted the 'Cruisers Act' allotting the whole of Droits of the Crown to the captors.[17] This provision was renewed by an act of 1739, the Prize Act of 1756 and the Privateers Act of 1759. These acts removed the financial interest of the crown in obtaining condemnation of prizes, and it might be supposed that the result would have been to improve the ability of the prize courts to reach judgments which satisfied international norms. In practice, the importance of the Cruisers Act was that it demonstrated the power privateer interests had acquired in parliament, the chief court.

Disputes over the interpretation of the rights of belligerents to intercept neutral ships and neutral cargoes as part of its naval action against an enemy can be simply categorised. Carlton Savage, writing for the United States Department of State in 1934, listed six areas of dispute.[18] Was it legal for a belligerent to seize enemy property being transported in a neutral ship? The concept of neutral ships being immune to arrest and inspection has been known as the principle of 'free ships make free goods'. Were neutral goods, if being transported by an enemy merchant ship, liable to seizure by a belligerent? The English position has generally been that the neutral ship may be required to surrender enemy goods which will be lawful prize, but that neutral goods captured in an enemy ship will be released. The exception made by all states has been a class of goods known as 'contraband', warlike stores destined for the armed forces of the enemy, but there has been little agreement about what constitutes contraband. Are 'naval stores', timber, cordage, tar, and the like contraband? Industrialisation exacerbated the problem of definition. When is a cargo of contraband considered to be destined for the enemy? The principle of continuous voyage allows seizure at any point outside neutral territory even if the items are manifested to a neutral *entrepôt* and are the property of a neutral. Is the principle of continuous voyage good law? Neutrals might not object to belligerents stopping neutral ships if an 'effective' military blockade were mounted in the vicinity of an enemy port which made it impossible for neutral ships to enter without interception. However, what test should be accepted of the effectiveness of a blockade? In the late eighteenth century the final question began to be asked, by the French *philosophes*, and by the American government: was it legal to seize any private property at all? Should the wars of governments be permitted to interfere with the flow of commerce? The answers to these questions had profound significance for naval strategists. The practicalities of naval operations, and neutral resentment, affected the answers which were given at different times.

LOW-BUDGET NAVIES – PRIZE MONEY AND PRIVATEERS

Economic warfare is concerned with the relative wealth of the belligerents, the one measured against the other. Accordingly, the war strategy of a belligerent is interested in maximising national wealth, while minimising that of the enemy. Conceptually these instrumental objectives are the two sides of the same coin, but practically speaking the positive and negative objectives are pursued by different means. Naval forces may be employed for both ends, but their targets will differ, as must their tactics. Largely for practical reasons, the principal interest of economic warfare up to the mid-nineteenth century lay in its positive capacity to enrich the belligerent. This rapacious objective eventually reached a high degree of sophistication in the mercantilist strategy of the Napoleonic War in which British manipulation of trade served to pay for the armies that brought Napoleon to bay. In a simpler form, the seizure of enemy cargoes and ships served a strategic function by subsidising the naval forces of the belligerent.

The simplest form in which the positive mode of naval economic warfare was manifested was the licensing of naval forces, by means of letters of marque, to earn their own keep by raiding shipping. Private war at sea was transformed into public war by the need of early modern states to have resort to low-budget navies. While the monarch sometimes shared with the subject a simple motive for pillaging enemy shipping, as Queen Elizabeth I invested in Francis Drake's expeditions, the state also had a strategic motive for permitting subjects to make a profit out of war. A medieval or early modern monarch could dispose of very little revenue. Medieval armies were summoned to provide a traditional and legally required unpaid service. Naval forces had to be mobilised in the same way. Medieval English city corporations provided shipping as a feudal due to the crown, but only a limited number of ships could be obtained in that way, and they could be retained on state business only for a limited time. Some monarchs owned a few ships, but even they depended upon their legal rights to 'arrest' ships for war purposes. The English fleet which fought the Spanish Armada in 1588 was composed of 34 royal ships and 163 belonging to private persons. Clearly it was a hardship for a merchant to have to take his ship out of trade and provide it to the crown, which might or might not pay wages and damages.[19] If an adequate war fleet was to be made available the hardship of the shipowner had to be mitigated. This could be done if he were issued a letter of marque authorising him to raid enemy shipping. As late as the eighteenth century, letters of marque were issued to naval auxiliaries as well as to professionals with purpose-built commerce raiders. The transports used to carry British soldiers to America during the revolution there were issued with them as a perquisite of government service.

As the seventeenth century progressed, the distinction between warships and merchant ships grew to the point where privateers were of no value in a battle fleet. By the mid-eighteenth century, privateers could not operate without a screen of heavy warships. In 1738 the British government tried to persuade British privateersmen to take out letters of marque even before the formal commencement of hostilities, but investors were not tempted by that anachronistic idea. Despite their limitations, however, privateers remained necessary for operations against enemy shipping, which had come to be valued by states for more important reasons than for the direct market value of the capture. Unless a state could mobilise private capital by providing incentives, it could not finance a fleet of commerce raiders at the same time as it maintained a battle fleet. Nor could it provide adequate defence for its own shipping. Privateers not only raided the enemy, they also contracted to convoy merchantmen, and recaptured merchantmen which had been taken by enemy privateers. Privateers continued to be a necessary part of a naval establishment into the nineteenth century. The most recent assessment of the role of privateers in Britain's eighteenth century wars against trade is that made by David Starkey, who has revised considerably the earlier calculations made by Richard Pares, and others. In the five wars between 1702 and 1783 in which the British attacked trade, privateers accounted for 40 per cent of the prizes. Their performance was well below average in the Seven Years' War when regular naval forces accounted for the greater number of captures, but in the American Revolutionary war privateers took more than half the total number of prizes.[20] The French, after the defeat at La Hogue in 1692, went so far as to lay up the battle fleet altogether and depend entirely upon their privateers, which took a great toll of English shipping. Jonathan Swift wrote approvingly in his 1712 pamphlet 'The Conduct of the Allies' that King Louis

> is at no Charge of a Fleet, further than providing Privateers, wherewith his Subjects carry on a Piratical War at their own Expense, and he shares in the Profit; which hath been very considerable to *France*, and of infinite Disadvantage to us, not only by the perpetual Losses we have suffered to an immense Value, but by the general Discouragement of Trade, on which we so much depend.[21]

Privateering was not necessarily a very remunerative undertaking, but the return was evidently enough to keep the raiders at sea throughout the wars of the sixteenth to eighteenth centuries. In the sixteenth century, before the Spanish government perfected its convoy system, privateering certainly had a strong appeal, although Kenneth Andrews doubts that it yielded a net return on national investment in England.[22] At the beginning of the seventeenth century, James I of England was reviled by the privateer interests for making peace with Spain, and William Pitt used them as a source of political power in the eighteenth century. Carl Swanson has shown that the outbreak of war between England and Spain in 1739 was enormously popular throughout the principal ports of the English

Colonies in America because of the prospects of prize taking. Newport Rhode Island and New York were especially active in the privateer war. Swanson's statistics, however, show that 23.6 per cent of the privateers outfitted in American ports during the war took no prize, 13.6 per cent took one, and 48.9 per cent took between two and four prizes. Because many of the successful privateers worked with a consort, the value of many of the prizes had to be divided at least two ways. The rewards must not have been great for the majority; 61.6 per cent of Rhode Island investors in privateers did so for only one of the ten years of war, and another 31.5 per cent for only two to four years. Swanson writes that

> For the majority of [Rhode Island's] investors, privateering appears to have been only of passing interest, and perhaps, only minimally rewarding. It is unlikely that men would have invested in only one year of the war if they had received substantial gains.

He concluded that 'a definitive pronouncement concerning the profitability of American privateers during the War of 1739 to 1748 remains elusive'.[23] James G. Lydon's estimation of the profitability of New York privateering during the American Revolutionary War, on the other hand, was that investors obtained a return, over all, of 100 per cent.[24] David Starkey shows that the declaration of war against the Dutch in 1780 was as popular in England as had been the Spanish war of 1739. However, he believes that it is not possible at this stage of research into the subject to assess the profitability of privateering. Its value as counter-index activity to compensate for wartime trade stagnation has to be taken seriously, but so do the problems which were generated by the privateers competing for maritime resources, and flooding markets with prizes and prize-goods.[25]

Studies of French privateering in the eighteenth century have suggested that the profits made from it by the *armateurs* were not enough to divert capital from other investments. It was only when formal naval operations made maritime commerce difficult that ships were converted into privateers. Few ships were built from the keel up for that purpose. When British warships raided the St Malo fishing fleet on the Grand Banks, the Maloese turned to privateering. The proximity of British naval forces based on the Thames and Medway, which prevented the Dunkirkers conducting maritime trade, had the same effect. When in the wars at the middle of the century the merchants of Brittany found ways of keeping their ships in trade, they virtually abandoned privateering. In the period 1695–1713 they licensed 2657 privateers, a notional 147 per year. In the four years between 1744 and 1748 only 206 were licensed, and in the Seven Years' War only 113. The pattern for Bayonne was reversed. Due to tax privileges, Bayonne had been able to sustain a profitable trade during the war of the Spanish Succession. The port did not begin to convert its assets into privateers until trade declined in the middle of the century.[26] The French government's provision of practical assistance for the privateers in the war of the League of Augsburg was very much an exception, and it only occurred after defeat at sea had led to the battle fleet's being laid up.[27]

The prospect of prize-taking was important, not only because it encouraged merchants to invest in ships which could be used for war purposes, but also because it provided the motivation for enlistment. Sailors on a privateer often received no pay, but were entitled to a share of the value of the prizes they captured and to 'Bounty Money' which was paid by the English crown for enemy warships which were sunk at sea. In New York, market forces determined the owner's share of prizes, and privateersmen generally received a larger share than did their English counterparts.[28] English privateersmen, who in the war of 1739 to 1748 divided amongst themselves two thirds of the value of any prize after the costs of Admiralty justice had been paid, could nonetheless expect much better returns than could their brothers in the navy.[29] Inevitably, the privateers became successful competitors for scarce naval manpower, although perhaps contemporary sources exaggerated the problem. John Hattendorf has shown that the Cruisers Act of 1708 did no more than arrest a declining investment in privateers, and suggests that its intention may have been as much to encourage enlistment in the navy as it was to support interest in privateers.[30]

The picture is not entirely clear. In Zeeland in 1691–92 a list was drawn up of the privateer force which at that time numbered no more than 31 vessels and 948 men. It was uneconomic to send large privateers to sea when smaller ones could glut themselves on smaller merchantmen without the expense of investing in the armament which was necessary for reducing large, defensively armed, traders. David Starkey, on the other hand, has shown that in the War of the Spanish Succession London's privateer crew lists totalled 29 000 men. There were a total of 671 vessels in London's fleet, and 50 per cent were ships of between 100 and 250 tons, which meant that there were an average of 4.9 tons of shipping per man. In the Seven Years' War the most successful group of London's privateers were those most heavily manned, with less than a ratio of 1.9 tons of shipping per man, which took 29.9 per cent of the prizes.[31]

Prize money was an important means of attracting men into the navy, although changes in the nature of naval service in the late seventeenth century reduced the incentive. Life in the navy became increasingly hard when warships stayed in commission throughout the year. As warships increased in size, the work of prize-taking was increasingly left to the privateers, and when naval ships did take prizes the size of their crews reduced the profits. The system employed for the division of prizes worked against the interests of the common seamen in a large warship. The Cruisers Act of 1708 established that prizes should be divided into eight shares, three of which went to the captain, one to the commander-in-chief, one to the officers, one to the warrant officers, and two to the crew. The eight hundred odd seamen on a first rate line-of-battle ship would receive little. Frigates' crews could expect better returns.

Whatever its limitations as an inducement for seamen to enlist, without question prize money or looting was an important inducement for officers. Alberto Tenenti credits the contemporary view in late sixteenth-century Venice that the failure of the navy to eliminate the threat posed by north European merchantmen-cum-pirates was to be attributed less to the technical problem of galleys operating against ships than to the fact that captains were not permitted to pillage the ships they captured.[32] A hundred years later, the system of prize division could ensure that a young captain in the English Royal Navy, if he were on a small ship cruising in an area where there were prizes to take, would become comfortably wealthy. An admiral, if he deployed his squadron with an eye to making captures, could become rich. The incentive provided by hope of such windfalls ensured that the fortuneless younger sons of the aristocracy would seek a career in the navy despite the hardships of a life at sea away from home. Lord Cochrane was one of many such who made his fortune as a naval captain. When in 1808 the prize regulations were altered to reduce the captains' proportion, he left the service, or so he told the House of Commons to which he had been returned in 1806. 'Prize money', he declared, 'ever formed the principal motive of seamen to encounter the perils of war'. Lord St Vincent, Nelson's early patron, although he was the target of Cochrane's attacks, agreed.[33] Only at the conclusion of World War II, long after the provision of pension plans to naval officers who were expected to be able to live on their incomes, did the British navy abolish the distribution of prize money.[34] Bounty money was paid for exploits in World War I, but not in World War II.[35]

The result of the navy's dependence upon the incentive of prize money was that governments found it difficult to exercise control over war on trade. Even when it was clearly counterproductive from the point of view of grand strategy to permit attacks on shipping, technical naval considerations urged the necessity for it. Control of policy was further diminished by political influence possessed by the owners of privateers who insisted upon the right to exploit war for private profit. English law, which made prizes the legal property of their captors, and even lent them the protection inherent in the extra-national nature of prize law, obstructed government control. The 1403 treaty between England and Flanders can be construed as a device for strengthening the control of the crown over its own 'privateer' navy.

In England all privateer captains were required to post bonds not to exceed their instructions, but it was not until the Privateers Act of 1759 that they were obliged to swear that they were worth the sum of their bond. Putting a bond in suit was a slow and unsure way of disciplining a privateer. It has been observed above that the successive English acts regulating the privateering business in the seventeenth and eighteenth centuries reflected the growing political power of privateersmen. When an English Secretary of State claimed that he could not authorise the release of a neutral ship before the case was heard by the prize court, he was no more than stating the truth. In the Seven Years' War, the Duke of Newcastle felt unable to alter the law to restrain the privateers, or even to act decisively to oblige them to conform to their instructions. John Locke's view, that the right to private property was the only control over despotism, was so generally believed in England that no restriction was possible on the right of the captors to 'their property'. William Pitt vigorously defended the privateer interests in parliament. After Pitt himself became prime minister, his Attorney General, Lord Hardwick, decided to interpret belligerent rights as enabling privateers to capture neutral ships which were undertaking trade as a service for the enemy. 'The Rule of War of 1756' unleashed the privateers against Dutch and Spanish shipping.

Sometimes the necessity to defer to the courts could be a convenience. The neutral could be deterred by the knowledge that, although he would probably obtain the release of his ship, the case would not in all probability be heard for several years. It might be preferable to compound with the captors and settle out of court. The expense to the neutral trader of such a proceeding made blockade more effective than it would have been if the law had been more perfectly reflected in fact. If the neutral state was powerful enough to declare war as an ally of the enemy, however, as Spain did in 1760 and the United States did in 1812, then the attacks on trade could be counterproductive indeed.

Clearly the dependence upon private capital created paradoxical results. Although privateer warships were necessary if a state were to attempt a sea denial strategy, the privateer interests had acquired the power to insist that commerce raiding form a part of any war strategy, even if the likely consequences appeared to be undesirable. In 1794, for instance, the British station commander in the Eastern Mediterranean refused a request from the British ambassador to the Porte to permit French grain ships safe passage to neutral Constantinople.[36]

The eventual decision to outlaw the use of privateers in the international convention known as the Declaration of Paris, 1856, was the result of new economic principles, and of experience of the effects of trade war on relations with neutrals. As such it was part of a comprehensive change in the laws of war. The ban against privateers was included both because they were the only means then available for the conduct of sea denial operations, and because of the difficulty which had been experienced over the centuries in controlling them. The Admiralty appears to have hardened its heart against privateers by the end of the eighteenth century, possibly because they were taking too much of the spoils.[37] By 1856 the political power of the privateer interests had been reduced to the point where it was possible for states to master them. Ironically, the development in the nineteenth and twentieth centuries of monolithic governments, which either democratically or arbitrarily are able to control most facets of the lives of their citizens, made it possible for the first time for states to fight naval wars without making concessions to the private profit motives of their peoples.

An end was not made to the payment of prize money to the Royal Navy until after World War II, but the professionalised navies of the nineteenth and twentieth centuries were able to prevent the motive of prize money distorting national strategies. In World War I there was considerable protest both within the Royal Navy, and amongst the public, that ships brought in for inspection were being released without resort to the Prize Courts. Not only did it appear, erroneously, that the civil service were frustrating the effective use of maritime strategy, but it was objected that navy officers and men were being robbed of their spoils. Bowing to pressure, the Asquith administration did create a Ministry of Blockade. Naval officers continued nonetheless to be denied day-to-day control of naval interceptions. The personnel of the Ministry of Blockade was drawn from the Foreign Office, and it continued to manipulate blockade operations in the interest of British war strategy, rather than in that of naval prize money. In Germany the civilians were less certain of their capacity to control the military during World War I, and German prize courts, according to J. W. Garner, were principally concerned with the problem of controlling the navy. 'They are established by their state to determine whether the legal instructions to which the naval authorities should conform are observed or not.[38] In contrast, British prize courts had come to regard their task as the protection of neutrals, which led the British government to find means of avoiding resort to them.

BULLIONISM: THE ANGLO–SPANISH WARS

In the sixteenth century states began to perceive that raiding trade could pay, not only for the naval forces engaged in it, but also for the entire war effort afloat and ashore. At the same time, the wealth taken from the enemy would deprive it of the capacity to pay its forces. The introduction into maritime commerce of relatively large, ocean-going, ships freighting very high value cargoes stimulated the creation of this new rationale for the ancient practice of commerce raiding. The entire profit of a year's trading and raiding by the Portuguese in India and Indonesia was brought home in a single voyage by a great carrack sailing from Goa to Lisbon. The *flota*, a convoy of treasure ships, annually carried home to Spain the products of American silver mines of which the government's one-fifth share amounted possibly to as much as 25 per cent of the royal revenues. The wealth Spain derived from its empire transformed it into a great naval and military power. Madrid was able to raise large armies and galley fleets quickly because it could purchase the new gunpowder weapons that did not depend upon the careful training of long-service soldiers.[39] The wealth of the Portuguese empire financed Europe's first ocean-going fleet of heavily-gunned sailing warships. In contrast, when Henry VIII's break with the Pope obliged England to acquire a first-rate battle fleet, the expenses could only be met by the seizure of monastic assets. There was no regular source of income on an adequate scale. The oceanic revenues of Spain and Portugal transformed commerce raiding.

It was to take all of the sixteenth and half of the seventeenth century to develop a doctrine of 'sea denial' out of the private warfare of reprisal, and the positive objective of seizing valuables from the enemy never lost its importance. It was the Huguenot Admiral Coligny who showed the English how privateer attacks in the English Channel could affect Spanish military operations in Flanders by obliging Spain to rely upon the difficult supply route overland across the Alps. The most dramatic incident occurred in 1568. Privateers drove Spanish pay ships into English harbours where they were released only after the money which was still technically the property of Genoese bankers had been taken by the English treasury as a loan on the English account.

Posterity has been more interested in the idea that the entire Spanish war-machine could be stalled by the interdiction of the Spanish silver route from New Spain across the Atlantic. Spanish royal revenue from the Indies was the foundation of Spanish financial credibility which enabled Spain to raise the loans needed to finance the war. Foreign observers were aware of Spain's vulnerabilities. On 7 August 1581 the Venetian ambassador to France, Lorenzo Priuli, wrote:

> If they could seize the Indian fleet they would produce a crisis such as that which took place when her Majesty seized the money of the King of Spain which was destined for Flanders under the name of private merchants. And this is the true way to humble the pride of Spain by plucking their pen feathers.[40]

After the defeat of the first Armada in 1588 the idea was seriously taken up of pursuing the war by attacking Spanish trade. John Hawkins, the Treasurer of the Navy, had redesigned English warships for greater speed and endurance, and now urged their employment in a continuous blockade of the Iberian peninsula. An experiment was made in 1590.[41] Sir Walter Raleigh was an advocate of maritime strategy.[42] In 1596, however, Elizabeth's beloved Earl of Essex was still urging without effect that

> The hurt that our State should seek to do him [that is, Philip] is to intercept his treasure, whereby we shall cut his sinews, and make war upon him by sea, whereby Her Majesty shall be both secured

> from his invasions, and become mistress of the sea, which is the greatness that the Queen of an Island should most aspire to.[43]

The aspirations of Elizabethan naval commanders had been ahead of technological realities. Elizabeth showed in 1594 that she valued the loot her sailors might seize, but regarded as casuistry their strategic arguments that the Spanish bid to conquer the Netherlands could be defeated by interdiction of the silver fleets. She limited the time a squadron could be away from home 'however profitable it might be' because she preferred 'surety before profit'.[44] When Essex was sent his orders to sail with the force under his command, no mention was made of depriving Spain of its source of power; rather the emphasis was that he should give strict orders how the treasure ships should be assaulted,

> and by whom, and not suffer any captains with any ships to attempt the boarding of them in any other sort than you shall appoint, lest by rash attempts, upon greediness for the spoil, they may perish with the treasure in them, before they are taken.[45]

Having very limited resources, Elizabeth was not even prepared to give royal support to the private attempts that were made by Christopher Carleill, Sir Humphrey Gilbert, and finally Sir Walter Raleigh, to found privateering colonies in North America within striking range of Spanish–American trade.[46] Instead she repeatedly sent relief expeditions to the continent which just barely succeeded in keeping Spanish forces out of the Channel ports. Her strategic judgment was certainly sound. Essex's raid on Cadiz destroyed the *flota* ships at their moorings and thereby severed the supply line from New Spain, but the result was disappointing for the advocate of sea power. Madrid was obliged to declare bankruptcy in 1597, but was not obliged as a consequence to seek peace.

In the long run, however, the Anglo–Spanish wars were significant in the development of the strategy of trade interdiction. Hawkins, Essex, Admiral Monson, and Sir Walter Raleigh, to name the most important, had established the strategic idea of making war by attacking trade. Fifty years later it was accepted by Cromwell's Commission of Admiralty as good doctrine.[47]

In the seventeenth century, economic thinking developed crude bullionism into the more sophisticated mercantilism. Economic warfare, however, often retains use for otherwise outdated practices. While this has been especially true of mercantilist trade war, it was also true of bullionism. For a century and a half after the defeat of the Spanish Armada in 1588, bullionism continued to drive English maritime strategy when the enemy to be defeated was Spain. Cromwell exhibited a strict strategic conservatism in 1656 when he brought to an end the First Anglo–Dutch war in order to reopen the Anglo–Spanish one which he considered to be more appropriate for conservative, religious, reasons. Using Lisbon as an advanced base, Cadiz was blockaded. Five treasure ships were captured and the rest were burnt at anchor in the Canaries. Spanish merchants did not have much political influence. Their losses could not bring Spanish capitulation. The arrest of the treasure, however, was not without military significance. Spanish armies in Portugal and Flanders could not be paid. They melted away, Portuguese independence was preserved, and, with the aid of France, an English garrison was installed in the privateer port of Dunkirk.

There was a penalty to be paid for making war by intercepting trade. For one thing the Spaniards reciprocated by attacking English merchantmen, hundreds of which were captured. Furthermore, the interception of the Spanish treasure ships played havoc with European markets for English goods. Attack on trade also led to trouble with neutrals. The determination of the English that the Spanish treasures landed in the Canaries should not be brought to Europe in neutral bottoms led to trouble with the Dutch, who denied the right of English warships to search and arrest.

The Spanish decision in 1701 to ally themselves dynastically to France presented England with a chance to use attacks on the Spanish treasure fleets as a means of disabling the French army. In 1702 Admiral Rooke burned a *flota* with its French escort in Vigo harbour, and was thanked for his exploit by the House of Commons in the following words: 'France has endeavoured to support its ambition by the riches of the Indies: your success, Sir, hath only kept them the burden of Spain and stripped them of the assistance of it'.[48] However, Henry Kamen has shown that the Spanish Treasury did not in fact suffer from the raid. Most of the merchandise seized or destroyed belonged to English, Dutch and French merchants, and the bullion was safely landed before the attack. The Spanish Treasury took the opportunity to seize $4 million owned by Dutch and English interests, and, despite the losses which had been suffered by Spanish merchants, the Indies trade was conducted with more vigour in the following years than it had been for some time.[49]

In 1708 Admiral Wager met the Spanish treasure galleons at sea, captured three, and drove the rest into Vera Cruz. By that date the protracted expenses of war had virtually exhausted the French treasury. The repercussions in international politics produced by the capture of the galleons, however, were inconsiderable. In 1710 and 1712 the French safely escorted home treasure fleets.

Despite these appointments, which may only seem inevitable with the benefit of hindsight, the direction of maritime strategy against the treasure fleets continued to find strong advocates in England. Jonathan Swift may have been chiefly motivated by revulsion at Marlborough's continental strategy, but in his 1712 pamphlet, 'The Conduct of the Allies', he complained that not enough emphasis had been placed on maritime operations.

> I have sometimes wondered how it came to pass, that the Style of *Maritime Powers*, by which our Allies, in a sort of contemptuous manner, usually couple us with the *Dutch*, did never put us in mind of the Sea; and while some Politicians were shewing us the way to *Spain* by *Flanders*, others by *Savoy* or *Naples*, that the *West-Indies* should never come into their Heads. With half the Charge we have been at, we might have maintained our original Quota of Forty thousand Men in *Flanders*, and at the same time by our Fleets and Naval Forces, have so distressed the *Spaniards* in the North and South Seas of *America*, as to prevent any Returns of Mony from thence, except in our own Bottoms.

By failing to blockade bullion shipments, Swift wrote, the English had enabled the King of France to make war:

> the Supplies he hath received from the *Spanish West-Indies*, which in all are computed, since the War, to amount to Four hundred Millions of Livres, (and all in *Specie*) have enabled him to pay his Troops.[50]

Interdiction of Spanish treasure fleets was again made the hinge of British strategy in 1726 when British security appeared to be threatened by a plan of Ripperda, the minister of Spain, to provoke the Holy Roman Emperor into war. Flanders had been transferred to the Empire following the Treaty of Utrecht, and at Ostend had been established an Imperial East India Company. Not only were Dutch and English investors distressed by the competition posed by the Ostend Company in a depressed market for oriental commodities, but the British government was also worried that the Company would provide the infrastructure for an Imperial navy based on the English

Channel. It was clear to everyone that Britain would fight to prevent that happening. The decisive element in the plot, accordingly, was the war subsidy which Ripperda offered the Emperor. The English response was to send Admiral Hosier with a fleet to blockade the Spanish treasure ships at Porto Bello. At the cost of 4000 men dead of illness, including the admiral, the blockade was sustained for most of a year, until Ripperda was disgraced.

Bishop Hoadly wrote at the time that

> no man who is the least conversant in the affairs of Europe can make any doubt but that this incident has been the only thing that has hitherto prevented a war in Europe, by depriving the Courts of Vienna and Madrid of the means of putting in execution the dangerous schemes they had projected.[51]

However, as a large part of the Spanish silver had been smuggled out of Porta Bella, it may be presumed that Hosier's blockade had more of a moral than an economic effect. No doubt it was an important part of the diplomacy which led to the conclusion of the Treaty of Seville which was later signed by Britain, France, Spain and the Netherlands. The general interest of those powers in averting a European war over the disposition of the Imperial throne on the death of Charles IV, was the dominant consideration. Nonetheless, the Ostend Company was suppressed.[52]

INTERDICTION OF CONTRABAND

The negative end of economic warfare, that of denying wealth and resources to the enemy, has the greatest hold on the twentieth-century mind, perhaps because it is further removed from the simple predatory motives of the pirate. Its exercise is of a considerable antiquity. Wallace-Hadrill has described the manner in which the Roman emperors and dynasts in the third and fourth centuries exploited the need of their Gothic invaders for food supplies from North Africa to control them, and to assimilate them. When in the early fifth century the Vandals conquered North Africa, the Romans' capacity to coerce the Goths was at an end.[53] However, only an empire as extensive and powerful as that of Rome, even when in decline, could hope to succeed in an act of economic warfare in which the economic and political focus was so diffused. Efforts by the successor states to conduct negative economic warfare on anything like that scale were universally unsuccessful. It was far more practicable to focus efforts upon denying the enemy's armed forces the specialised manufactures, raw materials, and rations needed for campaigning. Even campaigns limited to blockade of contraband, however, faced difficult if not impossible diplomatic and technical obstacles.

The strategy of interdiction of contraband could not be effective against an army which was equipped with reusable weapons, and which depended upon foraging for rations. Even when armies began to expand their logistic requirements in the early modern period, they did not automatically become vulnerable to naval action. The utility of naval forces for campaigns against logistics depends upon circumstances, and its early history is relatively limited and specific. It was most notably a strategy employed by naval powers against other naval powers. The development of the great gun-armed sailing warships in the sixteenth century strengthened the technical military reason for naval action against trade because they depended for their construction and maintenance upon the transport of materials at regular intervals to a few well-defined dockyards. Because all transport of heavy or bulky material had to be by water, and usually by sea, the obvious place to intercept the enemy's supplies was in the trade routes.

There were serious diplomatic difficulties which impeded naval action against contraband. In order to deny an enemy access to strategic *materiél*, navies had to be free to intercept, not only enemy shipping, but also the merchant ships of neutral states. Inevitably, this placed a great strain on relations with those neutrals. In 1587, Francis Drake established a blockade of traffic around the Portuguese coast to Lisbon where the first Spanish Armada against England was being fitted for sea. In justification, Lord Burleigh, Queen Elizabeth's Secretary of State, noted that

> It hath bene in all former tymes known, and is notably known to all persons that haunt the navigation and cost of Spayn that without havyng of masts, boords, cabels, cordag, pitch, tarr and copar out of the Eastlands, all Spayn is not hable to make a navy redy to carry the meanest army that can be ymagined.[54]

In November, after the destruction of the first Armada against England, London protested to the Hanseatic towns that the provision of naval stores to Spain was an 'unfriendly action'. They were urged

> to forbeare . . . upon paine of confiscation of the same goodes and the shippes upon which they should be laden, in case they should be taken with any such warlyke provision of any of her majestie's shippes or of her subjects.[55]

In June 1589 a fleet of 60 Hanseatic ships were captured as they approached the Tagus. Their cargoes, including naval stores 'which are manifestly of the proper nature of victualls and of munitions', were confiscated. The Queen's government produced precedents in defence of its action, and proclaimed that:

> Her Majesty thynketh and knoweth it by the rules of the law as well of nature as of men, and specially by the law civil, that whenever any doth directly help her enemy with succours of eny victell, armor, or any kynd of munition to enhable his shippes to maintain themselves, she may lawfully interrupt the same; and this agreeth with the law of God, the law of nature, the law of nations, and hath been in all tymes practised and in all countries betwyxt prynce and prynce, and country and country.[56]

A similar proclamation was issued in 1596, and in July 1597 Elizabeth defended English actions to the Polish ambassador by asserting

> that when kings are at war it is lawful for one side to intercept reinforcements or supplies sent to the other, and to see that no harm comes to them from that source.[57]

In 1601 the principle was proclaimed once again.

In asserting their claims, the English government were battling uphill. In the sixteenth century there was no general acceptance of the idea that a legal distinction should be drawn between general cargo and contraband. It was neither accepted that neutral states should respect the right of belligerents to seize cargoes of contraband, nor that belligerents should confine themselves to contraband control. Neutrals were concerned by the confusion which inevitably existed between the negative objectives of contraband control and the positive ends of economic warfare. They were also inconvenienced by the more comprehensive claims of belligerents which expanded contraband control to the extent of trying to besiege the enemy state, as Rome had besieged the Goths. The neutrals were right to be careful of their interests. As Professors Philip Jessup and Francis Deak remarked,

> When possible a belligerent banned all trade with the enemy; when

neutral pressure was too strong to permit him to do this, he confined himself to prohibiting trade in things most useful to the enemy.[58]

Not even English prize law accorded contraband control much legitimacy; the rapacious principle of reprisal remained at its heart. In order to enhance its claims to intercept shipping, the English crown in the sixteenth century began to use a French legal principle that the 'Robe d'enemy confisque celle d'amy', the doctrine of 'Robe' which entitled a belligerent to seize any cargo found in an enemy ship. At times French prize courts judged that the carriage of enemy cargoes also rendered a neutral ship liable to seizure. This principle might have served indirectly to justify a measure of contraband control, but apparently it was quite simply intended to make war more profitable. It proved to be unacceptable to the international community. The doctrine of Robe was renewed in the French *Ordonances de la Marine* of 1681 and 1704. English prize law was not amended by statute, the theory being more consistently sustained that the crown had no power to amend Roman Law. The English High Court of Admiralty confined itself to 'interpretation' of the law. It soon became evident, however, that the doctrine of Robe went beyond that which neutrals could accept to be valid law. The Anglo–Dutch treaty of 1674 establishing the immunity of Dutch ships from inspection when they were neutrals in English wars, the 'Free Ships make Free Goods' clause, set a precedent to which other states could aspire. Even Hambourg ships, despite the fact that the Germanic Empire was part of William of Orange's 'League of Augsburg', could only be persuaded to submit to the blockade by threats of force.

During the second and third Anglo–Dutch wars the High Court of Admiralty, in which the great Sir Leoline Jenkins presided, established many of the precedents which make up the course of Admiralty. D. J. Llewelyn Davies has shown that the interest of the court was not primarily in whether the captured cargo was contraband, but simply whether it, or the ship carrying it, was the property of the enemy. The principal aim, apparently, was to destroy the enemy's trade, and to take control of it. In determining whether cargo was or was not the property of neutrals who nominally 'owned' it, Sir Leoline was prepared to hear statistical evidence which supported a probability of fraud. The onus of disproof was on the victim, who usually presented his transaction books if he were honest. The court was interested in evidence of the ultimate destination of the cargo, wherever it may have been captured.[59]

During the seventeenth century a concept of contraband gradually developed, and the right of belligerents to intercept neutral ships carrying it was promoted. The concept, however, was not neatly or logically defined. Definition depended less upon pervasive law than upon treaties between different states which had different interests. As Jessup and Deak put it, the vicissitudes of contraband rule depended as much upon cannon, and bribery, as upon logic or learned theories.

The English generally favoured suppression of trade in contraband, but even they were not consistent in identification of naval stores as such. A treaty with France in 1677 excluded naval stores from the contraband list, no doubt because Colbert's efforts to develop the French merchant marine were so unfruitful that the English had little to fear from the French supplying an enemy navy. Freedom for English trade when France was at war would facilitate the development of the English merchant marine in the cross trades. In the late seventeenth century the domestic supply of masts and timber in England and France became difficult and the High Court of Admiralty began to condemn cargoes of naval stores, using as justification the practice in former wars. It was able to do so because relatively few neutral states were injured commercially by the inclusion of naval stores in contraband lists, but nevertheless it remained British policy to purchase the stores at invoice price plus 10 per cent and freight. The inclusion of food on contraband lists was no more consistent, although victuals and drink such as cheese and beer, which could be used to supply ships of war, were more often found by courts to be lawful prize. Grain, which might be used to feed armies, was less certain to be considered contraband. By the end of the seventeenth century the commercial treaties of European states had generally established that provisions were not contraband.[60]

Lacking a strong basis in international law, belligerents' action to deny their enemy access to contraband had to be restricted if the resentment of neutrals was to be avoided. In the sixteenth century the English had to be especially careful in dealing with French ships because of the power of France, and because Elizabeth wished to bolster French resistance to Spain's anti-Protestant crusade. In 1599 Elizabeth found it expedient to pay for the cargoes of wheat seized from Hamburg ships. The Spanish ambassador to Denmark encouraged that kingdom to protest at the seizures, and a restricted contraband list was agreed upon. The Poles were permitted to carry grain to Spain, but not material of war. In 1599 the shipping of

Venice and Tuscany was, by proclamation, made exempt from spoliation by English privateers.

Ninety years later, the attempt to intercept all neutral traffic bound for France during the War of the League of Augsburg got William III into trouble. He viewed the war as a Protestant crusade, but at the end of the seventeenth century that attitude was anachronistic. It was the realities of neutral interests and international law with which he had to cope. Locke's suggestion that internation relations existed 'in a state of nature' which Hobbes had described as 'nasty, brutish, solitary and short', was symptomatic of the breakdown of common political purposes amongst the states of Europe, which in practice meant that belligerents found few mercantile nations which were prepared to tolerate uncontested naval control of shipping.

During the campaigning seasons of 1689 and 1690 the English and the Dutch tried to enforce their convention against all French trade. William's determination, however, did not last long. In March 1689 the Danish envoys in London and the Hague presented memorials challenging the prohibition of French commerce, and in May it was announced that Sweden and Denmark intended to co-operate in convoying their trade. English and Dutch naval strength was not great enough to command Nordic respect, or to protect Nordic shipping from French reprisal. A Swedish convoy of naval stores was intercepted and brought into port, but Swedish resentment was minimised by the offer to purchase the cargoes for English use. The convention was not really enforceable, especially immediately after the battle of Beachy Head, in which an allied fleet under Torrington had to avoid a decisive encounter with a superior French fleet. Only the limitations on the ability of the Nordic states to co-operate with each other enabled William to obtain any results from his naval blockade. In 1691 and again in 1693 Denmark concluded treaties with Sweden for the joint defence of trade, but Sweden was not really prepared to co-operate. Accordingly, the northern kingdoms had to reach separate compromises with the belligerents. In 1691 Denmark seized six Dutch ships in reprisal for Danish losses, and this led to an accommodation, signed 20/30 June 1691. In May the King of Denmark had prohibited shipment to France of naval stores, and he agreed to prohibit Danish ships carrying cargoes between French ports. In the spring of 1692, in return for the payment of money in compensation for Swedish ships which had been seized, the Swedish commercial treaty of 1661 with England was renewed, apparently with the mutual understanding that it amounted to Swedish lip-service to English views on trade with France.

The controversy with the neutrals was renewed by William's attempt in 1692 to exploit the failure of the corn harvest in France. He first attempted to buy up all the northern exports for English use, England having suffered a failure in its own harvest. He issued instructions to privateers, dated 2/12 May 1693, declaring grain to be contraband. He had to withdraw before Swedish protests that summer, but in the following summer the declaration was enforced, although it was necessary to minimise the resentment of the neutrals by purchasing the cargoes. His willingness to pay compensation prevented a rupture on the question of neutral rights, but it is evident that William's attempt to dispense entirely with the right of neutrals to continue trading had failed. Having been obliged to negotiate, and to justify his actions, he had in effect enhanced the need of belligerents to observe legal forms, which amounted to an abandonment of the doctrine of 'Robe'.[61]

G. N. Clark has pointed out that the coincidence of the War of the Spanish Succession with the Great Northern War restrained the claims of states to belligerent rights. Not only was the danger of lateral escalation more than usually great, but the belligerents of one war served as neutral carriers supplying the needs of belligerents in the other. Britain greatly valued the service of Sweden in supplying naval stores. When the Treaty of Utrecht was concluded in 1713 the British commissioner, Bishop Robinson, persuaded France to agree to a provision that if either state were ever a belligerent against a third party in a future war the other could act as neutral carrier.[62] This limited move towards the principle that Free Ships make Free Goods did not significantly impede British exercise of belligerent rights later in the century when Britain's naval strength was greater.[63]

The strategic utility of naval effort against contraband trade appears to be obvious, but the actual results were not impressive. No doubt Spain was somewhat inconvenienced by English raids on supply ships during the Anglo–Spanish war of the sixteenth century, but they did not have decisive strategic significance. Drake's 1587 blockade delayed the sailing of the Armada by a year, and when it did make the voyage it was to encounter dreadful privation due to inadequate supply of barrel staves. Drake's success, limited as it was, could not be sustained. After the failure of the 1588 Armada, Spain was able to fit out three others in 1596, 1597 and 1599–1601. Their repeated failure was due to command decisions rather than to *matériel* weakness. The Spanish navy was able to sustain regular convoy operations across the Atlantic despite English efforts to deny access to naval stores.[64]

Both sides in the Anglo–Dutch wars made strenuous efforts to deny the other access to naval stores. The Dutch had geographical advantage for that purpose because they lay nearer to the Skagerrak. For the English, the most pressing problem was the shortage of masts.[65] However, neither side succeeded in disabling the other's fleet by that means.

Naval operations against the logistic needs of the enemy fleet did at least serve to precipitate naval battles in the Anglo–Dutch wars, which in turn produced political results. Both England and the Netherlands were economically dependent upon maritime trade, and hence were politically sensitive to threats against their naval power. France was less vulnerable to sea power. William III's war against France provides a measure, not only of the problem posed by neutral reaction to the exercise of seapower, but also of the utility of seapower in continental warfare. The technical naval and administrative difficulties were formidable.

William's motive for accepting the crown of England had been to acquire the services of an English army to help defend the Dutch frontiers against the armies of Louis XIV. Naval forces were of value to the extent that they contributed to the battle ashore, and the Anglo–Dutch fleet was ordered to interdict French trade with the Baltic, whence came grain needed to provision the French army. During the nine years of the war 490 letters of marque were issued to a total of 406 ships.[66] It is remarkable how similar in some respects was the strategic use of sea control during this period to that during World War I in the twentieth century. An attempt was made to ration imports into neutral Flanders. The Flemish state, however, was too decentralised to be able to control its traders, presuming that it wanted to, and England did not develop as it did in 1915 a technique for dealing directly with the foreign traders themselves. A treaty with the Spanish Netherlands and the principality of Liège stopping the trade in horses was ineffectual and had to be amended twice. The quantity of raw wool imported into the Spanish Netherlands was restricted to the amount which could be used there in manufacture, and grains were rationed. On 12/22 August 1689 a treaty was concluded between the English and Dutch stipulating a cessation of trade with France. Both the English and the Dutch governments attempted to block trade with France by means of a series of acts and *plakkaat*s. The merchant communities, however, perhaps especially the Dutch merchants, proved themselves adept at evading the controls.[67] It was found in 1694, the year that the greatest effort was made to prevent the importation by France of grain, that large quanities were still finding their way across the border by way of Aachen and elsewhere. The ration allowed the Spanish Netherlands was reduced by a third and a new system of inspection was introduced, but there was little success in stopping the flow. A renewed attempt in 1709 to blockade French supplies of Baltic grain was no more successful, defeated in part by conflict with the mercantilist motives of Dutch merchants who insisted on selling to the enemy at inflated war-time prices.

Strategy is an art of the possible, and the seventeenth century Anglo–Dutch alliance was not up to the comprehensive negative strategy employed by ancient Rome against the Goths. In the abortive Flanders operations the Anglo–Dutch strategy of logistics control converged with that of a general campaign against trade. The vastness of the latter target made the primary objective unobtainable. Seventeenth-century naval technology, and seventeenth-century political conditions, ensured its failure, but the record in the twentieth century is not much different. The convergence between trade warfare and interdiction of logistics was to be the principal characteristic of Germany's World War II 'tonnage war', in which attack on shipping was intended to undermine both the Allied war economy, and the strategic mobility of Allied armies.

In contrast to the failure of the comprehensive strategy attempted in the north, English use of naval forces to control logistics in the Mediterranean, where geography was more accommodating, had such powerful local effects that its tactical results produced systemic, strategic, results. Eighteenth-century armies had come to depend on elaborate commissariat arrangements in order to facilitate control of the soldiery. At the same time, the improvement of fortification meant that armies depended increasingly upon their siege trains. The heavy guns had to be transported by water, and water transport was preferable for bulk stores. In the Mediterranean area, it was often necessary to make use of the sea for the supply ships because there were few major rivers, and this gave navies the opportunity to influence, or even determine, the outcome of campaigns ashore. Improvements in naval architecture in the late seventeenth century, and the alliance with Portugal, enabled the governments of William III and Queen Anne to employ naval forces in the Mediterranean.

Admiral Sir Herbert Richmond credits the fleet of Admiral Russell with defeating a French assault on Barcelona in 1694 by interception of French supply ships moving along the Spanish coast. Twelve years later Admiral Leake defeated another French attack on Barcelona by the same means. This latter episode was but one part of the Duke of Marlborough's brilliant exploitation of his capacity to move logistics by sea while denying that capacity to the enemy. In 1704 English forces sent by sea to support the Duke of Savoy had been used to divert disproportionate French military resources away from the decisive campaign in the north in which the battle of Blenheim was fought. From that time, naval control of the Mediterranean was central to England's strategy for sustaining a balance of power in Europe.[68]

Scholarship on later eighteenth-century wars does not provide enough evidence to be able to make any general assessment of the extent to which naval action against seaborne logistics was a major determinant of the outcome of wars. Some observations, however, can be made. In the Northern War, which continued until Charles XII's death in 1718, the Dutch, and for the first time the British, sent fleets into the Baltic to protect their shipping. Especially important were the supplies of hemp coming from the Baltic states which had been captured by Russia. British commerce with the Baltic increased substantially despite the privateers commissioned by Sweden, and despite a retaliatory British embargo on trade to Sweden.[69]

The utility of attack on naval logistics may have been greater in the Seven Years' War, but its significance is far from clear. Paul Bamford believes that the battle of Quiberon Bay took from the French even the will to contest British control of sea communications, and that the French fleet at Brest fell into disrepair as a result of British interception of naval stores. Reconstruction could not be begun by Choiseul until Spanish involvement in the war in 1762 diverted British naval resources. In James Pritchard's opinion, however, collapse of the French naval supply organisation was not occasioned by 'the appearance of enemy vessels off the French coasts, but from the financial collapse of the government'.[70] The British navy enjoyed repeated success against the French, and took a great toll of French merchant shipping, but Pritchard has shown that French supply ships had little difficulty reaching the St Lawrence so long as that theatre of operations held any potential for France.[71] At all events, the destruction of the French Brest fleet at and after Quiberon Bay, and the subsequent loss of New France, did not prevent France continuing to be a major belligerent for two years.[72]

A decade and a half after the conquest of Canada, unavowed support by France of the American Revolution made it a difficult and dangerous task for Britain to intercept the gun runners sailing from France, and from French colonies.[73] Between 1775 and 1777 90 per cent of the 2.3 million pounds of gunpowder issued to the Continental Army was carried by munitions ships from France. This failure to control seaborne military logistics may have been a principal cause of Britain's failure to crush the revolution. The British themselves had great difficulty sustaining their forces in America during the American Revolutionary War, but as David Syrett shows, this was a result of weak administrative machinery at the beginning of the war, and shipping shortages later on.[74] The limitations imposed on strategic mobility through shipping shortages were not so much the result of French *guerre de course* as of the inadequacy of the mid-eighteenth-century shipping industry for the task. The inability of the British army to live off the land in America created an unprecedented logistical problem.

Thirty years later, on the other hand, the Iberian campaign against Napoleon was valuable to British grand strategy because Britain could move logistics by sea, whereas the French had to rely upon very inadequate roads. In northern Europe, however, the construction of canals and turnpikes made the armies of Napoleon even less vulnerable to naval control of supply than had been those of Louis XIV. That situation was so evident to the British that their naval strategy was based on entirely different, mercantilist, principles. From the 1830s railways began to be built, which in the American Civil War and the Franco–Prussian war proved to have the decisive potential for deployment and support of troops.

THE SHADOW OF MERCANTILISM

The attitude of neutrals in the seventeenth and eighteenth centuries to the suppression of contraband trade was stiffened by the fear that it was little more than a pretext for general economic warfare. In 1692 William Duncombe, British minister in Stockholm, reported that the Swedish college of commerce were concerned that if England felt free to prohibit trade with France in wartime, when it needed the neutrals as a source of supply, there would be no restraint on English policy in time of peace. It might close the Straits of Dover entirely in order to collect a toll, as Denmark did on ships entering and leaving the

Baltic, or simply as a measure of mercantilist trade war. Robert Molesworth, the English minister at Copenhagen, reported that Danish friendliness with the French

> is because they know of no other naval force able to contest the entire dominion of the sea with the English and Dutch; and they are willing to keep the dispute about that dominion undetermined between the French and us, that no laws may be laid on traffic, but that they may reap their share of the trade of the world, which they think would be but small should this point be finally decided to our advantage.[75]

Eli Heckscher has shown that mercantilism was essentially conceived as a system of power. It was the ultimate expression of sophisticated rapacity which sought the impoverishment of the enemy only insofar as it contributed to the increase of the belligerent's own wealth, which in turn multiplied the belligerent's power. It was more sophisticated than the bullionism of the Anglo–Spanish wars because it saw that the wealth a state needed for the purpose of war was derived from all trade, including trade in low-value products. Indeed the volume, not the value, of trade goods determined the scale of investment in the merchant shipping fleets which were an index of national trade and also provided the technical infrastructure for naval forces. Seaborn trade was therefore doubly valued as the source of naval power. An anonymous pamphleteer wrote in 1672:

> The undoubted Interest of England is Trade, since it is that alone which can make us either *Rich* or *Safe* for without a powerful Navy, we should be a Prey to our Neighbours, and without Trade, we could neither have sea-men or Ships.[76]

Neutrals had to insist upon limiting belligerent rights to manipulate trade. Definition of contraband was one means. Another was restriction of the right to seize general mercantile cargoes to warships guarding the entrance to a formally blockaded port. When it was in their interest to do so, as in 1711, the English admitted this restriction. The English minister to Sweden was given instructions about the legal restraints on naval war.

> If those towns were actually besieged, or blockaded, it would be allowed to be a just reason for prohibiting a trade with them, but the case is not the same in respect to a few ships of warr ordered to cruize before the ports and her Majesty does insist to have a free trade thither for her subjects.[77]

This legal nicety was a little unrealistic given the contemporary limitations in naval technology. Until the middle of the eighteenth century the blockade of even a single port for a protracted period was virtually impossible.[78] However, any specious constraint upon the capacity of belligerents to effect what might be permanent changes in economic power, and which probably would not be in the interest of neutral states which had reason to fear monopolies, was welcome.

THE SPANISH–DUTCH WAR

The prolongation into the late 1640s of the war between Spain and the Netherlands is a good, and perhaps the first, example of a war fought for mercantilist reasons by mercantilist means. It was not a war in which navies played the dominant part, but its history is important to the study of attack on maritime trade because of what it shows about the total picture of mercantilist warfare. Johnathan Israel's account of it provides an excellent example of the interaction of economic and political factors in a mercantilist struggle.[79]

Naval forces served mercantilist purposes most directly by their capacity to transport the armies which were needed to secure control of resource colonies, or obtain access to important markets. Naval action against shipping contributed to mercantilist objectives by denying to the enemy trade with their own colonies, and by blocking its re-exports. Simpler, rapacious, reasons for raiding shipping continued to provide the incentive for naval officers' and privateersmen's participation in the mercantilist war. The Netherlands employed naval forces for all these purposes.

The government of Spain, in contrast, was obliged to pursue its ends by other means. It recognised that the Spanish fleet had little chance of defeating in battle the navy the Dutch had created. Neither did direct attack across the land frontier between the Spanish Netherlands and the Netherlands Republic have any appeal. The experience of the Spanish army indicated that any attempt against the Dutch fortress line would be nothing but an expensive frustration. Accordingly, the Spanish high command decided upon an administrative campaign against Dutch trade, especially the north–south carrying trade, the rapid growth of which had in any event been the principal reason for the renewal of the war in 1621 after a nine-year's truce.

The offensive efforts of the Spanish navy were confined to raiding operations from Ostend against Dutch fisheries with the objective of forcing up the price of the Dutch staple product, herring, and from Gibraltar to undermine the economics of Dutch trading by obliging the Dutch to convoy their Mediterranean trade. The principal means by which the Spanish government sought to cripple Dutch commerce was by port embargo to deny it access to markets. The authority of the Spanish crown could be exercised in Flanders, the Franche Conté, the entire Iberian peninsula, and much of Italy. Dynastic alliance with the Emperor of the Holy Roman Empire extended Spanish influence throughout Germany. The history of this war makes it obvious that, to the Mahanist trinity of navies, trade and colonies, must be added – markets. Markets are the *sine qua non* of trade war.

Administrative conditions in the Spanish empire made it a slow business to ensure that loopholes in the embargo were stopped up, but the embargo was given priority over every other concern, including Spain's own naval forces which experienced shortages in the naval stores usually supplied by the Dutch. Ships entering Spanish-controlled harbours had to produce a certificate from a magistrate of its port of lading stating that the cargoes were not of Dutch origin or owned by Dutchmen. Spanish officials were sent repeated orders to scrutinise ships and cargoes with care. In October 1624 Philip IV set up a new customs organisation called the *almirantazzo de los paises septetrionales* which effectively closed the ports of Andalusia to Dutch commerce under any disguise. Similar success was achieved in eastern Spain where the market for northern grain was cut off and the Dutch denied access to the salt pans of la Mata and Ibiza. In Navarre and Portugal local administrations were set aside by Castilian officers who were determined to endure depression in the local markets provided the Dutch too were injured. The Dutch grain trade to Italy was partly stopped, Dutch shipping was kept out of Flanders, and in July 1625 for four years the import of Dutch produce into Flanders via the inland waterways was put to an end. The market price in Dutch cities of cheese, butter and herring fell dramatically, but the inability of the Flemish authorities to find alternative sources of food supply obliged a relaxation of the embargo with respect to cheese, butter, herring and grain, although not of sugar, wine, and other produce. In April 1629, however, the river blockade had to be abandoned because it was too injurious to Flemish commerce. The Dutch had quickly seized control of the waterways into Germany, and Spanish efforts to finance a German

Imperial navy were frustrated by the Swedish invasion of Germany in 1630. In return for establishing the Hanseatic League as the principal carrier of Baltic produce to Spain, however, Spain was able to establish resident officials in Hanseatic ports to ensure that Dutch ships and cargoes no longer could masquerade under the Hanseatic flag.

Israel writes that the Spanish embargo had depressed important branches of Dutch commerce, especially the grain trade and the textile industry, but also that the economic dislocation of war had acted in favour of some sections of the Dutch community. The farmers benefited by the existence of rival army garrisons which purchased food for cash payment, except for the period 1625–29 when the Spaniards tried to dispense with Dutch agricultural produce. Most important, the war had benefited Dutch enterprises overseas. The West India Company had been formed after the breaking of the truce, and in 1628 it captured a Spanish silver fleet. In 1630 the Dutch declared a blockade of the coast of Flanders, bringing down on their heads the protests of neutrals, and established themselves in the Pernambuco region of northern Brazil.[80] In 1639 the Spanish navy suffered two shattering defeats, off Pernambuco, and in the Downs. France joined the war in Flanders against Spain. In 1640 Catalonia revolted and Portugal broke away from the crown of Castile.

The re-establishment of Dutch trade with Portugal, however, did not put an end to the effectiveness of the Spanish embargo. Spanish naval forces in Flanders continued to exact great losses on Dutch shipping and fishing, and Dutch shipping and insurance rates rose to their highest point during the war. The hardship this caused began to find a stronger voice and more listeners because of the growing realisation during the early 1640s that the West India Company could not make a profit while fighting Spain and Portugal in Brazil. In 1643, a Dutch expedition to Chile ended in fiasco and by 1645 West India Company shares reached half their 1640 value. Simultaneously the Calvanist, 'Counter-Remonstrants', war party lost political power in the town councils of Holland. In 1648 the Treaty of Munster was concluded between Spain and the Netherlands, forced through, according to Israel, 'almost entirely owing to the pressure of the great commercial centres of Holland'.

Because of the decentralised nature of the seventeenth-century state, even in such comparatively absolutist states as France and Spain, it is no surprise that it was the intimidating effect the mercantilist strategy had upon merchants which led to the realisation of the political objectives. States were badly equipped themselves to appreciate the economic effects of a campaign against their trade, unless it was brought to the attention of the government forcefully by merchants' protests. The decentralised nature of the state economy meant that local shortages or local trade depressions would have relatively little effect upon the overall national economy, and as was the case during the Spanish war, the depression in overseas trade could be balanced by prosperity in agriculture. Accordingly, the effectiveness of the strategy would depend upon the political importance within the state of the overseas traders. In the seventeenth century the Netherlands was clearly the state most vulnerable to the strategy because of the importance of Dutch traders in the States General. Where traders had such influence, the strategy had some prospect of success, because it did not have to attempt complete severance of trade. Merchants are intent on making a profit and complain as soon as profit-making becomes difficult. Obviously, it is easier for an enemy to make trading unprofitable than it is to prevent it altogether. Few governments in the seventeenth century, however, were as responsive as was that of the Netherlands to the complaints of merchants. England, despite its growing importance in trade, and despite the representation of its townspeople in parliament, was not in the seventeenth century an easy target for mercantilist attack, as was to be shown during the Anglo–Dutch wars. It also proved itself, however, to be the greater naval power, a fact which naturally complicates the evidence.

The effects of the limitations on the power of central government were not all antagonistic to the use of trade control as a means of coercion, although they did favour a mercantilist objective. It was the very limitation upon the power of the Spanish central government in the seventeenth century which more than anything else made the employment of a strategy of trade control desirable. The Spanish government's inability to raise a substantial tax revenue from its independent-minded subjects for the purpose of equipping armies, without a resort to the Cortes which the crown wished to avoid, made it all the more good policy to exploit the established royal authority over customs. Even that exercise of royal power, however, had its dangers. The Catalonian and the Portuguese revolts may be attributed to the loss of trade and colonies occasioned by Castilian imposition of wartime customs restraints, and by Dutch attack.

The long-term results of the Spanish–Dutch war were not consistent with the short-term effects of Spain's economic campaign. The Dutch share of trade to Spain continued to grow, as did Dutch trade to the Indian Ocean. The Treaty of Munster continued the wartime closure of the Schelt river to trade, thus ensuring that for three centuries, until after the treaty of 1839, Antwerp was kept from replacing Amsterdam as the principal centre for north European commerce.[81] Spain did limit Dutch penetration of its American empire, but that only left the field clear for the French and English to fight for its control in the eighteenth century.

THE ANGLO–DUTCH WARS

Mercantilist considerations ensured that the maritime states of Europe engaged in continual warfare for the next century and a half. Administrative means were used to divert trade, most notably in 1651 when Cromwell's Navigation Act consolidated earlier legislation intended to promote the English shipping industry, and thereby to enable English woollen manufactures to find markets across the North Sea. Administrative means, however, could result in war. The Navigation Act was intended to undermine the capacity of the Dutch to offer lower freight rates by reducing their role in the cross-trades. It led directly to the first Anglo–Dutch war.[82] 'What matter this or that reason?' remarked one of Cromwell's Generals-at-Sea, George Monk. 'What we want is more of the trade which the Dutch now have.'[83]

The Anglo–Dutch mercantilist wars were pursued primarily by naval means, although in the end the army of France was to be the decisive factor. English attacks on Dutch shipping injured the very Dutch trading interests for which the war was being fought, and in doing so helped to make possible the competition of English merchants in European markets. Geographic factors enhanced the capacity of the English to defend their own trade, while attacking that of the Dutch, much of which normally passed through the English Channel. Dutch admirals had to find necessarily imperfect means of combining the tasks of convoying trade and seeking battle with the enemy.[84] With less shipping to defend, and much of that sailing from western ports, the English could concentrate on offensive action. A contemporary saying was that the Dutch were a mountain of gold making war on one of iron. In 1665, during the Second Dutch war in which France was allied with the Netherlands, the Venetian ambassador to France, Marc Antonio Giustinian, reported that

> The abundance of ships which the English possess permits them at the same time to trade and to fight. The Dutch and French suffer from greater deprivations, losing the profits of trade and being forced to consume themselves with expenses, without hope of gains.

During the winter of 1652–53 the Dutch successfully blocked London's coal supply by attacking the colliers sailing down the coast from Newcastle. The English navy, however, captured large numbers of enemy merchant ships. Ralph Davis writes that the lowest estimate of prizes taken by the English in the First Dutch war was 1000 vessels, against which the Dutch took relatively very few. The English merchant marine was transformed. English tonnage nearly doubled, and their Dutch prizes were ships built along more commercially valuable lines than were traditional English designs. Losses to Spain in Cromwell's religious war somewhat reduced the English gains from the Dutch, but total English tonnage rose from 115 000 tons in 1629 to 340 000 tons in 1686.[85]

Dutch commercial houses had great political power. Accordingly, the Netherlands were a good target for a strategy of trade interdiction. Technical naval problems, however, prevented the English being able to exploit to the full the Dutch Achilles' heel. The English fleet could not depend upon adequate logistic support to sustain a protracted blockade. Although John Hawkins had experimented with the deployment of squadrons to blockade Portugal in the 1590s, the number of ships involved had been small. English and Dutch fleets in the 1650s and 1660s, by contrast, could include more than a hundred ships each. It was the inability of the Navy Board to supply victuals in good condition to so large a number of ships that led to the formation of the Victualling Office in 1654. The administrative strain, and the wear and tear on ships which is produced by blockade operations, continues to be one of its principal disadvantages.

The ability of the merchant, and of the state, to survive naval attacks on trade was to some extent the result of the ponderous nature of the trade organisation of the early modern period which enabled it to outlast the more evanescent threat of naval action. The ocean trades of the sixteenth to eighteenth centuries sailed in annual cycles. On some routes, there was only one well established time of year for departure from home port, and on no route would it be expected to make more than two or three return trips per year.

Sailing dates were derived from annual weather cycles, but nonetheless there was considerable slack in the system. Merchants were accustomed to stockpiling goods for extended periods and so could endure protracted delays, or even the cancellation of one year's enterprise. The out-bound ocean trades, therefore, were in a relatively strong position *vis-à-vis* a naval blockading force which might be able to keep station for a month, but would then have to leave the coast unguarded for weeks. Where the ocean traders were more vulnerable was in the return voyage when ships would be expected at certain seasons. Blockading forces could time their own cycles in order to be able to intercept the home-coming merchant fleets. However, defending naval forces could do so as well. In effect, the expected arrival of the ocean trades was the signal for the encounter of hostile naval forces. The coastal traders were more vulnerable to blockade because they were less accustomed to keeping large stockpiles, and were in any case the suppliers of the staples which were needed in large quantities. Dutch naval action against England's coasting trade, however, had not obtained political effects anywhere near commensurate to the effort put into it.

The political effects of the seizure of Dutch shipping contributed to Cromwell's ability to bring the First Dutch war to a close, but Dutch losses did not prevent the outbreak of the Second Dutch war. On 20 April 1665, Giustinian wrote:

> Since the declaration of war it is estimated that sixty merchantmen of this nation and Dutch ships have fallen into the hands of the English, a very serious loss to the people of these two nations who raise loud cries to heaven at the injuries which they suffer. It is not easy to see any remedy at hand, indeed they fear even greater perils.[86]

For both sides, however, it is apparent that operations against trade were most significant as means of obliging the enemy to offer battle, and that it was the outcome of battles which carried political force. When Charles II attempted to lay up the battle fleet and depend entirely on commerce raiders, the Dutch raided the Medway and burned many of the battleships 'in ordinary'. The humiliated English sued for peace.

The first two Anglo–Dutch wars had served to defeat Dutch efforts to obstruct English commercial development, but they had left the mercantile wealth of the Netherlands virtually intact. The third round of fighting which started in 1672 as a result of the Anglo–French Secret Treaty of Dover was to produce a more dramatic change in national fortunes, largely because the French changed sides, for mercantilist reasons. Louis XIV's Finance Minister, Jean Colbert, had estimated that the Dutch had 16 000 merchant ships, the English 4000 and France but 200. For a decade, he attempted to develop New France into a resource colony capable of supporting a French marine. Eventually tiring of the drain of resources with little in return, Colbert decided to emulate the English by attacking Dutch shipping directly.[87] English and French fleets operated together in the Channel, but the decisive force in the war was the French army. The war was a nightmare for the Dutch, who only survived a French invasion attempt by giving military authority to William of Orange, who opened the dykes to flood the invasion route. Immediate needs of territorial defence prevented them giving much attention to trading and colonial interests.

Although French shippers eventually were able to pose a serious competition to the Dutch in the Mediterranean, it was the English who gained most from the war. English parliamentary pressure led to Charles II concluding a separate peace with the Netherlands. The Treaty of Westminster of 1674 was in the long term of great value to the Dutch, in the middle years of the eighteenth century when England was at war with France. In the shorter term, in the interval between the signing of the Anglo–Dutch treaty and the conclusion of peace between France and the Netherlands in 1678, English shippers were able to profit by the 'free ships make free goods' clause. Ralph Davis shows that the English rapidly moved into the carrying trade, displacing Dutch shippers. During a three-year period before the war, between 1668 and 1671, an average of only seven English ships had entered the Baltic each year, in comparison to 158 Dutch. In the three-year period following the Treaty of Westminster, between 1675 and 1678, the English found it profitable to send an average of 128 ships per year, while the Dutch sailed no more than 28. Once peace was re-established between France and the Netherlands, Dutch shippers returned to the ascendancy, sailing an average of 179 ships per year in the period 1679 to 1682. The English felt they had suffered commercially by the war. In fact, however, their Baltic trade now employed 47 ships per year, an increase of nearly 700 per cent over the pre-war period. The Dutch had also lost colonies to the English, especially New Amsterdam which was finally and permanently transferred to England.[88]

THE ANGLO–FRENCH 100-YEAR MERCANTILIST TRADE WAR

King William's war was the first military phase of a great mercantilist trade war between England and France which lasted until the destruction of the First French Empire in 1815. Charles II had renewed the Navigation Act when he returned to England in 1660, and the apparatus for exploiting a protected colonial trade was developed with the Staple Act of 1663 and the Plantation Duties Act of 1673. The results appeared to be those intended. Between 1660 and 1688, according to Davis, the English merchant marine doubled in size. Between 1663–69 and 1699–1701 English export trade expanded by about 56 per cent, and 30 per cent of the whole was re-export trade in colonial products.[89] War with France could be used to further that growth by seizing control of the colonial sources of profitable trade goods, and by directly reducing the size of the enemy merchant fleets. It has already been shown that William III's objectives were not mercantilist. He was a politician with little interest in commerce, and he was a soldier who needed to contain the military power of France. His English and Dutch subjects, however, were acutely aware of the association between economic and military power. William III's employment of naval forces was at least compatible with mercantilist objectives, although he was more receptive to what G. N. Clark refers to as the predatory instincts of his English subjects, taking the form of attacks on shipping, than he was to the more acquisitive traditions of the Dutch. His attempts to block supplies to the French army also served mercantilist purposes because it was thought at the time that English economic growth depended on a virtual elimination of trade with France.

What William III only pursued indirectly, subsequent British administrations sought conscientiously. The observation Carl Marie von Clausewitz was to make when writing during the Napoleonic wars, that 'war is simply a continuation of political intercourse, with the addition of other means', is most evidently applicable to the interaction of economic and political motives which determined British foreign policy in the eighteenth century.[90] Nicolas Magens, a German financier in London, wrote in 1775 in his *Essay on Insurance*:

> when we examine to the bottom of the thing, it appears very evident, that sea battles are fought not so much to kill people, as to be masters of trade, whereby people live; and by stopping their

supplies, to compel our enemies in the end to live in friendship with us.[91]

Only about half the century saw the countries and their transient allies actually at war, but the mercantilist struggle was continued in war and peace until the advent of *laissez faire* economic principles in the last quarter of the eighteenth century began to draw distinctions between the strategies for wealth and those for security.

The Dutch were secondary players in this struggle. The wars of the second half of the seventeenth century had served the mercantilist purposes of France and England by reducing Dutch economic pre-eminence. English shipping had moved into trades hitherto dominated by the Dutch, and French shipping had acquired markets, especially those in the Mediterranean. Perhaps more importantly, the cost of the wars themselves had undermined the profitability of Dutch business. Alice Clare Carter observes that the war debts of Dutch towns were serviced by increased customs charges, which produced price and wage inflation, and priced the labour-intensive aspects of Dutch business out of the markets. The Dutch were drawn into the war of the Spanish Succession in 1701 because of the desperate need to prevent France acquiring sovereignty in Flanders, or command of the economic resources of the Spanish empire, but they were dominated by their more powerful English allies. After the Treaty of Utrecht was concluded in 1713, the Dutch sought with some success to avoid war for the rest of the eighteenth century, and profited from the need of belligerents for neutral shipping. The part taken by the Netherlands in the suppression of the Ostend East India Company in 1726–30, a mercantilist move to destroy competition, was an exception. On the whole, the Dutch had to be content with a more passive foreign policy, which was possible because the need for neutral Dutch shipping ensured there would not be a renewal of French invasion threats. The British also found it expedient to tolerate the activity of Dutch shippers because it was a guarantee against the danger of French occupation of Flanders and Netherlands ports from which Britain could be injured by attacks on trade, or by invasion.[92]

Following the failure of Colbert's efforts to create a French commercial and maritime empire to replace that of the Dutch, Louis XIV's objectives were primarily dynastic and political. These, however, had profound economic implications. The English had profited by the earlier defeat of the Dutch in which a major role had been played by the French army, but they needed the economic and military survival of the Netherlands to prevent France acquiring 'universal monarchy' in Europe. Of no less importance was the question of the succession to the throne of Spain upon the death of Charles II of Spain in 1701. The prospect of a Bourbon successor presented the threat, amongst many threats, that France would gain control of the trade of Spain and of the Spanish empire.

The wars of Louis XIV are notoriously a showcase for virtuoso French *guerre de course*. After the Battle of La Hogue of May 1692, which put an end to plans to invade England, the French attempted to employ attack on shipping as a major coercive force. Marshal Vaubon made himself the spokesman of the privateering interests. He invested his personal capital with privateer *armateurs*, as did many French courtiers. Unlike Colbert who hoped that attack on Dutch shipping would permit the expansion of French trade, Vaubon viewed peaceful French commerce as an irrelevance. His purpose was not directly mercantilist. The *guerre de course* instead should provide for France at once a means of coercing England, a source of wealth, and a source of needed imports. In his *Memoire sur la Caprerie*, 30 November 1695, he urged that the legal impediments to profit-taking by French *armateurs*, and their backers, should be reduced by changes in prize court procedures, and taxation.[93] When a grain famine led to a fall in tax revenue the French went so far as to lay up the battle fleet altogether and rely entirely upon privateers. State resources were put behind the privateer effort, although Vaubon's recommendation that three naval squadrons should support the privateers was rendered impossible by the run-down of the royal fleet.

Dependence upon private commercial motive reduced the strategic and macro-economic utility of the French *guerre de course* because *armateurs* did not co-operate with each other.[94] However, the Anglo–Dutch losses were substantial. G. N. Clark lends his support to the estimate of a contemporary Venetian that in the period 1688–95 French privateers captured more than 900 English and Dutch ships.[95] The English Admiralty itself claimed the losses had amounted to 4000 ships, but Ralph Davis discounts that evidence because the Admiralty only produced it in 1707 as 'proof' that its convoy arrangements had improved. Samuel Pepys states that some 500 ships were lost during the early years of the war, and all the rest were taken in the last four years after the French battle fleet had been laid up. The greatest disaster occurred in 1693 when faulty naval intelligence led to the loss of a convoy sailing to Smyrna. This led to a revolt of the

Commons, who tacked onto the 1694 Land Tax bill a requirement that naval forces be created for the defence of trade.[96] In the next two years the Admiralty improved its system and, although French privateering activity expanded rapidly, the Levant Company at any rate suffered no further losses.[97] English privateers had also had their successes, which offset those of the French. 1289 French prizes were condemned in the High Court of Admiralty during the first phase of the war.[98]

Geoffrey Symcox believes that the strategic effectiveness of the French *guerre de course* was assessed unfairly by historians because of the Mahanian dictum that commerce raiding could not decide the outcome of wars.[99] The more conservative view expressed by G. N. Clark was that the attacks on shipping did not further the strategic purposes of either side, but were mutually war-losing. Clark wrote:

> there is a general consensus of contemporary and later judgments that, on all sides, the nations ended the war in part because, indecisive as the campaigns had been, economic resources were worn out. It would be vain to look for any discussion by the statesmen of that war, how such a prevention of a military solution, could be averted in future . . . [but] it may be inferred from the general course of events in the next two generations that the war on French trade had, in its outcome, disappointed.[100]

The peace of Ryswick was concluded on 20 September 1697, and when war broke out again in 1701 over the succession to the throne of Spain neither England nor the Netherlands renewed its war on French trade immediately. When later England led the Dutch into making an effort against French trade it was, in Professor Clark's view, less vigorous, and occasioned less protest from neutrals. Admiral Rooke's 1702 attack on the *flota* in Vigo harbour, and Admiral Wager's 1708 action at sea against the Spanish treasure galleons, were a return to a bullionist strategy, which had less impact on relations with neutrals. As we have seen, the spoliation of Spanish treasure was counterproductive from the mercantilist point of view as it undermined England's objective of developing trade with Spain. The effort in 1709 to blockade French supplies of Baltic grain proved to be no more useful.

French privateers continued their depredations upon English shipping after 1701, although they no longer were supplied from the royal arsenals. The English Admiralty acknowledged that 1146 English ships had been lost by 1707. The merchants claimed that the figure was much higher, and began a serious clamour in the House of Lords. Ralph Davis suggests a minimum loss of 2000 ships to French privateers, but John Bromley puts the figures up as high as 4544 prizes with a further 2118 ships ransomed.[101] Jonathan Swift wrote in his 1712 pamphlet 'The Conduct of the Allies' that losses to French privateers 'hath been . . . of infinite Disadvantage to us, not only by the perpetual Losses we have suffered to an immense Value, but by the general Discouragement of Trade, on which we so much depend'.[102] The British ministry withstood the merchants' protests until 1707, but in the end Parliament forced upon them an act 'for the better securing the Trade of this Kingdom by Cruisers and Convoys'. It stipulated that 43 ships were to be earmarked for trade defence. Freight and insurance rates, according to John Bromley, were not greatly affected by the passage of the act. Insurance rates homeward from Venice were the same in 1710 as they had been outbound in November 1707, although much less than they had been homebound that month. Freight rates homeward from Barbados stayed above £6 per ton until 1711, reaching £8–£10 per ton in 1708 and 1710, which was three times the peacetime rate. The passage of the act, however, did defuse the political crisis, and the government did not have to make any further concessions as a result of French successes at sea.

As the century advanced, it became increasingly clear that mercantilism, coercion, and simple rapacity, were the dominant motives for attack on shipping. The manner in which privateers, especially those of France, came to accept ransoms for their prizes indicates that very little consideration was given to the possibility of denying supplies to the enemy. Anglo–Dutch blockade forces made it difficult for French privateers to bring in their prizes for condemnation. Accordingly, they adopted the practice of accepting a ransom for all but the biggest prizes while still at sea. The privateersmen earned a profit by taking ransoms, but the effect on the enemy of their depredations was reduced to the level of a war tax. The merchants' sufferings might evoke pity, and could in the long term lead to important loss in government revenue, but in the short term they could hardly make the enemy's prosecution of the war impossible. The French government forbade acceptance of ransoms for the largest prizes because their cargoes were needed, but apparently that fact should not be taken as an indication that the Anglo–Dutch blockade was a war-winner. Pitt's Privateers Act of 1759 (32 Geo 2, c.25) made ransoming of prizes an act of piracy, not because it conflicted with economic war strategy but because it was leading to problems with neutrals.

The easy availability on the London market of war-risk insurance for ships of all nations makes it clear that the British had come to regard a limited, predatory and mercantilist, strategy as the only practicable objective of sea control. Many factors go into determining the extent of the impact attacks on trade may have, but certainly the existence of an effective way of spreading the risk through marine war-risk insurance is one of the most important determinants of an ability to survive attack. In the eighteenth century London became the principal centre for marine insurance. London insurance markets kept, not only the British merchant marine at sea, but also that of France. The loss of the Smyrna convoy in 1693 had caused many bankruptcies in London insurance circles, but from that experience London learned how to cover war risk by accepting insurance on vessels engaged in different trades. French insurers were not able to make that compensation because their business, instead of being located in a centre of world trade, operated out of a number of smaller ports, each of which specialised in a different trade. Consequently, French and Spanish ships were insured abroad in wartime. Because the Dutch preferred to supply the French with neutral Dutch bottoms rather than sell them insurance, that insurance was often taken out in London. There was some feeling that it was unpatriotic to send compensation to the enemy owners of ships taken by British naval forces, but there were no second thoughts about accepting the wartime premiums. Acceptance of insurance on enemy vessels was made illegal in 1748, but 1748 was the last year of one phase of the Anglo–French war, and the legislation was not renewed until 1793.[103]

In effect, the war on trade not only lost any strategic function of denying the enemy cargoes, but also lost the capacity to drive enemy traders out of business. British insurance kept the French merchantmen at sea, and British naval forces served British interests by keeping insurance premiums high. The capture of a French ship did indeed bring about the transfer of the flag to Britain, but the financial sufferings of the French ship-owners was limited by the insurance they were paid. It could be reinvested in other ships which in their turn might be captured by British cruisers and privateers. As British markets for mercantile tonnage became glutted, prices fell, and French shippers would replace lost tonnage with purchases from British dealers. Shippers could instruct agents in London to buy back from their captors the captured ships. Together with the practice of privateers of ransoming captives while still at sea, the marine insurance system ensured that war operations against shipping became a sophisticated system designed to funnel the profits of a lively international commerce into the pockets of the merchants of the more successful state.[104]

The famous work by George Beer on British colonial policy revealed the difficulty the British government experienced in controlling trade with the enemy.[105] Richard Pares's more recent work has shown that the apparent difficulties were, at least in part, the result of mercantilist policies.[106] The conduct of mercantilist trade war required the British Treasury Board, the Board of Trade, and the Admiralty, to make pragmatic decisions. When in 1739 Britain and Spain drifted once again into war, in part because of the inability of the Spanish government to control the privateer *guarda costas* which were preying on British shipping, British efforts at blockade were directed primarily at facilitating British trade to Spanish settlements in the West Indies, by seizing Spanish shipping and by destroying the harbours from which the *guarda costas* operated. In 1739 Admiral Vernon attacked Porto Bello and destroyed its fortifications so that it could not be used for the annual galleons fair. Queen Anne's act for encouraging privateers had a clause safeguarding the smuggling trade to Spanish America, continuing the restraint ordered in 1707 against marauding activity in the Spanish settlements between Rio de la Hacha and Chagre. The galleons were successfully blockaded into Carthagena, except in 1744, but the export to Spain of British finished products was excluded from the 1740 ban on trading with the enemy.

When France joined the war, a primary British objective became interdiction of French colonial trade so that British merchants could dominate the European market for colonial produce. The re-export of West Indian rum and sugar was a valuable aspect of French trade, and as it undercut British prices, British planters were eager to carry on their policy of ruining their French competitors 'by other means'. The French West Indian Islands were peculiarly vulnerable to blockade, and British raiders blocked direct shipments from France of provisions for the French West Indies. However, export to the French colonies of victuals from British colonies in North America was only prohibited, as it was in 1740, when there was a need to stockpile for an intended military operation. No restraint was placed on the import into Britain of French wine. It was recognised that French merchants had to be permitted some sales on the British market if they were to be able to finance imports from Britain. Virginia and Maryland were licensed to sell tobacco to France.

Analysis of mercantilist strategy has to cope with the limitations of eighteenth-century government. Mercantilist trade war was clearly a strategy rooted in the instincts of people who had not yet learned to find value in injuring an enemy unless the result was at the same time of direct profit. Those instincts could be difficult to control for the ends of the state. Nowhere was the effect of political decentralisation more evident than in the inability of the British government to stop trading with the enemy, even to the extent that that appeared desirable to mercantilist strategic ideas. Eighteenth-century constitutional thinking and administrative practice placed severe limits upon the ability of government in Britain to impose its laws. It was high treason to 'aid and comfort' the King's enemies (25 Edward III) but that was not an adequate deterrent because selling goods to the enemy on favourable terms was held to injure the enemy. In the reign of William and Mary it was made high treason to export arms and ammunition to the French, but the act expired with the war. It was renewed in the next (3 and 4 Anne c.14), but not subsequently. Having established the need for such temporary enactments, there could not be said to be any customary law about trade with the enemy, and such prohibitions as were made by royal proclamation did not have the same force. A merchant trading with the enemy stood to have his goods condemned as a lawful prize if taken by a privateer or warship, but so long as the goods were not contraband weapons of war he was only held to be guilty of a 'high misdemeanor' which incurred little penalty. Furthermore, convictions were almost unobtainable, especially in the colonial courts which had jurisdiction over misdemeanours. The difficulty was increased by the need to prove that a merchant had actually completed a trade transaction; it was not enough to prove that he intended to undertake trade with the enemy for in English law the intention to commit a crime was not itself a crime.

Besides the legal pitfalls, the government was faced with the collusion of colonial officials in those colonies which could profit by trading with the enemy. The smuggling trade from Jamaica to Spanish America was actively supported by colonial administration in peacetime and war. North American colonists used every possible subterfuge to permit their trade with the French colonies, and were sometimes helped by customs officers who were venal, though they were often non-existent in the smaller ports. Colonial governors issued flags of truce to merchants to return exchanged prisoners of war, with permission to off-set the expense of the voyage by selling their cargoes to the enemy. Often the prisoners were doled out in ones or twos to provide for all the ships wishing to make the passage. Another trick was to arrange a collusive capture of a ship by an enemy privateer which would then sell the ship back to the owner for a nominal sum. It was impossible to prevent export to the neutral West Indian islands, and from there, perhaps after a collusive sale of the ship, or the naturalisation of the ship's captain, the cargo could be smuggled into the enemy port where the local governor might 'force' it to be sold. Only the British sugar planters had an interest in stopping traffic with the French islands, in order to protect their markets from French competition. The inability of the government to ensure that all the colonies were enforcing the proclamations against trading ensured that there was tremendous public opposition to enforcement where it was effective, as in Ireland. Ireland depended heavily upon its trade in salt beef to the navies and colonies of the world. It was a terrible hardship to cut off the trade, and yet it was not possible either to countenance it, or to purchase all the production for government use.

As the eighteenth century progressed, and the British navy and merchant marine increased their size and relative strength, losses inflicted on British shipping by the French *guerre de course* gradually diminished in scale. The political significance of French attacks on British trade fell accordingly. No doubt competition for political influence by British shipping interests, City insurance brokers and underwriters, and privateering interests affected the trend. Lucy Sutherland's account of the business dealings of William Braund show the extent to which an individual businessman might have investments in more than one of those aspects of the affair.[107] In the opening three years of the 1739–48 war Spanish ships effected little damage to British trade. When France joined the war in 1742 shipping losses increased, to a level of 500 ships per year. The *Gentlemen's Magazine* listed losses totalling well over 3000 British ships taken by the enemy during the war. Nevertheless, this number did not represent an increased loss over that suffered in the period 1702–12 in proportion to the much expanded British merchant fleet. In the Seven Years' War between 1756 and 1763 according to C. P. Crowhurst, no doubt in part because of improvements in convoy organisation, there was little protest in Britain at merchant shipping losses.[108] The 3386 ships which were estimated lost during the American Revolutionary War represented, because of the increased size of the British merchant marine, a loss-rate of half that suffered in 1702–12.[109]

Scholarship has not yet come to a conclusion about the utility of mercantilist trade war, or rather it has come to several conflicting ones. The complex motives which lay behind the operations against merchant shipping makes it difficult to assess the success or failure of the campaigns. Michael Howard observes that the appearance in France early in the eighteenth century of anti-mercantilist economic treatises indicates that the French had discovered that it was difficult to make a profit out of warfare.[110] There continued to be advocates of *guerre de course* in France. The Comte de Broglie, French ambassador in London, wrote in 1731 his opinion that trade attack should be the central focus of French naval strategy. He was primarily interested in the coercive effect of trade warfare, although he certainly was not in conflict with the predatory objectives of Vaubon: 'A captured vessel belonging to a merchant or to one of the English companies makes the nation cry out more than does the loss of ten battles'. He urged that the French fleet be broken up into cruising squadrons which could be deployed in support of the privateers. After the unsatisfactory battle of Toulon in February 1744, Maurepas, the minister of the marine, did just that with the naval forces in the Mediterranean.[111] De Broglie, however, did not claim that attacks on British trade could serve French mercantilist purposes.

Carl Swanson shows in a recent work that the entry of France into the war in 1740 reduced England's commercial prosperity to an extent which probably was not offset by the wartime profits of privateers.

> England's imports and exports fluctuated with the vicissitudes of the prize war. In the first phase of the conflict, the War of Jenkin's Ear, England's total trade with her American Colonies was affected very little. The limited nature of the Anglo–Spanish prize actions did not seriously interrupt the British Empire's commerce. In fact, exports and imports were actually larger in 1741 and 1743 than they had been in 1740, the first full year of the conflict. France's entry into the conflict signaled a sharp escalation of the prize war. This produced a marked decline in the volume of England's colonial commerce. Exports from the British West Indies to the mother country fell by 17.6 per cent in 1744. English

imports from North America registered a decline of 24.9 percent. Colonial imports also suffered. Caribbean purchases from England decreased by £162,681 sterling (official prices – a decline of 36.6%) while North American consumption of British goods dropped by £201,511 (official prices – a decline of 23.3%) . . . England's total trade with her colonies declined even more in 1745, the busiest year of the prize war. British commerce revived in the later stages of the conflict, but it did not return to pre-war levels until after the peace of Aix-la-Chapelle.[112]

James Riley, however, in his recent work on the economic and financial toll on France during the Seven Years' War, has concluded that the impact of war on trade has been grossly exaggerated by those who regarded only the sudden drop in trade movement at the outbreak of war. Throughout the eighteenth century the volume of French trade grew steadily, perhaps at a faster rate than did that of Britain. The dramatic fluctuations apparent in the graphs depicting French maritime trade are to be explained by the compensatory activity of merchants who frequently had to cope with maritime war. In anticipation of war, trade would be artificially expanded in order to secure a stockpile; on the outbreak of war, merchants would withdraw their assets from the sea; but with the return of peace they would again rush to build up stocks and to fill overdue orders. France did lose large numbers of merchant ships to *guerre de course*. Marseilles records show that 688 Marseilles and Provençal ships were lost during the period 1744–49, 716 in the period 1755–63 and 424 during the period 1778–83. During the Seven Years' War marine insurance rose from 2–4 per cent to as high as 50–60 per cent. The incidents of bankruptcy amongst the merchants of Marseilles, however, indicates that the economic problems of maritime war could be supported by the community. In fact, bankruptcy peaked in 1730 and 1744, years of peace. During the active phase of the War of the Austrian Succession bankruptcies declined. After a high in 1755 before the Seven Years' War reached the Mediterranean, the rate of bankruptcy continued to decline during the war. Because of French invisible earnings, the French balance of trade remained favourable throughout the war.[113]

The relatively small insurance premiums charged on British shipping even in wartime indicates the extent to which business could accommodate itself to war. Premiums on English East Indies voyages in the 1680s rose to eight guineas per cent, reduced to six if the ship accepted convoy. Homeward from Alexandretta, insurance was two guineas per cent in peacetime, and five in the war years of 1710–12. Insurance from London to Leghorn which in the 1730s was only one and a half guineas per cent, increased in 1739 on the outbreak of war with Spain to six or eight guineas per cent. The wine trade from London to Madeira paid 6 per cent premiums during the Seven Years' War, reduced to 3 per cent if the ship sailed in convoy. Ralph Davis concludes:

> it seems evident that the wartime rise in freight rates, coupled with the probability that those ships that did venture to sea would secure fuller cargoes in war than in peace, far more than covered all the possible risks and costs which arose out of the danger of losing a ship to the enemy.[114]

The British parliamentary government, which was deeply committed to mercantilist growth, had been a good target for the French *guerre de course*, although it was found in the end to be inadequate to defeat Britain. France was much less vulnerable because of its predominantly continental orientation, and strong agricultural base. Neither the French nor the Spanish government were especially sensitive to the problems of merchants. It appears that British raiding of Bourbon shipping in the periods between 1739–48 and 1755–62 failed to disable the enemy in any vital way, and it did not create intolerable political pressure to seek an accommodation with Britain. Apparently 69 of the 118 neutral ships Spain registered to carry silver home from New Spain were captured between May 1740 and June 1745, but Spain proved to be capable of getting along without the treasure. Richard Pares, the premier authority on this campaign, writes that the impact of British marauding upon the ability of the French to pursue the war was no greater.

> The combined value of imports and exports to the French colonies, which had risen to its highest at 24 million livres in 1743, was reduced to 7 in 1748, although the war was finished half-way through that year. In the years 1753 to 1755 it rose well above 30 millions, but fell below 8 in 1758 and 1759 and below 4 in 1760. The next year it rose to nearly 7, and in the last year of the war almost touched 15.

He concluded:

> The Seven Years War demonstrates to my mind the impotence of

> blockade and colonial conquests to break the will of France. The French colonial trade did not slowly decline until in 1762 it reached vanishing point and so forced the Government to make peace. On the contrary, it collapsed quickly in the spring and summer of 1757, and in the last two years of the war it was reviving a little. The colonial merchants simply went out of business, and contented themselves with getting home their old debts if they could . . . [The French Minister Choiseul] proved, with the circumscribed help of the neutrals, how easily a nation can live without colonial trade, and even without colonies. Pursued by the imprecations of the seaports and manufacturing towns, he continued a losing war at sea and kept his hold of Germany the better to recover the colonies and trade of France. If she made peace in 1763 on terms not unworthy of her, it was because her Minister would not yield to a form of pressure which only touched the circumference of her economic life.[115]

It was unfortunate for Britain, and for the advocates of sea power, that naval force and the economic strength it produced could rarely be translated into political influence without the agency of an army. In the war of the Spanish Succession England's most necessary victories were won by the armies of the Duke of Marlborough in Germany and Flanders. The very scale of Britain's naval victories in the Seven Years' War serves only to emphasise their relative political insignificance in the short term. The military campaign in Europe had not been mounted or directed on a scale equal to those of Marlborough, and to the European neighbours of France it appeared that Britain had not played a major part in achieving it. Once the immediate threat was passed, Britain's wartime subsidies were far less influential than had been Marlborough's armies. In the years of 'peace' which followed, the Duc de Choiseul was careful to avoid posing any threat to the German states. As a result, Britain's attempts to renew its alliances with Prussia and Austria, or to conclude one with Russia, proved futile. The subsidies were only influential while they were being paid, and the continental states had seen that British attacks on French trade and French colonies did not arrest the French army in the field. Without an army, Britain was largely without influence in Europe. It was not even consulted when Poland was dismembered by Russia, Prussia and Austria. Nor did those states conceive their own interests to be threatened when Choiseul rebuilt the French navy, or when Vergennes intervened in the American revolution in hopes of undermining Britain's commercial and naval power.[116]

Despite the difficulty of converting wealth into effective power, however, it is clear that the British did relatively well during the eighteenth century in their mercantilist war, and that in the long term the mercantilist gains transformed Britain into a world power. British and French trade suffered depredations in time of war which were not compensated by the small profits of privateering, but in terms of mercantilist economic warfare the important considerations were those of which nation of traders suffered more in time of war, and which acquired greater long-term advantages from the conflict. It is evident that the British, who devoted more of their resources to promoting mercantilist success than did the French, came off best. Marlborough's victories would have been unobtainable had England and the Netherlands not been able to pay the costs of the armies in the field. That ability to pay was the product of successful mercantile competition, and of parliamentary constitutions which enabled the Stadhouder-King William, and his successors, to raise tax revenue. English mercantile success was in part a product of the ability of the English navy to promote English trade, and the eventual triumph of the English battle fleet over French and Spanish enemies was very much the product of the access the English crown enjoyed to tax revenue. Parliamentary government, which ensured an effective relationship between the navy and the mercantile interests of England, was an important key to English success.[117]

The experience of the Dutch in the seventeenth century, and of the French at the beginning of the eighteenth, that it was difficult to make war with a great power directly profitable in the short term, was also the British experience in the mid-eighteenth century. The short history of Britain's occupation of Manila in the Seven Years' War provides a case study of the difficulty experienced in turning war to profitable ends.[118] The picture of Britain's long-term economic growth throughout the century, however, is more important. From 1699–1701 to 1772–74 British exports and re-exports increased 244 per cent. Exports as a proportion of imports rose from 1.09 per cent to 1.23 per cent.[119]

A. H. John's assessment is that 'war in the first half of the eighteenth century exerted, on the whole, a beneficial influence on the development of the English economy'.[120] John ascribed the development to increased demand, and to the resultant willingness to introduce new technologies, not to the triumphs of British arms. The greatest growth area in British trade was in manufactured goods to Britain's North American colonies. Exports to America increased in that period 604 per cent while imports only increased 430 per cent. Ralph Davis points out that the war with France may have been the reason for some of the exports, but not for the majority of it. By 1774, furthermore, it would no longer be true to say that trade with the colonists took place exclusively as a result of the protectionist legislation which the navy enforced. British manufactures were already becoming competitive in quality with continental production. Nevertheless, the war with France was not irrelevant to the growth of British economic strength. Ralph Davis's analysis is that mercantilist legislation ensured the 'take off' of British commerce in the late seventeenth century, and that successful colonial wars subsequently ensured that there was no foreign interference in the development of Britain's colonial trade.[121] After the initial impetus of the Dutch wars, English merchant shipping was not directly increased by the wars with the much more dangerous French. Ultimately, however, the colonial conquests which led to expansion in British trade also produced new growth in English mercantile shipping.

The Treaty of Utrecht which concluded the War of the Spanish Succession in 1713 ensured that France would not have exclusive access to the economic resources of the Spanish empire. In the subsequent fighting with Spain and France in the 1730s and 1740s, Britain gradually expanded its colonial sources of supply, and established its naval position. In the Seven Years' War Britain's naval triumphs ensured that the wealth Britain derived from its overseas and colonial trade did not diminish, even if it did not greatly expand as a result of the war. That wealth enabled Britain to subsidise the armies which turned back French attacks in Germany. The French were less successful. The Seven Years' War deprived France of its Canadian and Acadian colonies and reduced the French position in India to one fortified post at Pondicherri. While the French economy could sustain the losses inflicted at sea by the British, the cost of the French war effort in the Seven Years' War was unprecedented. The war was paid for by credit, and the failure of the *ancien régime* to devise an adequate method for resolving that debt in the post-war years led directly to the French Revolution.[122] In the 1760s the Duc de Choiseul found his every effort to re-establish the French colonial empire frustrated by British naval power, and only in the 1770s did the American revolution provide the Duc de Vergennes with an opportunity to redress the balance. However, that war added to the indebtedness of the *ancien régime* and stimulated the growth of a revolutionary reform movement.

Both Britain and the Netherlands benefited significantly by the effective restraint placed on French commercial and territorial expansion. Britain, however, became the wealthiest state in Europe, able to afford the unparalleled naval strength and to subsidise the allied armies which were required to limit French power and influence. The Dutch were able to do no better than stave off disaster and accept the jackal's share.

THE PROBLEM OF LATERAL ESCALATION: THE LEAGUE OF ARMED NEUTRALITY

The difficulty William III had experienced in obtaining neutral acceptance of restraint upon maritime trade was typical of the problems Britain experienced throughout the eighteenth century, and into modern times. If an attempt was to be made to deny an enemy the use of the sea, it was also necessary to impose severe controls on the activity of neutral traders. In effect, trade war was a strategy which had to be conducted against neutrals for the ultimate discomfiture of the enemy. Mercantilist objectives required less interference with neutral shipping than did attempts to block access to supplies, but mercantilism had more profound long-term implications for neutral trading nations. Only evidence that the belligerent was able to defend his claims, and dispense with the services of neutral carriers, would persuade neutrals to acknowledge belligerent rights. The conclusion of bilateral treaties by states from the middle of the seventeenth century, providing for the immunity of shipping from arrest, was a reflection of the military weakness of the signatories. When circumstances changed, such treaties ceased to be respected.

The role of neutral states in eighteenth century wars did not conform to the ideas developed in the nineteenth century that neutrals should be strictly impartial, and carry on their affairs according to pre-war patterns. Nor did they retain medieval ideas of common objectives for all Christian states. The neutral did not acknowledge any restraint upon the promotion of its self-interest. Carl Kulsrud believes that the underlying reason for the conflict which developed between belligerents and neutrals was the mounting mercantilist ambitions of neutral states which wished to exploit the wars of the great powers to develop their own trade.[123]

The activity of the Dutch neutrals was especially annoying to the British. The Dutch were bound to Britain by a defensive alliance, and in 1743 Britain invoked it, largely because it was easier to control the shipping of a co-belligerent than it was that of a neutral. Nevertheless, in 1745 168 vessels entered the French island of Guadeloupe from the Dutch island of St Eustatius, in comparison with 16 ships from France in 1743, four in 1744 and one in 1745. When war broke out again with France in 1755, and the British fleet began to seize French merchantmen preparatory to a declaration of war, the Dutch were very careful to avoid taking an active part. Dutch merchants, however, were again active in providing shipping services for the French. In 1758 the British Lord Chancellor Hardwick established the 'Rule of the war of 1756' which declared that a neutral lost his protection if he undertook to serve trades of the enemy in wartime which were closed to him in peacetime by navigation acts or comparable legislation. This formulation was indeed in keeping with 150 years of legal precedent in the High Court of Admiralty, and in French and Dutch courts, but its enforcement was fatal to the mercantilist ambitions of the neutrals.[124]

Inevitably, enforcement of the Rule of 1756 led to international dispute. In 1758 there was a crisis when British privateers nearly opened fire on a Dutch convoy in the North Sea. In 1759, however, London agreed to receive three specially commissioned officers from the Hague to 'assist' Dutch shippers defending themselves before prize courts. In effect their function was to negotiate with London a compromise which would enable Dutch shippers to remain in business. The colonial trade of France was abandoned by the Dutch, and trade in naval timber was circumscribed, but many other European trades remained open. Agreement was facilitated by the real service Dutch ships were providing Britain, by keeping open the Virginia tobacco trade to France and the French wine trade to Glasgow. The Dutch also furthered their case by voting the quick construction of 25 warships, which ultimately were only employed convoying traders on European routes. In return, Pitt's Privateers Act of 1759 tightened controls over privateersmen by restricting letters of marque to ships of 100-tons burthen, and by making ransoming of prizes an act of piracy.[125] The whole diplomacy has significant parallels to the pragmatic arrangements the British Ministry of Blockade made with neutral shippers and their governments in the 1914–18 war.

The rule of 1756 lost its importance when states lost their mercantilist empires in the nineteenth century, or deregulated their shipping. Of more enduring importance was the simultaneous re-establishment of the principle of continuous voyage. Although the principle was admitted in the seventeenth century in the High Court of Admiralty it had apparently fallen out of use. In 1756 it was permitted in connection with contraband control, and in 1804 its use was extended once more to general economic blockade.[126]

The Danes, having less to offer Britain than the Dutch, and less capacity to threaten, had no choice but to accept British decisions. Spain, however, proved to be more difficult to reconcile to British exercise of sea power. Initially, the Spanish government had not been a belligerent in the Seven Years' War. However, in 1760 the Marquis de Grimaldi concluded the *Pact de Famille* by the provisions of which Spain was committed to joining the war against Britain. The counter-productive diplomatic effects of sea denial operations had this time gone so far as to add significantly to the forces arrayed against Britain. As 'a Spaniard' later said to the British *chargé* in Madrid: the British 'as Masters of the Sea, [were] too powerful not to be oppressive'.[127]

A decade and a half later, the American Revolution was so destructive of British prestige that Britain's use of naval force to intercept contraband was circumscribed. Before 1778 the perceived need to avoid war with France at all costs was the principal factor in the failure of the British navy to stop this traffic, which was a major reason for the success of the Revolution.[128] After the declaration of war with France, 2670 privateers were fitted out in British ports, but these failed to prevent the American Revolutionaries maintaining vital trade contacts with Europe.[129] Nantes successfully established a trade with the American colonies at the height of the war.[130] Furthermore, the attempt to impede the use of St Eustatius as an *entrepôt* supplying the Americans, and to repeat the efforts of the Seven Years' War to deny France and Spain access to Baltic supplies of naval stores, led to serious trouble with the northern neutrals.

Nicolas Magens had written in 1775 in his *Essay on Insurance*,

> Might not those who fought the battles ask, what signifies our being masters at sea, if we shall not have liberty to stop ships from serving our enemy?[131]

As early as April 1778 the British ambassador at the Hague was instructed to renegotiate the marine treaty of 1674, because 'we can never permit the subjects of the Republick to become the carriers of our enemies and the old claim of free ships free goods can never be admitted'.[132] Britain had some excuse for demanding renegotiation, for the Dutch were in no condition to honour their alliance obligation to Britain. The treaty was unilaterally abrogated, and in October 1778 an act of parliament was passed, and was implemented by order-in-council, authorising the seizure of all ships carrying naval stores. The order also authorised the purchase of the seized cargoes for the Navy Board, and the payment of freight and damages, but that provision was inadequate to prevent serious trouble with neutrals. In 1778 Britain did not appear to be entitled to the privileges belonging to 'masters at sea'.

The neutrals, led by Catherine II of Russia, refused to accept British control of trade. In the summer of 1778 both Denmark and Russia began to consider taking naval action in defence of trade, as much against the rebel privateers as against Britain. Naturally, France gave the idea every encouragement. At first Catherine contented herself with ordering her fleet to keep privateers off the Russian coast. She did not trust Sweden, which was a French satellite, and she did not want Britain defeated. Her coastal patrols were at least as much in the British as the French interest. In December 1778, however, she warned Harris, the British ambassador in St Petersburg, about the activity of British privateers. Early in 1780 she mobilised a Russian squadron and began negotiations for a League of Neutrals to defend the freedom of maritime trade, choosing a moment when the Spanish declaration of a blockade against Gibraltar made the move less clearly anti-British. In March Catherine issued a declaration demanding that the belligerents recognise the rights of neutral ships to navigate freely and to convoy the property of belligerents without risk of seizure. Exception was only to be allowed for seizure of contraband, but that term was not extended to include naval stores. This was no more than Britain had granted Russia in the commercial treaty signed in 1766 during Britain's attempt to negotiate a military alliance, but Britain was now reluctant to state explicitly that the treaty would be honoured. Catherine was claiming for all neutrals what Britain was only prepared to give unofficially to the tiny Russian merchant marine, by means of intervention (which was now found to be politically just possible) in the prize courts. In July 1780 Denmark signed a convention with Russia and issued a declaration of its own to the belligerents. The Danes were vulnerable to British reprisal, however, and were prepared to suppress Danish trade in naval stores in return for British agreement to permit that in provisions. Sweden issued a declaration on 21 July, and signed a convention with Russia on 1 August.

A trial of strength could not be avoided, although British diplomats were able to use stalling tactics to prevent an outright confrontation with the League. Bowing to Russian pressure, a means was found to release all Russian ships from British prize courts. In 1780, on the other hand, an excuse was found for declaring war against the Netherlands before the adherence of that state to the League became effective. Dutch willingness to make commitments which led to war with Britain was a result both of Britain's increasing economic dominance and of the reduced military threat posed by France.[133] The prestige of the League was injured by its shuffling failure to support the Dutch, who suffered severely in consequence. A Dutch convoy escort was defeated at the Dogger Bank in 1781, obliging the traders to put back to the Baltic. St Eustatius was captured with 30 merchant ships in the harbour and full warehouses ashore. Britain, however, failed in its objective of blockading naval stores. Prussia had also joined the neutral league, and Austria and Russia had concluded an alliance. Britain could not fight all the world, and so had to accept on face value the 'naturalisation' of Dutch ships under Prussian and Austrian flags. In 1780 only 671 Prussian ships passed the Sound, but in 1781 the number rose to 1507. The measure of Britain's failure is that between 1778 and September 1782 Riga exported 996 masts to Britain, 868 to France (with an additional 29 sent via Genoa), 405 to Spain, and 1855 to the Netherlands, only 600 of which were on the account of the Dutch navy.[134]

Only the recovery of the British navy in the 1790s prevented the effective re-establishment of the Armed Neutrality in the war against Napoleon. That war was to see the last great exercise of mercantilist strategy, but was also to see one neutral, the United States, driven by it to abandon its neutrality.

French experience with the problem of lateral escalation was not dissimilar to Britain's. Eventually the French came to claim that they had always respected the immunity of all neutral flags, but the facts are otherwise. The old French doctrine of 'Robe', that both ships and goods were liable to seizure if either were enemy property, was abandoned in the seventeenth century. However, whenever French power appeared to allow it, French prize courts imposed a severe interpretation of belligerent rights. The instructions given by the French crown to warships in 1681, 1692, and 1704 all ignored the treaties and reverted to the doctrine of Robe. Only in 1744 did

France undertake to conform to the now 80-year-old treaty with Denmark and the Netherlands. Even then, a proviso was made that Britain must do so as well. For a while during the French Revolution, French interpretation of law reverted again to something very like the doctrine of 'Robe'. This led to two years of quasi-war with the United States.

THE CONTINENTAL SYSTEM AND BRITISH ORDERS-IN-COUNCIL

In the mid-eighteenth century advanced economic theorists in Britain had began to call in question the entire mercantilist system. Josiah Tucker questioned the value of colonial possessions in the 1730s, and was an opponent of Britain's imperial conquests during the Seven Years' War. In 1752 Hume published his *Jealousy of Trade*, and in 1776 Adam Smith published *The Wealth of Nations*, which attacked the idea that states should seek to monopolise wealth. Only wealthy states, he argued, had the capacity to be good markets. Turgot, the French Finance Minister, greatly approved of Tucker's work. The growing awareness of the value of free trade, however, did not immediately lead to an end of the great mercantilist trade war. Choiseul's attempt to re-establish the colonial strength of France was followed by Vergennes' intervention in the American Revolution. Turgot was dismissed. In 1786 William Eden negotiated with France a lower level of tariffs which encouraged trade, but French manufacturers objected that freer trade benefited the more advanced British industry, and the Eden tariffs became one of the grievances in the French Revolution. The wars of the French Revolution and Empire were fought with unswerving mercantilist purpose, and with mercantilist means.

The continuation of French economic policy along mercantilist channels was more than the triumph of reaction. Although restraints on trade have come to be seen as destructive of total world wealth, military power is a product less of absolute than it is of relative wealth. It makes sense in military strategy to attempt to deny the enemy access to wealth, and to maximise the resources of the belligerent. Adam Smith himself, asserting that 'defence is of much more importance than opulence', did not include the Navigation Act in his criticism of restraints on trade. Tucker was more radical. In

1781 he published a pamphlet, *Cui Bono?*, in which he argued that Britain should take the opportunity to be rid of the American colonies. In the short term he proved to be right. British trade with the Americans continued to increase after the legislative separation. It can be seen now, however, that Tucker was correct largely because of the extent to which Britain was becoming an indispensable source of high technology. Legislative mercantilist protectionism, defended by the military power it generated, remained the central economic means of advancing the political power of the state.[135] In effect, a gulf was for the first time being driven between the economic policies for peace and those for war. Clausewitz's maxim, that war is the continuation of policy, became less self-evident when peacetime policies had to be amended in anticipation of the needs of war.

French strategy against Britain was directed primarily at the objective of ruining their enemy by denying it the ability to sell its products. Hopes had been fed by grave doubts felt in the most respectable banking quarters about the stability of the British economy. To a Frenchman, the British economy seemed to be fundamentally unsound because it lacked the strong agricultural base which France enjoyed. The size of the British national debt, which in 1775 had been £124 million, was £230 million in 1793. At the time of the peace of Amiens in 1802 it was no less than £507 million, which was only £80 million less than it was to be in 1914. It appeared to be inevitable that a campaign against British trade would lead to the failure of Britain's international credit. No less an authority than Adam Smith had drawn attention to the vulnerability of Britain through trade war by demonstrating that it had been exports of manufactured goods, not of bullion, which paid for the Seven Years' War. The handwriting appeared to be on the wall when in 1797 the Bank Restricting Act released the Bank of England from its obligation to redeem paper currency. To Frenchmen the evils of paper currency were all too obvious. Napoleon viewed the British funded debt as a fatal weakness. He did not permit his own bankers to make comparable arrangements, preferring to leave his bills unpaid. Precarious credit, and blockade of a narrow range of manufactures, were expected to put much of Britain's 'over-specialised' labour out of work, and thus lead to revolution.[136] In fact, the resort to unbacked currency made not the slightest difference because British bankers continued to have complete confidence in all things British.

Napoleon did not need naval strength to effect his policy. He had to impose control upon consumption, and that was most easily done by his army. Prohibitive customs duties were placed on goods which normally, or because of the war, came only from British sources. The import of goods from the enemy was prohibited. The principle of excluding British cargoes from French-controlled territory was maintained even during the brief peace of Amiens, 1802–3. For the first time in the Anglo–French wars the political dispute between states was used to justify the arrest of British nationals found on the continent upon business or personal affairs.

Enforcement of the regulations was sporadic until the defeat of Prussia gave Napoleon control of virtually all western Europe. Then he issued his 'Berlin' decree of 21 November 1806 by which he proclaimed Britain to be blockaded. A year after the battle of Trafalgar, British naval control of the seas around the island was undisputed, but Napoleon's blockade was enforced by the imposition of customs control ashore. The Hanseatic towns were occupied by the French army, and the vassal states of Italy and the Netherlands hurriedly passed ordinances against British trade to forestall French intervention. When the treaty of Tilsit was concluded in 1807 between Napoleon and Czar Alexander, the customs control was extended to cover all Europe from Turkey to Sweden, which latter was compelled to give nominal compliance by the force of Russian arms.

At sea, the French navy and privateers did not depart from the rapacious objectives of Vaubon, but French mercantilist purposes were also served by the draconian decree of 18 January 1789 by which French prize courts were instructed to determine the nationality of ships according to the presence or otherwise of British products in their cargo or equipment. The vigorous enforcement of this principle drove neutral carriers well away from the French coast.

In defence of American shipping, Congress authorised the US Navy and privateers to attack any French raiders. An embargo was placed on trade with France, and for two years the United States was at war with France in all but name. In December 1799 Napoleon repealed the decree and returned to more normal prize law. Compensation for American losses was eventually included in the Louisiana Purchase, and paid by the United States government a hundred years later.[137]

The depredations made during the 17 years of war on British commerce by French privateers, and by privateers of states allied to France, cannot be said to have had any major strategic effect. Some naval resources were diverted to trade protection, and there was dislocation of commercial patterns. British shipowners and insurers, however, retained their capacity to make compensations for marine war risk. Insurance rates were pushed to unusual heights, with Baltic rates reaching 40 per cent in 1808. The homeward rate from Jamaica in the first half of 1812 was 6.8 per cent, but the depredations of American privateers after the American declaration of war that year pushed it up to 11 per cent. These rates were paid, however, and trade continued. The system was entirely capable of managing the risk. The British navy provided convoy for merchants, but they often preferred to sail alone so that their British nationality could be disguised by using false colours.[138] Lloyds Coffee House had grown into an institution capable of policing its members, as well as providing the Admiralty with advice on shipping organisation. When the Berlin and Milan decrees put neutral shipowners at unusual risk, Lloyds published deliberately deceptive shipping lists.[139]

French resources were not well suited for an attempt to deny Britain access to supplies, and in fact that was never the focus of French strategy. Political attention was focused on the question of Britain's vulnerability to blockade of food supplies in 1795, when there was a poor harvest that reduced yields by 20–25 per cent, and in 1800 when the harvest was also a poor one. In the judgment of Freeman Gilpin and Mancur Olson, however, the war was not the principal cause of the distress although the blockade of supplies from abroad had a psychological effect. The supply of food in the country was not greatly reduced, but panic and speculation led to hoarding, which pushed up the average price of wheat from 50 *s* per quarter to 156 *s* in mid-March 1801. The poor rioted, and the politicians looked for scapegoats. A House of Commons select committee was appointed, which recommended several measures of substitution for wheat, and increased importation from the United States. The decision to send a fleet into the Baltic, which destroyed the Danish fleet in Copenhagen harbour, was influenced by the food shortages, and did in fact put an end to the crisis. Once the threat from Denmark was eliminated, British convoys were able to escort neutral grain ships from the Baltic. In 1809–10 Britain experienced another severe harvest, but Napoleon was more concerned to sustain the French farm economy than to attempt starvation of England. He licensed export of the surplus French crop.

Napoleon was right to discount the political utility of trying to stop British imports. In 1812–13 Britain endured another dearth, and there was large-scale rioting. The rioters, however, directed their wrath at the machines which were taking their jobs. Measures which had been taken to increase domestic investment in agriculture, and to avoid waste, proved adequate. Food shortages were in fact of so little consequence during the wars against France that the population of the British Isles rose by an unprecedented 14.3 per cent between 1801 and 1811.[140]

In Geoffrey Ellis's view, the focus of historians upon the anti-British aspects of Napoleon's Continental blockade has been misleading. It is true that French documentation of the blockade concentrated on analysis of the impact it was having on Britain. Nevertheless, Napoleon's focus was always a continental one. He sought to defeat Britain primarily because Britain threatened his control of central Europe. The 'Continental System' was intended to develop the economy of France at the expense not only of Britain, but also of French vassal states, and of neutrals. This objective was a commonplace of the mercantilist system, and was the all important means of paying the expenses of war. The problem for the historian, as it was for Napoleon, is that limitations upon bureaucratic control of economic functions meant that measures taken to disable enemy trade did not necessarily benefit French production.[141] The British response to the Continental Blockade, because it was directed entirely toward multiplying British trade, and wealth, can be analysed more simply.

At the beginning of the war Britain did attempt, as in the war of the Spanish Succession, to blockade French supplies of grain. Between June 1793 and August 1794 a ban was placed on all grain shipment to France and many American grain ships were brought into port where their cargoes were forcibly purchased. Only by sacrificing the Brest fleet at the battle of 'The Glorious First of June' were the French able to convoy grain ships home from the United States. In the end, Britain had little difficulty in sweeping from the sea the flags of France and of its allies because the revolution had effected such injury to the French naval officer corps. The attempt to starve France was soon abandoned, however, and the emphasis of British policy was focused on the mercantilist concept of forcing trade upon the enemy, while denying him the ability to export his goods, upon the sale of which depended his ability to pay the expenses of war.

The appropriate British response to Napoleon's measures of mercantilist trade war was to force trade upon France, and especially to circumvent French restrictions on trade with its satellites. A series of orders-in-council were issued in November and December 1807, and were added to later, which obliged neutral shipping to submit to inspection at sea, and forbade it the right to carry enemy cargo anywhere except to the neutral country itself, or to Britain. The orders were given vague wording which facilitated later modification. The 'paper blockade' was not to be enforced by warships stationed off enemy ports but by warships and privateers operating on the trade routes. A high customs duty was charged on enemy colonial products when they were landed by neutrals in England, in order to reduce their competitiveness with English goods. The mercantilist objective was made quite apparent by the clearance that was given to American traders to carry home-grown grain directly to the continent. There was no thought of starving the continent. Raw cotton and medicinal cinchona bark were made prohibited exports, in part to sustain British domination of the cotton product market, but licenses were issued permitting re-export to France of those commodities provided the French also agreed to take other British goods. The same proviso was made on licenses permitting imports, generally of luxuries, from France. In 1810, 18 000 licenses were issued, totally transforming Britain's pro-forma trade blockade into a system of protected trade.[142] Enemy shipping interests were encouraged to trade to British ports, and even provided with convoy.[143] When President Madison finally decided to resort to war in 1812, he described the British strategy in mercantilist terms.

> It has become . . . sufficiently certain that the commerce of the United States is to be sacrificed, not as interfering with the belligerent rights of Great Britain; not as supplying the wants of her enemies, which she herself supplies; but as interfering with the monopoly which she covets for her own commerce and navigation. She carries on a war against the lawful commerce of a friend that she may the better carry on a commerce with an enemy – a commerce polluted by the forgeries and perjuries which are for the most part the only passports by which it can succeed.[144]

Madison was quite correct. The President of the Board of Trade, Lord Bathurst, described in 1812 British objectives: 'France by her decrees had resolved to abolish all trade with England: England said, in return, that France should then have no trade but with England'.[145]

Because of the weakness of the French navy, and because of the threat posed by the revolution to all the neighbours of France, Britain had little difficulty overcoming neutral objections during the first years of the war. In December 1800 Sweden, Denmark, Russia and

Prussia reformed the League of Armed Neutrality, but it did not survive beyond the next spring because of the murder of Czar Paul I, and Nelson's destruction of the Danish fleet at Copenhagen. An Anglo–Russian naval convention was concluded, to which Denmark and Sweden gave reluctant assent. The doctrine of 'Free ships make free goods' was signed away, and the neutrals went so far as to agree that British warships could inspect their merchantmen even when they were being convoyed.

The Americans were the only neutrals to whom Britain had to make concessions. Early in the war the American government sent John Jay to London to negotiate a settlement of Anglo–American disputes. From the time of the revolution the Americans had tried to establish the validity of the doctrine of 'free ships make free goods'. Jay was unable to obtain agreement to the principle, but accepted a compromise which exempted American trade with the French colonies from the 'Rule of 1756', even though such trade was illegal in peacetime according to French law. A joint commission awarded damages to American shippers amounting to $12 million. Britain was also brought to acknowledge that food could not be considered contraband.[146]

The compromise collapsed because the concession was abused by the American government, which simplified American re-export arrangements so that goods of French colonial origin could be sold, indirectly, to European markets. In 1806 British courts decided that the exception which had been made could no longer justify the flagrant violation of the principle of continuous voyage, although the American commissioner in London, James Monroe, reported that British courts were continuing to employ every possible excuse to release American ships.[147] Napoleon's response exacerbated American problems. On 17 December 1807 Napoleon issued his second 'Milan' decree, which extended the self-blockade to the sea and authorised prize courts to condemn as 'de facto British' any neutral ships which had called at a British port, paid British duties, or even had the misfortune to be inspected at sea by a British cruiser. As Napoleon intended, the Americans were obliged to choose between permitting the British to act as middlemen to the continental markets, or resisting the extension of British authority to the high seas.

President Thomas Jefferson chose to resist, and resort was made to non-importation as a means of reprisal. Legislative self-blockade had first been used during the Stamp Act crisis before the American

Revolution. It had a strong appeal to American strategists, and in connection with Napoleon's Continental System it did pose a serious threat to Britain. In 1805, 30.5 per cent of British export trade went to the United States and 37.8 per cent to Europe. If Napoleon could really enforce his decrees, Britain could hardly hope to survive without access to the American market. The Americans passed in 1807 a 'Non-Importation Act' prohibiting most British imports, and after the Milan decree this was replaced by an 'Embargo Act' against all foreign trade. It was not, however, a successful measure. It proved to be impossible to enforce it against American businessmen, and Napoleon used it as an excuse for ordering the seizure of all ships carrying the American flag, many of which were British using false colours as a *ruse de guerre*. In March 1809 the Embargo Act was replaced by the 'Non-Intercourse' act, which banned trade only with France and Britain. American merchants made vast profits supplying the British army in Portugal, and, with the help of British convoys, running the gauntlet of Danish privateers into Russian ports.[148] All restraint on American trade was lifted by the Madison administration in 1810, conditional upon the belligerents mending their ways. Napoleon obfuscated. London grudgingly decided to exempt American traders from the provisions of the orders-in-council regulating trade, but there continued to be incidents of American ships being stopped at sea and searched for deserters from the British navy. In 1812 Washington declared war on Britain. The political pressures on Washington to exploit Britain's embarrassment, which might make possible annexation of Canada, added to the motives for war.[149]

The British navy quickly established a *guerre de course* off the American coast, but did not attempt to block all American trade. New England was spared, partly because the New Englanders were hostile to the war, and partly because of the need in the British West Indies for provisions. British naval forces purchased their own provisions from American farmers. In 1812 grain ships from the Chesapeake sailed to the West Indies, and American grain continued to supply the needs of Wellington's army in Portugal. Licenses were issued by local British commanders, and confirmed in London. 500 had been issued by August 1812. Jefferson justified the American commerce on grounds of expediency, and mercantilism: 'A truth . . . not to be lost sight of is, that no country can pay war taxes if you suppress all their resources'.[150] In May 1813 Congress made it an offense to employ a British pass, but this served only to divert the traffic into British bottoms sailing under neutral colours. Of more importance was the reopening of the Baltic in late 1812, and the enormous reserve of flour which had been collected in Lisbon. In consequence, British forces off American harbours tightened their grip in 1813, and the Chesapeake was formally blockaded.[151] The effect of British raids on coastal traffic can be measured by the price of flour which, according to Admiral Mahan, sold in August 1813 for $6 per barrel at the grain centre of Baltimore, fetched $7.50 in Philadelphia, $8.50 in New York and $11.87 in Boston. West Indian sugar cost $18.75 a hundredweight at Boston, which was not blockaded, $21.50 at New York, and $22.50 at Baltimore. The re-export trade in West Indian products from New England was eliminated, but these figures do not suggest that even the most vulnerable US cities were in danger of being starved into submission.[152] In 1814 the blockade became so effective that Robert Greenhalgh Albion characterised it as virtual strangulation. All the same, it was an accountants' war which sought to make the American resort of violence unprofitable.

In a proclamation in June 1814, President Madison pointed out that no 'blockade' of the 2000-mile long American coastline was possible which conformed to the accepted principle that it must be effectively enforced. The fact that merchant and naval ships did continue to enter American ports disproved the existence of an effective blockade.[153] Technically, Britain was conducting a *guerre de course* campaign from a position of strength. The American navy could inflict the occasional defeat on isolated cruisers but could not risk battle with the supporting ships of the line. More effective was the work of American privateersmen, who drove up insurance rates for British shipping, and produced a storm of protest in parliament.

Neither the British nor the American government was greatly influenced by the injuries suffered by their traders. A government which could order a trade embargo was hardly likely to be coerced by enemy blockade. More significant to the American government were British raids made against the American coast, and the failure of their own campaign in Canada. The British, for their part, were able to make commercial and naval adjustments to compensate for the American attacks. Had the Continental System not already been weakened by the Iberian revolt, and by Russian withdrawal, however, the impact of the new war on Britain might have been much more serious.

Napoleon failed to obtain the degree of compliance with his regulations which would have been necessary if he were to eliminate that 37.8 per cent of British exports which were normally taken by European markets. In the course of 1808 French control had been extended over Leghorn, Rome and Trieste. British trade had been excluded from southern Europe. In that same year, however, Napoleon's efforts to force Portugal to boycott British trade produced an insurrection in Spain which opened all Iberian ports to British ships, and opened great prospects for the redirection of British exports to Spanish America. The defection of the Spanish colonies from Napoleon's empire also facilitated the British capture of the French West Indian Islands.

No less important than the variation in the external boundaries of Napoleon's control was thè distinct limits that there were to the acceptance of his orders. The vassal states had no motivation for obedience save the knowledge that manifest refusal to comply would lead to the intervention of the French army and French customs officers. French governors of subject cities were happy to make a private fortune out of bribes. When in 1810 Napoleon ordered the destruction of British goods, there were bonfires lit in every city presided over by French officialdom, but the flames were fuelled by the least valuable but most bulky of the British manufactures and produce. In order to reduce the leakage, Napoleon in 1810 extended the borders of France along the Dutch coast to the Hansa towns and Holstein. In December of that year, however, Czar Alexander enforced a customs *ukase* which in effect amounted to defection from the system. It forbade imports except by sea, and gave encouragement to ships which were nominally American but really British.

Napoleon's inability to exact obedience to his decrees can be explained in part by his inconsistency, and by his failure to comprehend how monumental a task he had undertaken. He was convinced that British exporters offered supplies for credit, and accordingly they could be intimidated if the goods were destroyed before they reached the hands of whoever was eventually to pay for them. In reality British industrial products were so much in demand that British traders could ask for cash in advance. Consequently the seizure of even a large proportion of British exports did nothing to discourage British exporters. Furthermore, Napoleon destroyed any incentive there might have been for the vassal states' whole-hearted compliance with his decrees by offering seized British goods for sale. The revenue so obtained clearly amounted to tribute from the vassal states to the French overlord. Smuggling became such an established system of trade that quotations were offered for exporting to any country, the highest prices being paid for smuggling into France.

In 1810 Napoleon altered his system in order to cash in on the high fees that smugglers could charge. The Trianon Tariff dropped the ban on colonial products. British manufactured goods were still in theory to be burnt, but a licensing system was introduced. The licensee was permitted to import British manufactures provided Britain took French items in return. This change of strategy transformed the Continental System into something more nearly resembling Britain's effort to monopolise trade, but, given the relative weakness of the French economy, it had no chance of success. Napoleon had apparently begun to lose interest in the struggle to defeat Britain through trade war, and was increasingly focussing on augmenting imperial revenues. The licenses for trade to Britain became an important source of revenue, and Napoleon began to regard his conquests in Europe less as a means of denying markets to Britain than as a means of ensuring them for France. Italy in particular was singled out as a protected source of raw materials and a market, thus dislocating the traditional German and Swiss connections with Italy. French manufactures were so uncompetitive on the British market, however, that Continental traders were prepared to qualify themselves for an import license by loading inexpensive rubbish which could be dumped on arrival in Britain.

Napoleon could not make such sweeping alterations to international trade patterns without having some impact upon the British economy, but it was remarkably little, and was matched by the distress felt in France. In July and August 1810 there was a severe economic crisis throughout Europe which lasted, in diminishing degree, until 1812. Britain suffered a glut of colonial products which brought their price down to about one half. Many merchants who had speculated unwisely in the South American market were ruined. The closure of cotton mills led to the Luddite riots. The value of the pound had begun to fall in 1808, and gold began to leave the country. However, that was probably the fault of the poor machinery the British government had for handling the massive subsidies it was paying to the states fighting France, and for paying the British army in Portugal. The Luddite rioters directed their wrath more at the machines which were taking jobs than at the government, despite the refusal of the government to act upon their petitions for relief and for regulating the conditions of work. The closest the British came to revolutionary activity was the popular refusal to comply with the regulations the government imposed on the use of grain to ensure its availability. There was in consequence a shortage of grain, especially in 1810, but Napoleon's licenses for the export of all the grain that he did not need for his army and for French domestic needs minimised civil unrest in Britain.

The measure of the success of Britain's mercantilist strategy, and the failure of Napoleon's, were the subsidies London was able to pay its allies. Between 1806 and 1816 the British population of 14 million paid £142 million in income tax alone, and three times that amount in customs duty.[154] This revenue paid, amongst other things, for subsidies to continental states which rose from about £2.6 million per annum in the early years to £20 million for the ten month Waterloo campaign of 1814–15 alone.[155]

For Napoleon the mercantilist strategy had been a costly failure. It was Russian resistance to the Continental System that led to the 1812 invasion of Russia. It was the need to garrison the Hanseatic towns to prevent them violating the customs embargo which prevented Napoleon having the army he needed for the Russian campaign in which he was defeated. Britain's orders-in-council had also created an expansion of Britain's military problems, by bringing the United States into the war, but that was more than compensated by the capacity the mercantilist controls had given Britain to pay for the mobilisation of Napoleon's foes.

Not only had the Continental Blockade failed to impoverish Britain, and stimulated military opposition to France, but it had also failed to support French economic development. Napoleon's mercantilism had proven itself almost as crude as Hitler's was to be 130 years later. The French economic crisis of 1810–11 was the result of French overproduction. Napoleon's efforts to keep out colonial products needed as raw materials for manufacture had failed, and his protectionist tariffs had impoverished the continental market for French exports.[156] François Crouzet writes that the stagnation of ports and loss of overseas markets and raw materials brought about the collapse of industrial production in port cities, and an actual reduction in population. 'In Marseilles, the value of industrial output fell from 50 million francs in 1789 to 12 in 1813.'

> Because of the permanent injury inflicted on many Continental industries by interruption of overseas trade, the war brought about a lasting deindustrialization or pastoralization of large areas (with in some parts of France and Holland, a definite shift of capital from trade and industry towards agriculture). Seaboard districts failed

> generally to attract the new industries which developed during the wars . . .

Only the French cotton industry profited enough from the constraint of trade to establish itself on a permanent footing.[157]

FREE TRADE, THE CRIMEAN WAR, AND THE DECLARATION OF PARIS

In the wake of Napoleon's defeat, *laissez faire* principles began to influence economic thinking so strongly that new strategic ideas were generated. Secretary of State Adams approached the British government in 1823 with a project for a treaty to abolish altogether 'private war' at sea. The idea had originated with the French Enlightenment. Rousseau, in his *Social Contract*, established that war is a relationship between states, not one between the individuals which constitute them. It followed that private property at sea should be as safe from pillage as convention had established it to be on land. In 1780 Benjamin Franklin adopted the idea, and in 1783 it had been suggested to the British government by the American commissioners negotiating a peace settlement.[158] It was the American view that it was in the interest of civilisation that the practice of seizing merchant ships should be abandoned altogether. The logical parallel between private property at sea and that ashore obscured the consideration that attack on oceanic trade was a means of economic war which was technically possible whereas attack on the economic resources within a state was impossible unless the territory in which they lay had already been captured. Air power in the twentieth century was to change the strategic possibilities, and put an end to the respect for private property within hostile states. It must also be said that armies ashore claimed foraging rights which parallel the need of small-budget navies to pay their officers and men with prize-money.

Behind this attempt to deny the belligerent the strategy of economic warfare lay a hope that war itself could become a thing of the past. Adams pointed out to London that the collapse of the colonial systems of France and Spain meant that a mercantilist strategy could no longer be conducted by naval operations against enemy ships. Colonial products now reached most European countries freighted on neutral ships laded in neutral harbours.[159]

The United States concluded, between 1824 and 1850, a series of treaties with the successor states to the Spanish Empire in South America, which recognised the principles that 'free ships make free goods', and that neutral cargoes in enemy ships might be seized. These treaties provided an exception in the event that the neutral in question should conform to British practice, in which case their ships would be lawful prize in wartime but their goods might safely be freighted onboard the shipping of an enemy. American policy respecting the inviolability of neutral commerce made the United States the principal obstacle to British use of naval force after 1817 to suppress the slave trade.[160]

A vigorous campaign in Britain led to the repeal in 1846 of the protectionist 'corn laws' which were the basis of Britain's mercantilist empire. David Ricardo argued that it was unnecessary to protect home production because business interests would always seek to supply a market, even an 'enemy' one in wartime.[161] There was no comparable public demand for repeal of the Navigation Act, because it was generally recognised that naval defence depended upon a substantial merchant marine. Nevertheless, the reforming spirit of government led to the virtual repeal of the Navigation Act in 1849.[162] As the prospect of war with Russia loomed, the free-trade lobby group who had become known as the Manchester School began to agitate for a right to conduct trade freely in wartime.

This objective on the part of business interests in the only state which had significant naval forces, and which had financed the recent war against Napoleon by trade control, appears to be quixotic. No doubt the merchants were self-serving. Their demands, however, were a logical consequence of the faith with which *laissez faire* principles were held. Mercantilist trade war was a system aimed less at injuring the enemy than at maximising national wealth for all purposes, including those of war. If free trade was indeed a significant multiplier of wealth then to many contemporary minds it appeared that free trade should be regarded as the correct means of paying for war, or at least it should be by states such as Britain, which had the commercial and technical resources to play a dominant role in international trade. Free trade in wartime, in that context, was a modification rather than an abandonment of the mercantilist strategy. It re-established a Clausewitzian unity between the economics of war and peace, and it enjoyed the very great attraction as a strategy that it could not provoke conflict with neutral traders.

The arguments of the Manchester School were not specifically intended to augment the power of the state. The reverse was true.

Their case was that the state existed to serve its people, and the wars of states only made sense if they furthered that purpose. Accordingly, every effort should be made to reduce the adverse impact of war upon the people. The 'Philosophical Radicals' supported the Manchester School's position on the grounds that a belligerent, in pursuing the objective of the general good, should seek to avoid injury to enemy civilians. Furthermore, private property was still regarded as a bulwark against state power. The political eclipse of the privateer interests in England left the property of merchant traders in a position of unchallenged political importance. Perhaps these political and domestic considerations distorted the strategic thinking of British statesmen. Nevertheless, the arguments of the free traders did have a basis of sense in the last generations before states regeared themselves for total war.

Although the economic liberalism of the Manchester School represented only a minority view, practical considerations ensured that their objectives were more or less satisfied by the policy adopted by the Earl of Aberdeen's government in the Crimean War. No attempt was made to conduct comprehensive operations against trade. Britain's Foreign Secretary, Lord Clarendon, more than half agreed with the parliamentary demands of the free traders. The First Lord of the Admiralty, Sir James Graham, advised the cabinet that Britain had more to lose than to gain by severe restraint on Russian trade. As tension mounted in the months before the outbreak of war, Clarendon expressed in private his opinion that British prize law would have to be changed, if only to prevent conflict with neutrals. It was a real possibility that any return to ocean warfare to control trade would lead to conflict with the United States. Some amendment of British belligerent practice was in any case unavoidable when war was declared in 1854 by Britain and France. French and British practices had to be brought into line. The French would not adopt the 'Rule of War of 1756' which had become the foundation of Britain's right to prevent neutrals supplying the needs of an enemy. On the suggestion of the French Foreign Minister, Drouyn de Lloys, it was agreed to waive for the duration some of Britain's belligerent rights, specifically the Rule of 1756. A declaration to that effect was made on 28 March 1854. The French agreed to suspend their practice of condemning neutral cargoes captured as part of the cargo of enemy merchant shipping.[163]

It was also agreed not to employ privateers. This self-denial was conceived of primarily as an inducement to neutrals not to admit

Russian privateers into their ports.[164] Given the decision not to undertake a general sea-denial campaign, the suppression of privateering did not significantly reduce British and French naval power. Its importance, in the opinion of C. I. Hamilton, lay in the precedent thereby established. In conducting their negotiations, the British and French governments were less interested in the Russian war than they were in the prospect of a future war between themselves. For that reason, the French agreement not to issue letters of marque was made against the objections of the Minister of Marine, Theodore Ducos.[165] Suppression of privateering was entirely consistent with the belief that war would be won the more quickly if commerce were as little impeded as possible. American Secretary of State Marcy would not agree to ban privateers from American ports, and urged that the doctrine of 'free ships make free goods' should be made a permanent doctrine of British prize law. In July the United States concluded a treaty with Russia establishing that principle.[166] During the war, however, no privateers operated out of American ports.

The overwhelming naval strength of Britain and France combined ultimately made it possible to blockade every Russian port, although the Manchester School's point of view prevailed to such an extent that no blockade was declared until February 1855, and the priority given to Black Sea operations reduced the capacity of the French and British navies to enforce a blockade in the Baltic. Until the blockade was effective, the only trade restriction imposed was an order in council forbidding the entry of British ships into Russian ports. Britons were permitted nonetheless to conduct trade with Russia via neutral carriers. When a close blockade of Russian ports was declared, preventing access by neutral shipping, Britons were still free to route their commerce through neutral ports. Prussia facilitated the trade by constructing a railway from Danzig. The British government despaired of finding means to close the loop-holes, but the Manchester School insisted in any case that loop-holes were necessary so that Russia could continue to supply British industry with raw materials.[167]

The Anglo–French blockades did have a fiscal effect on the Russian war economy. Russian exports fell by 80 per cent between 1853 and 1855, to the consternation of British importers of Russian raw materials, and Russian imports fell by 33 per cent.[168] In consequence, Russian customs revenue was injured. However, J. L. Ricardo, son of the great economist, was not alone in viewing the blockade as useless.

> To blockade the coast of a country having such a frontier as Russia is a mere absurdity. Of what avail is it to seal up Reval and Riga, and leave open Memel, Dantzig, and Konigsberg? To guard one door and throw open others? What possible object can be gained – not by preventing, but by diverting, the enemy's trade? . . . The property of some few poor Findlanders has been destroyed, and some of our own, and the pretext is, that the damage to his commerce will put such pressure on the Emperor of Russia that he must consent to our own terms of peace.[169]

The failure of the Anglo–French blockade to coerce the Czar's government is consistent with the experience of three centuries. Ricardo *fils* should have been more interested in the success of the Anglo–French strategy in sustaining the cost of their own war effort. The President of the Board of Trade, Viscount Cardwell, vigorously opposed the demands within the British cabinet, and from the public, that Britain should revert to the traditional belligerent laws. He convinced the cabinet that Britain could suffer disproportionately from further restraints on trade.[170] Olive Anderson has characterised British economic strategy during the Crimean War as masterful and pragmatic. It

> was distinguished by an unaccustomed grasp of the interconnexion of military and economic strength, and a deliberate determination to preserve the latter to the utmost possible extent in order to increase the former.[171]

Pragmatism led to a return during the war to deficit financing, despite the nineteenth-century economic thinking which insisted that wars must be paid for out of taxation. Pragmatism also sustained the policy of virtually free trade in wartime.

Ricardo's impatience with the failure of Anglo–French sea power to deal direct lethal injury to the Russians is a foretaste of the development later in the century of ideas of total war. The more immediate result of the Crimean War upon maritime strategy, however, was reinforcement of the trend towards limitation of the impact of war upon trade. No doubt British policies were influenced by short-term phenomena, including the misleading circumstance that Britain was still the most highly developed industrial state, and therefore most able to profit from free trade. The abandonment of the Navigation Acts was followed by a great expansion of the British merchant fleets. Contemporaries too readily assumed that the latter was the effect of the former. It can now be seen that British shipbuilders' ability to adopt iron construction, and the dislocation of the American merchant marine caused by the Civil War in the 1860s, were the principal reasons. Similarly, the circumstances of war with Russia, which still had a continental and peasant economy, did not provide any support for arguments that trade control was strategically important.

After the conclusion of peace at a congress in Paris in 1856, Czar Alexander II invited the world powers to conclude an instrument redefining belligerent rights at sea. The *Declaration of Paris* established four principles of international law of war at sea which in effect made the pragmatic wartime agreement between Britain and France an international norm. Privateering was abolished. The principle that neutral shipping was inviolate was adopted; henceforth 'free ships' would indeed make 'free goods'. At the same time, the British principle that neutral cargoes carried by enemy ships should be restored to the neutral owners by prize courts became internationally recognised. The ancient principle that blockades were only legal when enforced by the immediate presence of warships at the approaches to the blockaded harbours was affirmed by states which over the centuries had recognised that naval technology made close blockade a less than effective way of attacking enemy commerce.[172] Collectively, these principles, in the technical conditions of the times, virtually put an end to the right of a state to use naval forces to control trade.

The Declaration of Paris, by outlawing privateers, greatly reduced the extent to which states could mobilise the private capital of citizens for the purposes of naval war. The incentive of prize money for naval officers was retained, and the elaboration of government which increased its power to raise revenue was already providing states with the ability to expand the regular naval forces of the state. Nevertheless, the fiscal incentive for selecting the strategy of attack on maritime trade had been greatly reduced. The United States did not sign because it believed that, unless a complete prohibition were placed on interference with private property, a ban on privateers would serve only to disarm the weaker naval powers or oblige them to increase tax levels to pay for regular naval forces. In reality, the great naval powers were no less affected by the regime. A result of the American decision, to the dismay of Washington, was that the Confederacy was free to resort to the use of privateers during the Civil War. In 1870 Prussia announced an intention to raise a volunteer navy, and France objected that this amounted to employing privateers. The Prussian scheme never materialised, however, and the employment of privateers by the Confederate government was their last significant appearance.[173]

There was no opposition in the British cabinet to ratification of the Declaration of Paris.[174] Clarendon justified in the House of Lords his signature of the convention by claiming that a refusal to do so would have turned every maritime power against Britain:

> and most properly so – because we should have been maintaining a law which was contrary to the public opinion of the world, which was hostile to commerce, and as unfavourable as possible to a mitigation of the evils of war.[175]

Although mercantilist strategy had paid for Britain's victories in the Seven Years' War and the Napoleonic War, it had also led to war with Spain in 1760, with the Netherlands in 1780, and with the United States in 1812. Clarendon received very little criticism for his decision. Lord Derby observed that, without a decisive economic weapon, Britain would be dependent upon an ally for influence over European affairs. In 1859 Lord Palmerston expressed strong disagreement with the American plan to immunise private property at sea, as it would deny British seapower its coercive influence.[176] However, when in 1860 the Horsefall Commission of the House of Commons reported on the significance of the Declaration of Paris to the safety of British shipping in wartime, the worst it foresaw was that British shipping would stay in harbour while British trade was carried by neutrals. They recommended that Britain press for a further diminution of belligerent rights in order to protect all private property at sea. Clearly the predominant contemporary opinion was that experience had shown the economic weapon of seapower to be ineffective and dangerous in its coercive form, and most effective in the supportive mode when pursued by free enterprise. The general agreement to abolish privateers appeared to Britons as justifying any loss of prize rights. The American failure to agree was regarded as unimportant because world opinion would deter resort to privateers. J. S. Mill was one of a very few who continued to demand the abrogation of the Peace of Paris, which he believed had crippled Britain's capacity to be the champion of liberal democracy.[177]

It was not until after the American Civil War that opinion changed in Britain about the value of blockade. In 1870 London refused to second French objections to the Prussian volunteer navy. In 1871

Lord Salisbury described the Declaration of Paris as 'reckless Utopianism', the result of which was that 'the fleet, valuable as it is for preventing an invasion of these shores, is almost valueless for any other purpose'.[178] In 1919, when Sir Francis Piggott wrote his monograph on the Declaration of Paris, he could hardly contain his indignation. It then appeared that Britain had only defeated Germany in World War I by wholesale evasion of the restraints on belligerent rights.[179] The recent scholarship of C. I. Hamilton perceives the events of the Declaration of Paris through the same perspective, but credits the British cabinet with a cynical intent of preserving the substance of seapower which they believed in the steam age to be less dependent upon techniques of ocean warfare than upon coastal blockade.[180] This view is in total contradiction to the earlier work of Olive Anderson and M. R. Pitt, which latter portrays the British attitude as influenced by the disappointing record of blockade in the Crimean War.[181]

TRADE WAR AS A STRATEGY OF CONTAINMENT

In the years following the Crimean War the Imperial Russian navy sought to devise a means not only to dissuade Britain from further interference in Russian foreign policy, but also to prevent a reoccurrence of the close blockade of Russian ports which had marked the last years of the war. In 1860 Csar Alexander II agreed to Grand Duke Konstantin's plan to construct sail and steam frigates designed for commerce raiding in distant waters. The peacetime coercive function of the Russian frigates was closely parallel to the latent threat of attack on British shipping, and invasion of Canada, which helped the Union government avoid British intervention in the Civil War. In the event of war between Britain and Russia, the strategic function of the Russian commerce raiders would become that of containing British naval power by obliging the British navy to devote so many ships to trade defence that the resources would not be available for blockade of Russia's widely separated sectors of sea coast. Russian naval missions were established in New York and San Francisco, and in 1863, fearing British intervention in support of Russia's Polish citizens, the distant-water squadrons were deployed to those neutral harbours. The deployment also made clear Russia's unequivocal support for the Union.[182]

The needs of trade defence have always imposed constraint upon the capacity of navies to act offensively. Admiral Richmond, in his 1932 monograph *Capture at Sea in War*, wrote that the privateers employed by the American revolutionaries had served a valuable strategic function by containing British naval forces, preventing them effectively blocking access to military stores manufactured in Europe.[183] The strategy of trade attack to contain enemy resources became technically more promising when the unit cost of warships was driven up by steam propulsion, shell guns, armour, and iron construction, and when the abolition of privateers obliged state treasuries to pay the full cost of naval armament. In the long years before the Declaration of Paris, the British navy was able to devote relatively little effort to trade defence because part of the function of British privateers was defence against those of the enemy. Privateers sometimes provided convoy for traders, they blockaded enemy ports, and recaptured merchant ships in enemy hands. By preying on enemy privateers, no doubt they also obliged enemy *armateurs* to fit more expensive, and hence fewer, ships. The demands of English merchants that the navy provide 'cruisers and convoys' could be met with a few ships escorting large convoys. Nineteenth-century fleets composed of smaller numbers of more effective units had much more serious problems in deploying forces to guard against every threat, as well as to carry out offensive operations. In the twentieth century the role of trade war as an aspect of 'grand tactics' on a world scale, or operational strategy, was to become one of the central motives for investing in that means of warfare.[184]

THE AMERICAN CIVIL WAR

The American decision not to sign the Declaration of Paris backfired almost immediately. With the outbreak of civil war, the Confederate States proceeded to demonstrate how the weaker naval power could use privateers against the trade of the stronger. Washington's support of the free-enterprise warriors disappeared immediately, but the efforts of Earl Russell to obtain Secretary of State William H. Seward's signature to the Declaration of Paris was defeated by the latter's attempt to use adherence as a means of obliging the European states to treat Confederate privateers as pirates.[185] The American merchant marine was all but destroyed because the privateer raids forced insurance rates up to the point where American shippers were priced out of the market. The success of Confederate raiders in avoiding battle with superior Union forces, especially the long career of the *Alabama*, impressed naval planners. The need for cruisers for trade defence was underlined.

In the long term this loss to the American shipping business proved to be permanent. In more immediate terms, however, the sufferings of American shipowners was not politically significant. Shipowners quickly divested themselves of an unprofitable enterprise. The warning given by the British government that it would not tolerate Confederate attacks on British-registered shipping precluded an economic blockade of the Union, and also encouraged the sale of American ships to British owners. In 1864 Cobden noted in the House of Commons that 609 ships had been transferred from American registry in the last three years. Perhaps even more significant was the dramatic expansion of new construction which took place in British North America to supply the needs of the Union. Towards the end of the war, the Confederate raiders found it increasingly difficult to operate because of the growing power of the Union navy, and the prestige of the Union government. By that time they were also having trouble finding American flag ships to prey on. The economic and strategic strain on the Union caused by the 'flight from the flag', however, was not great enough to produce important political effects.[186]

The Union blockade of the Confederate States initially enjoyed an unwarranted degree of success because of an attempt made by Confederate committees of public safety to use embargo of the cotton crop as a means of obliging Britain and France to intervene in the war. The strategy was similar to the use of embargo before the War of 1812, and to the 'self blockade' of Revolutionary France. Between 1840 and 1860 the United States had supplied 80 per cent of the raw cotton used in British manufacturies. The Confederates were convinced that Britain would be compelled to recognise the Confederacy to prevent revolution in the northern mill towns.[187]

The British business community as a whole was able to make adjustments to cope with the effects of the cotton famine. Cotton manufacture had to be reduced drastically, but not because of a lack of raw cotton, a great deal of which was warehoused in Europe, and which could at a higher price be purchased from India. Unsold supplies of pre-war production, wartime disruption of the market, and reluctance to make for stock at a time of high cotton prices did oblige large-scale closure of mills. The losses suffered by the cotton industry, however, were more than compensated for by war profits in other areas. Besides the great growth which took place in British and colonial shipping, great profits were made from the sale of munitions.[188]

British labour was less well insulated against the effects of mill closure, but the political effect of the privation was not that for which the Confederacy had hoped. In November 1862 three quarters of the Lancashire cotton mill hands were out of work, but British working men were developing a degree of political sophistication which was to have important consequences. Sympathies were strongly and vocally hostile to the slave states. Karl Marx brought the fact of this working-class solidarity to the notice of the world, and a *New York Times* editorial led to shiploads of American produce being sent across the Atlantic to the relief of the impoverished mill hands.[189]

Once the coercive power of the 'self blockade' was found to be inadequate for its intended purpose, it proved to be an embarrassment. When in late 1862 the Confederate states abandoned the embargo and tried to re-establish trade, it found that the Union government had little difficulty demonstrating that its blockade had been 'effective'. The blockade being 'effective', in the terms demanded by the Declaration of Paris, the Confederates were unable to persuade the British government to deny its legality. Policy also guided the British government's decision. A reaction having set in to the completeness of the Declaration of Paris, London found it expedient to recognise the blockade despite its defects. British shipping interests, in consequence, were given no support in their blockade-running efforts.

The Union government, a gamekeeper turned poacher, developed a principle of continuous voyage to stop the runners using Bermuda and Nassau as *entrepôts*.[190] Neutral shipping with clearances for those ports were stopped at sea, and information obtained by the American consuls in Europe was used to identify cargoes ultimately intended for the Confederate states. As recently as the Crimean War the American government had objected to the principle of continuous voyage, but President Lincoln ensured that the Supreme Court would not declare the interception of shipping on the high seas a violation of prize law. He delayed hearings on the first prize cases until vacancies occurred on the Supreme Court bench, which he filled with justices on whom he could rely. He even expanded the bench to ten justices in order to strengthen his hand. The bench did not let him down. The British practice was copied of deliberately obscuring the principles upon which the law acted, in order to extend the belligerent claims without openly admitting doing so. Secretary of State Seward added diplomatic procrastination to evasion, especially in order to retain some control over trade into Matamoras in Mexico, which was an easy river connection to Texas.[191]

Only fear of neutral reaction limited the scope of the blockade. Law had some part in defining how the neutrals would react, and power determined which neutrals had to be placated. With the Union fighting a desperate battle for its very existence the peril which had to be avoided above all others was that of driving Britain into the war on the Confederate side. Seward took a very strong line with London and Paris, warning that any recognition of the Confederacy would mean war with the Union. A European war, however, would have been the swan-song of the Union. When a Union naval officer boarded the British steamer *Trent* and took prisoner Confederate commissioners bound for London and Paris, the act had to be disavowed. The opportunity was taken to show that the violation was identical to the seizure of British deserters onboard American ships during the Napoleonic wars, which had been one of the reasons for the American declaration of war in 1812. Once the Confederacy was defeated, the American government abandoned its restraint. Claims against the British government for its laxity in permitting Confederates to fit out warships in British ports were pressed and London found it expedient to pay a substantial indemnity.[192]

Some contemporary accounts attribute the defeat of the Confederacy to the blockade. On the whole this idea can only reflect the enthusiasm of Union naval officers, including the future Admiral Mahan, and the reluctance of Confederate military leaders to admit that they had been defeated in the field.[193] There is no doubt that the Civil War caused severe economic dislocation in the Confederacy, and that the high freight rates which could be charged by neutral blockade runners because of the blockade played a part in this ruin. Poor administration, however, and the refusal of the states to pool their resources, probably had more to do with deficiencies in army supply than did the Union blockade. The Confederate states had never been in an economic position to compete with the North, and had not been able to create in wartime an administration capable of dealing effectively with their limitations. The dependence of Confederate finance upon inflation of the money supply is a striking example of short-sighted policies. The blockade merely exacerbated difficulties, and provided an excuse for failure to deal with them.[194]

During the course of the war, Union blockade forces took 1149 prizes and destroyed a further 355 vessels. However, it has been estimated that the blockade was successfully run 8250 times. Stanley Lebergott, working with evidence developed by Marcus Price, has calculated that the capture rates of blockade runners were:

	Steam (%)	Sail (%)	Combination (%)
1861	0.3	4.9	3.1
1862	24.4	46	40.9
1863	13.4	43.5	27.1
1864	15.4	51.4	27.8
1865	16.7	71.1	32.7
1861–65	16.1	42.6	29.7

The profits of blockade running evidently were not high enough, at about 40 per cent, to tempt many shipowners to try their luck more than once, but enough undertook the venture to sustain a small but important trade. Of 6.8 million bales of cotton grown during the war, perhaps 500 000 were sold to Europe and 900 000 to the North.[195] The figures would no doubt have been considerably higher but for the initial Confederate cotton embargo. F. L. Owsley says this export made possible the purchase of 600 000 odd stand of arms which were run into Southern ports to equip the Confederate army.[196] L. H. Johnson shows how fraud facilitated the export of war materials from New York to the South.[197] Failure to make more effective use of limited economic resources, not to mention the limited capacities of Confederate military leaders when faced with General Grant's Union steamroller, outweighs in importance the blockade. Frank E. Vandiver's assessment is that the

> blockade running was not one of the Confederacy's blunders. It was perhaps the most successful, large-scale campaign attempted by the South. Its failure was not due to any weakness in its own make-up, but to the collapse of its foundation – the collapse of the Confederacy itself.[198]

Considering the extent to which the Union had undermined the long-standing American objection to 'paper blockades', and the limited strategic utility of the blockade, F. L. Owsley concluded that 'Old Abe sold American's birthright for a mess of pottage'.[199] In World War I Britain was able to use Civil War precedents to justify comprehensive trade controls.

THE *JEUNE ECOLE* AND THE MAHAN SCHOOL

Despite the limitations hindsight can see in the utility of the Union blockade, the American Civil War was to be a turning point in the history of maritime strategy. A strong impression had been created that a major cause of the defeat of the Confederacy had been the sea denial operations of the Union navy, and specifically the impact on the Confederacy of stoppage of imports. It appeared that the aspirations of Elizabethan admirals had at last become technically possible, because of the greater sophistication of marketing arrangements which reduced stockpiling and local economic autonomy, and because of the development of steam-powered navies. There was consensus, however, only about the strategic importance of sea control. Concerning the technical requirements of the strategy, and hence which nations profited by the developments, there was less agreement. The French *Jeune Ecole* was sharply opposed by the analytic work of a new breed of British and American naval historians.

The *Jeune Ecole* was a group of anti-British officers in the French navy who in the mid-1880s promoted through publications a belief that Britain's capability to out-build the French battle fleet was no impediment to France defeating Britain in naval warfare. The new steam-powered torpedo boats could evade the battleships and cruisers and attack the merchant shipping upon which Britain was far more than ever dependent for imports. It was not thought that the enormous British merchant marine could be sunk or captured *en masse*. In that appreciation the *Jeune Ecole* and the British Admiralty were in agreement. It was the belief of people like Admiral Aube, however, that dramatic sinkings on the first days of war would force up insurance rates to the point where shipping would be kept in harbour. The result would be food shortages and unemployment, which would reduce the labouring classes to starvation, and to rebellion.[200]

The views of the *Jeune Ecole* were far from universally accepted in France. Admiral Bourgois, one of France's foremost sailors, warned that violation of the laws of war would inevitably lead to alliance of the neutral shipping states of Europe with Britain. The British public, however, was impressed by Britain's apparent vulnerability. The French blockade of rice in 1884–85 to bring pressure on the Chinese government was a warning that food supply might be at risk in wartime despite the laws of war. Agitation in parliament led by

J. C. B. Colomb and Admiral Lord Charles Beresford resulted in the formation in 1887 of the Naval Intelligence Division at the Admiralty. That decision neither allayed the public's fears, nor led to the rapid adoption of measures to defend trade. The naval manoeuvres of 1888 demonstrated how difficult it would be for a British fleet to blockade French commerce raiders into their ports. Admiral Sir George Tryon, in May 1890, pressed the idea of a national war-risk insurance, but the idea was rejected by the government on the grounds that interference in the enterprise of shippers would keep them from finding ways of evading attack. Another panacea solution with wide support was the establishment of national granaries and subsidies for home production of wheat.[201]

The Admiralty did not fully share the alarm, although they embarked on a major cruiser programme to defend trade. When in 1892 the Imperial Russian navy launched the fast cruiser *Rurik*, Britain responded by ordering the *Powerful* and the *Terrible* to track her and her sister ship *Russia* down in the trade routes. In 1902 a specialist Trade Division was established in the Naval Intelligence Division. The following year an association which numbered amongst its members 40 admirals, 30 peers, and 50 Members of Parliament, was formed to press for a Royal Commission on Food Supply in time of War. The Commission once formed, however, did little more than endorse the need for overall naval superiority, although it did decide that it was necessary for the government to indemnify shippers for war losses if they were to be persuaded to risk trading in wartime.[202] A Treasury Committee was appointed in 1907 with Austen Chamberlain as chairman, but it did not recommend any state intervention in the insurance business. Not until May 1913 did a sub-committee of the Committee of Imperial Defence take up the question again, and not until July 1914 was an arrangement made to provide some governmental reinsurance for mercantile hulls against damage caused by 'the King's enemies'.

An important factor in the complacency of the British government was the analytic work of the British naval historian Captain Philip Colomb, and the more influential work of the American Admiral Alfred Thayer Mahan. When Mahan published his *The Influence of Seapower Upon History* in 1889 he wrote eloquently of

> the noiseless, steady, exhausting pressure with which sea power acts, cutting off the resources of the enemy while maintaining its own, supporting war scenes where it does not appear itself, or

> appears only in the background, and striking open blows at rare intervals.

However, he was quite convinced that the advantages of sea power could not be obtained by forces which were unable to fight the battles necessary to ensure their freedom to occupy decisive areas of the sea.

> It is not the taking of individual ships or convoys, be they few or many, that strikes down the money power of a nation; it is the possession of that overbearing power on the sea which drives the enemy's flag from it, or allows it to appear only as a fugitive; and which, by controlling the great common, closes the highways by which commerce moves to and from the enemy's shores. This overbearing power can only be exercised by great navies . . .

A victorious battle fleet could blockade trade, and could also convoy its own merchants. Small squadrons operating in such a way as to avoid battle could not, on the other hand, disrupt trade to an extent which was strategically significant. The Comte de Broglie, and the *Jeune Ecole*, were wrong. On the basis of the historical evidence then available to him, Mahan insisted that only the dominant naval force could exercise sea power.[203] Geoffrey Symcox believes that Mahan was primarily motivated by the political objective of persuading Congress to build a blue-water fleet.[204] He certainly succeeded in reinforcing British convictions that the battleship was pre-eminent. The Royal Commission on Food Supply was concerned to make it clear that it was unsound for naval forces to be diverted by enemy attacks on trade from the principal task of fighting the decisive battle for command of the sea.[205]

In keeping with this thesis, the British refused to interfere with market forces affecting agriculture. By 1914 British farmers raised no more than 35 per cent of the calories consumed in Britain. Germany, in contrast, took seriously the need to promote national production. By 1914 80 per cent of German nutritional requirements were supplied from domestic sources. Capital investment in German farms permitted the feeding of 70–75 people per 100 acres, compared to 45–50 people supported by the same acreage of British farmland.[206]

PACIFIC BLOCKADE

At the same time as the defence community were debating the capacity of blockade to defeat a great industrial power in a major war, the great powers were actually employing naval control of trade as an instrument for policing their interests when these were threatened by the actions of lesser states. The use of naval blockade to promote limited purposes without resort to war, without abandoning the advantages of a non-belligerent relationship, is known as 'pacific blockade'. The practice was derived from the concept of reprisal, and was most properly directed at such problems as the failure of states to honour international debts. As an act of reprisal or 'self help', a pacific blockade was generally held to be directed only at the ships of the quasi-enemy. No right was usually claimed to interfere with neutral shipping. Private property seized during a pacific blockade might not be condemned. Once the dispute was settled, the property was returned to its owners. The objective of reprisal is by definition a limited one; one not involving the safety of either party.[207]

It is generally held that the first instance of pacific blockade occurred in 1827 when the navies of Britain, France and Russia combined to blockade the ports of Greece in support of the struggle for Greek independence from the Ottoman Empire. Perhaps, however, that date should be put back to Admiral Hosier's blockade of Porto Bello in 1726, or even earlier. About twenty instances of pacific blockade occurred during the nineteenth century, including the famous Don Pacifico affair in 1850 when the British fleet blockaded Greece to exact reparations for a number of injuries, including that suffered by a British subject at the hands of a Greek mob.[208]

In 1884 the French declared a blockade of Formosa, ostensibly to compel the government of China to pay compensation for an 'ambush' of French soldiers in Annam. French purposes were in fact political. The Premier, Jules Ferry, admitted in the *Journal Officiel* (27 November 1884) that

> There are great advantages to following the policy of reprisal without a declaration of war, to waging war as we are now doing without resorting to a prior declaration.[209]

The passivity of the blockade was thrown into doubt when the Port of Kelung was bombarded and captured. Later Foochow was shelled, Chinese ships were sunk, coal mines were seized, and rice ships were prevented from carrying their cargoes to northern China. After initial hesitation, Britain decided that French behaviour amounted to war. The Foreign Enlistment Act was enforced, with the result that the

French navy was denied the use of Hong Kong harbour. Britain did not declare neutrality, but France, in retaliation for what was taken as British intervention, informed the powers that it claimed the rights of a belligerent. The seizure of coal mines at Kelung was conceived in Paris as a means of enabling the sizeable French fleet in the Pacific to continue its operations. Admiral Courbet advised against the plan, but was ordered to carry it out nonetheless.

It appears that the blockade of Formosa was not instrumental in the eventual Chinese decision to negotiate, but the rice blockade is credited with having been an effective instrument of coercion. France did not obtain the indemnity demanded, but China signed away sovereignty in Annam and Tonkin.[210]

In 1902 the German, British and Italian governments imposed a pacific blockade on Venezuela because of the failure of the Venezuelan government to honour its debts. Inevitably the use of limited force was complicated by the political implications to neutrals, in this instance the United States. Secretary of State John Hay indicated that the United States 'understood that European powers were bound to claim the right to defend their interests in South America' but 'greatly deplored the intervention of a European power in the affairs of a South American republic'. A demand by the German government for protracted control of the Venezuelan customs house, ostensibly for collection of the debt, suggested an underlying motive of securing a political and possibly military foothold in South America.[211] To deflect that possibility, President Theodore Roosevelt assembled in the Caribbean the US Navy's North Atlantic, South Atlantic and North European squadrons under Admiral of the Navy George E. Dewey; 54 American ships including battleships to oppose 14 smaller European ships. The newspapers were kept well informed of American naval movements. Roosevelt explained the position tactfully but clearly to the German ambassador, and let it be understood that Canadian interests in the outcome of the Alaska boundary dispute were a hostage to British good behaviour. The United States asserted that a pacific blockade did not justify interruption of the commerce of third parties, upon which the blockading states declared a state of war to exist, and converted the 'pacific' to a belligerent blockade. The British, however, came to believe that Berlin was attempting to use the episode to exacerbate Anglo–American frictions, and withdrew from the blockade operation. In the second half of January 1903 the Germans commenced violent operations against Venezuela, but the limitations of the German navy were so apparent that there was no alternative to accepting arbitration to resolve the dispute.[212]

The use made of pacific blockade, in truth, was rarely without a political significance. The separation of Greece from the Ottoman Empire can hardly be described as reprisal. In 1831 Lord Palmerston used British warships to blockade ports in the Netherlands. War was not declared, but the British objective was nonetheless a political one. The blockade was intended to support the French army in the establishment of an independent state of Belgium.[213] British and French naval support for the Spanish–American struggle for independence was also political in purpose. At the very least, the use of force to effect reprisal amounted to a demonstration of the military reach of the quasi-belligerent. The ability of the French to continue their blockade of Formosa despite the loss of British facilities in Hong Kong was significant in the progress of French power in the Pacific.

Despite its name, pacific blockade amounts to the naked use, or abuse of power. It is an act of 'coercive diplomacy', falling within James Cable's category of 'Purposeful Force', which

> does not itself do anything: it induces someone else to take a decision which would not otherwise have been done.[214]

In the context of nineteenth-century international relations, pacific blockade was a relatively successful means of protecting the interests of the great powers. Albert Hogan wrote in 1908: 'during the last eighty years, pacific blockades have been the means of bringing a number of such disputes to a peaceful conclusion'.[215] The inchoate rules of pacific blockade minimised the resentment of the developed states which possessed ocean-going merchant marines, and the right of such states to use force to manage relations with less developed states was scarcely questioned. By the beginning of the twentieth century, public sentiment began to favour more restraint. Following the Venezuelan episode, pacific blockade did not appear to be practicable politics. At the 1907 Hague Conference the great powers agreed to the 'Porter Convention', which proscribed the use of reprisals to exact payment of debts.[216]

THE HAGUE CONFERENCES AND THE DECLARATION OF LONDON

In the last decade of the nineteenth century and the first of the twentieth a major effort was made to develop by international convention the restraints upon belligerent rights at sea. Both Britain and the United States were impelled by consideration of the need to ensure the safety and profitability of their shipping as neutral carriers in a world troubled by imperial wars. In 1871 the United States had concluded a treaty with Italy in which the two states agreed that their merchant shipping should be immune from capture should war occur between them. During the Spanish–American war the United States had declared a blockade of the north coast of Cuba, but Washington continued to seek a general ban on 'private war' against merchant shipping. The American delegates to the first Hague conference in 1898, who included Mahan amongst their number, proposed that

> The private property of all citizens or subjects of the signatory powers, with the exception of contraband of war, shall be exempt from capture or seizure on the high seas . . .[217]

The British government shunned the temptation during the South African war to intercept food shipments to the Boers because they had come to see their interest as excluding food from a contraband list. The inconvenience Britain and the United States experienced as neutrals in the Russo–Japanese war by Russian inclusion of food and fuels on the contraband list led Secretary of State Hay to circularise a protest amongst European diplomats.[218]

Support in Britain for restrain on belligerent rights came as much from those who doubted their utility as from those who feared foreign attack. Not all Britons were satisfied with Mahan's conviction that a dominant naval power could strangle an enemy by blockading his trade. The experience of the Civil War, which had founded Mahan's faith, was less convincing to Britons who knew that there had always been a good chance that suitable ships could run the Union blockade. The experience of the Crimean War had also suggested that the internal communications of Europe had developed to the point where the power of the British navy against trade could have little effect. In 1904 Sir George Sydenham Clark, Secretary of the Committee of Imperial Defence, drafted a paper in which he concluded:

> The sea pressure that can be brought to bear upon a continental enemy appears, therefore, to be far less effective than formerly. If this be admitted the advantage a belligerent state possesses from the right to capture contraband appear[s?] illusory.[219]

Eyre Crowe, the Senior Clerk of the Foreign Office in 1907, did not share Sydenham Clarke's doubts. He wrote that the publications of Admiral Mahan showed that 'Sea power is more potent than land power . . . No one now disputes it'. The inference Crowe drew, however, was that it was

> but natural that the power of a State supreme at sea should inspire universal jealousy and fear, and be ever exposed to the danger of being overthrown by a general combination of the world.

In consequence, he urged that Britain should be careful to avoid posing any threat to the trade of its neighbours.

> In proportion as England champions the principle of the largest measure of general freedom of commerce, she undoubtedly strengthens her hold on the interested friendship of other nations, at least to the extent of making them feel less apprehensive of naval supremacy in the hands of free trade England than they would in the face of a predominant protectionist power.

The same year he also advised against plans which, in the event of war with Germany, would seek to deny access for Germany to trade by blockading the coasts of neutral Belgium and the Netherlands.[220]

The growing prospect of war with Germany did not persuade the British government that it was necessary to reverse the trend towards limitation of belligerent rights. Between 1904 and 1907 the Committee of Imperial Defence and the Naval Intelligence Division reappraised Britain's interests, but concluded that a compromise could be reached between Britain's interests as a neutral, and as a possible belligerent against Germany, if the concept of contraband were eliminated altogether. Germany was not well placed to attack British commerce but had a substantial merchant marine hostage to British attack, the loss of which could be expected to have political effects in Berlin. If contraband control were eliminated as a motive for trade warfare, British shipping would be safe, but Britain would still be able to deny Germany access to military supplies by conducting a close blockade of German ports.[221] The Japanese warned the British government in 1907 that the experience of their late war had shown how difficult it was to enforce a close blockade, but it was not until 1908 that the policy of close blockade began to be modified. As late as 1911 Admiral Sir Arthur Wilson, when First Sea Lord, reverted to it.

At the conclusion of the Russo–Japanese war in 1907, Czar Nicholas II proposed a second conference at the Hague. Neither the

British aim to eliminate contraband as a reason for stopping neutral ships on the high seas, nor the reiterated American suggestion that private property should be considered immune from seizure in war, were satisfied.[222] Later, both countries were to be glad of that. Mahan had himself come to oppose according immunity to private shipping because he increasingly saw Britain's capacity to threaten German shipping as the only means available to confront Prussian militarism. He did not trust the British Liberal administration to sustain the practical means for its own defence and obtained Theodore Roosevelt's permission to publicise his views.[223] The Hague Conference did establish safeguards for merchant seamen by requiring warships attacking trade to search the ships they intercepted, and to provide for the safety of their crews. This amounted to a restraint, if respected, upon the worst excesses of the *Jeune Ecole*. The conference also agreed in principle to the establishment of an international prize court.[224] The Admiralty protested vigorously, but the Liberal administration were more interested in removing the causes of conflict than in preserving the legal ambiguities which had been used in the past to support British belligerent rights.

The Admiralty was confident of its ability to defend trade against cruisers, but the British public in general was impressed by the alarmist views expressed by Admiral Lord Charles Beresford that British trade was defenceless.[225] In 1905 Mahan himself had retreated a little from the position that only a dominant naval power could effectively execute economic warfare, accepting that *guerre de course* against commerce could form a useful part of an inferior power's strategy by haemorrhaging enemy resources.[226] The Foreign Secretary, Sir Edward Grey, feared that it would be impossible to obtain political support for the Hague convention unless the law of belligerent rights were clarified. Invitations were sent to the powers to meet in London in the winter of 1908–9 to complete the work of the Hague conference by drafting the 'Declaration of London' on the laws of war at sea.[227]

The Declaration of London served British interests by eliminating the application of the principle of continuous voyage to 'conditional contraband', commodities which only became contraband if they were freighted to the enemy armed forces, and by including food on the conditional contraband list rather than making it absolute contraband. Most of the primary products Britain imported were put on the free list. The greater precision imparted to the question of contraband would also benefit Britain as a neutral. The conference failed to resolve the question of conversion of merchant ships to war purposes, but at least it did not make the problem any worse. The right of belligerent navies to sink neutral prizes was conceded, but it was hedged with enough limitations to render it less of a threat.

Four successive directors of Naval Intelligence recommended that the Declaration be ratified by the government. The Admiralty's confidence in its ability to protect British trade found support in the analytic work of the naval historian Julian Corbett. He did not agree with Sydenham Clarke's skeptical opinion of the utility of contraband control, and wrote an article justifying 'Capture of Private Property at Sea'.[228] On the other hand, in 1911, in his *Some Principles of Maritime Strategy*, he asserted that the capacity of minor naval powers to injure a great one by attacks upon trade had been notably diminished by the new technologies which reduced the range of warships and provided merchantmen with wireless communication. The ban on privateers could be overcome by commissioning armed merchant ships as warships, but he believed it 'unlikely that such methods will extend beyond the larger privately owned vessels'. The capacity of regular cruisers to conduct trade attack was significantly limited by their range, and by the problem of providing prize crews.

> No Power will incur the odium of sinking a prize with all hands, and their removal to the captor's ship takes time . . . and the presence of such prisoners in a cruiser in any number soon becomes a serious check on her fighting power.[229]

General diplomatic considerations also urged the desirability for Britain agreeing to the Declaration of London. When it was introduced to Parliament as the Naval Prize Bill of 1911, Mr McKinnon Wood defended it on the grounds of diplomatic necessity. Critical naval officers, he said, 'forget what our interference with neutral trade then cost us – world-wide hostility and an extension of the field of war'.[230] Public opinion in Britain, however, reversed its earlier enthusiasm for limitations. It was feared that the conditional contraband clause, and the right which was conceded commerce raiders to sink blockade runners once their crew had been removed, could be used to permit destruction of neutral ships carrying food to Britain. Eventually the House of Lords voted against the bill.[231] M. R. Pitt comments that the Lords served British interests well, but for the wrong reasons. The Declaration of London was a threat not to the defence of British trade but to Britain's capacity to use naval force offensively. According to Marion Siney, only one or two Members of

Parliament had any understanding of the role of economic warfare, or appreciated the extent to which modern naval technology prevented close blockade of the German coast.

Captain Maurice P. A. Hankey began his life-long opposition to diminution of belligerent rights by submitting a paper to the Committee of Imperial Defence urging the need to impose a distant blockade of Germany at the Skagerrak.[232] However, notwithstanding the failure to obtain Parliamentary sanctions, the Admiralty incorporated the substance of the Declaration of London in its war orders. The First Lord, Reginald McKenna, was impressed by Hankey's defence of belligerent rights but may have been influenced by the consideration that the Declaration of London would benefit British interests in a war in which Britain was neutral, and could be denounced should Britain be at war and succeed in defeating the enemy battle fleet.[233] As Hankey wrote in 1927,

> When the war came we discovered at once how great a handicap the Declaration of London was. Although unratified, the Government were deeply committed to it, and it was not easy to shelve.[234]

This was a false dawn of international law, which persuaded Corbett to discount the value of cruisers for trade attack, and which also misled people like Admiral Sir Herbert Richmond about the utility of the submarine in trade war. In 1914, echoing common opinion, he wrote that

> The submarine has the smallest value of any vessel for the direct attack upon trade. She does not carry a crew which is capable of taking charge of a prize, she cannot remove passengers and other persons if she wishes to sink one.[235]

The needs of trade defence did not appear to be urgent. In 1909 the Trade Division of the Naval Intelligence Department had been abolished, and it was not re-established until August 1913 as the Trade Branch of the Operations Division of the recently formed War Staff. Even then it was given very limited resources.[236] In the light of the virtual breakdown of international law which occurred during World War I, the faith people had in civilisation seems somewhat incredible. The treaty laws which were developed in the wake of the Declaration of Paris lacked the vitality of even the disputed interpretations of the course of Admiralty and did little more than undermine respect for a pervasive international law. If indeed naval force put unlimited power into the control of a few favoured states it was improbable, to say the least, that international treaty would be able to preclude its use. The impact of the treaties limiting belligerent rights had less importance than did the enhanced reputation imparted to maritime strategy by the theorists.

It was a weakness of contemporary naval scholarship that it employed the results of two centuries of mercantilist trade war, in which navies had played a significant part, to support a belief in the capacity of modern navies to impose an economic blockade which would deny an enemy access to resources. The great wars of the twentieth century were to reveal that limitation, and to restore some of the respect given in earlier centuries to the positive objectives of economic warfare. Following World War I, efforts to restrict by treaty the strategic use of naval forces became hopelessly entangled by competing national interests, and instead efforts were directed to limiting the *matériel* of navies.

NOTES

1. Fernand Braudel, *The Mediterranean and the Mediterranean World in the Age of Philip II*, vol. ii, pp. 865–91, s.v. 'Piracy: A Substitute for Declared War'. See also: B. A. Wortley, 'Pirata Non Mutat Dominium', *British Yearbook of International Law*, 1947, p. 258; C. R. Pennell, 'Tripoli in the Late Seventeenth Century: The Economics of Corsairing in a "Sterill Country"', *Libyan Studies*, 16 (1985), pp. 101–12; and 'Piracy and Diplomacy in Seventeenth Century North Africa: The Diary of Thomas Baker, English Consul in Tripoli 1679–1685', read in manuscript, 1985; and Alberto Tenenti, *Piracy & The Decline of Venice 1580–1615*.
2. See Samuel Pyeatt Menefee, International Maritime Bureau, *A Third Report Into the Incidence of Piracy and Armed Robbery from Merchant Ships*, USA, October 1985; General Council of British Shipping, *Guidance Notes on the Protection of Shipping against Terrorism and Sabotage*, London, August 1986; and Admiral Ko, paper presented to the SIIA–NUS international conference on 'The Security of the Sea in the Asia–Pacific Region', 2–3 May 1985, Singapore.
3. Francis R. Stark, *The Abolition of Privateering and the Declaration of Paris*, pp. 49–57.
4. L. M. Hill, *Bench and Bureaucracy*, p. 49, and see pp. 30–53.
5. A. C. Bell, *A History of the Blockade of Germany, 1914–18*, p. 463; and James Wilford Garner, *Prize Law During the World War*, section 126.
6. Richard H. Cox, *Locke on War and Peace*, pp. 7–44 and 136–46.
7. William V. O'Brien, *The Conduct of the Just and Limited War*, chs. 1 and 2.

8. C. J. Ford, 'Piracy or Policy: the Crisis in the Channel, 1400–1403', *Royal Historical Society Transactions*, 1979, p. 63.
9. Hugo Grotius, *The Rights of War and Peace*, A. C. Campbell (ed.); and *De Jure Belli Ac Pacis*, (Francis W. Kelsey translation, Introduction by James Brown Scott).
10. J. W. Garner, op. cit., p. 201.
11. See CAB 21/307, 'The Law of Prize in Relation to the Dominions', *draft*, *circa* 1926.
12. R. W. Tucker, *The Laws of War and Neutrality at Sea*, pp. 3–10.
13. D. P. O'Connell, *The Influence of Law on Seapower*, p. 3.
14. Kenneth Raymond Andrews, *Elizabethan Privateering*, pp. 22–31, s.v., 'Regulation'; and Robert W. Kenney, *Elizabeth's Admiral*, pp. 33–87.
15. See C. H. Firth and R. S. Rait, *Acts and Ordinances of the Interregnum 1642–1660*, vol. II, p. 66.
16. William and Mary 4–5, 1692. The text of this act does not agree with the information given in Kemp, *vide infra*.
17. Peter Kemp, *Prize Money*; and *The Oxford Companion to Ships and the Sea*, s.v., 'Prize Money'; and Carl E. Swanson, 'Predators and Prizes: Privateering in the British Colonies During the War of 1739–1748', PhD, University of Western Ontario, pp. 31–56.
18. Carlton Savage, *Policy of the United States Toward Maritime Commerce in War*, vol. i, p. iii.
19. See Timothy J. Runyan, 'Merchantmen to Men-on-War in Medieval England', in *New Aspects of Naval History*, Craig L. Symonds (ed.), pp. 33–40.
20. David J. Starkey, 'British Privateering, 1702–1783, with particular reference to London', University of Exeter PhD, 1985, p. 366, Table 87, *et passim*. See also Richard Pares, *Colonial Blockade and Neutral Rights, 1739–1763*, p. 18.
21. Jonathan Swift, *Political Tracts 1711–1713*, Herbert Davis (ed.), s.v., 'The Conduct of the Allies', November 1711, p. 22.
22. Kenneth Raymond Andrews, *Elizabethan Privateers*, pp. 3–21, s.v., 'Privateering and the Sea War', and pp. 222–40, 'The Consequences of Privateering'.
23. Carl E. Swanson, loc. cit., pp. 3–11, 166–185, 300–4, 320.
24. James G. Lydon, 'Privateering becomes a Business: New York in Mid-Eighteenth Century', in *Commission Internationale d'Histoire Maritime. Course et Piraterie*.
25. David Starkey, 'British Privateering Against the Dutch in the American Revolutionary War, 1780–1783', in *Studies in British Privateering, Trading Enterprise and Seamen's Welfare, 1775–1900*, Stephen Fisher (ed.), pp. 1–18; and 'British Privateering, 1702–1783', pp. 362–5.
26. Patrick Crowhurst, *The Defence of British Trade 1689–1815*, s.v., 'French Privateering and British Trade 1689–1815'; and 'Bayonne Privateering 1744–1763', in *Commission Internationale d'Histoire Maritime. Course et Piraterie*.
27. John S. Bromley, 'The Loan of French Naval Vessels to Privateering Enterprises, 1688–1713', in *Corsairs and Navies, 1660–1760*, pp. 187–212.

28. Patrick Crowhurst, op. cit., p. 495.
29. Carl E. Swanson, loc. cit., p. 320.
30. John B. Hattendorf, *England in the War of the Spanish Succession*, ms pp. 235–43, Garland Press, 1987.
31. David John Starkey, 'British Privateering, 1702–1783', pp. 95–6, 243, and *passim*.
32. Alberto Tenenti, *Piracy and the Decline of Venice 1580–1615*, pp. 128–30.
33. Christopher Lloyd, *Lord Cochrane*, p. 100. See also John S. Bromley, 'The Profits of Naval Command, Captain Joseph Taylor and his Prizes', in *Corsairs and Navies, 1660–1760*, pp. 449–62.
34. 'The only award now payable under the Naval Prize Act, 1864, is for prize salvage for the recapture of British property in war'. England, Queen's Regulations for the Royal Navy, Chapter 51, 5101 para 2.
35. See ADM 116/1319, 1320B and 1715, subject files on distribution of Prize Money and Prize Bounty, 1914–18 war.
36. Patricia Crimmin, 'The Royal Navy and the Levant Trade, c.1795–c.1805', in Jeremy Black and Philip Woodfine (eds), *The British Navy and the Use of Naval Power in the Eighteenth Century*, pp. 221–36.
37. Colin Elliott, 'Some Transactions of a Dartmouth Privateer During the French Wars at the End of the Eighteenth Century', in *Studies in British Privateering, Trading Enterprise and Seamen's Welfare, 1775–1900*, Stephen Fisher (ed.), pp. 19–40.
38. J. W. Garner, *Prize Law During the World War*, pp. 8 and 195–9.
39. John Francis Guilmartin, op. cit., p. 156.
40. *Calendar of State Papers*, Venice, vol. 8, no. 40.
41. James A. Williamson, *Hawkins of Plymouth*, pp. 317–22.
42. See Agnes M. C. Latham, *Sir Walter Raleigh*.
43. *State Papers Domestic, Elizabeth*, CCLIX, no. 12.
44. Ibid., CCLIII, no. 70.
45. Ibid., CCLXIII, no. 102.
46. Kenneth Raymond Andrews, op. cit., pp. 187–95.
47. See R. B. Merriman, *The Rise of the Spanish Empire*, vol. iv, pp. 207, 436; J. A. Williamson, *Hawkins of Plymouth*, p. 159; Sir Walter Raleigh, *Three Discourses of Sir Walter Raleigh*, and M. Oppenheim (ed.), *The Naval Tracts of Sir William Monson*, vol. i, p. 46.
48. Quoted in Sir Herbert Richmond, op. cit., p. 291.
49. Henry Kamen, 'The Destruction of the Spanish Silver Fleet at Vigo in 1702', *Bulletin of The Institute of Historical Research*, vol. XXXIX (1966), pp. 165–73.
50. Jonathan Swift, *Political Tracts 1711–1713*, Herbert Davis (ed.), s.v., 'The Conduct of the Allies', November 1711, p. 22.
51. *An Enquiry into the Reasons of the Conduct of Great Britain with Regard to the Present State of Affairs in Europe*, Dublin, 1727 (quoted in Sir Herbert Richmond, *The Navy as an Instrument of Policy*, p. 397).
52. Alice Clare Carter, *Neutrality or Commitment*, pp. 53–8. See also N. Laude, *La Compagnie d'Ostende et son activité coloniale au Bengale 1725–30*.
53. J. M. Wallace-Hadrill, *The Barbarian West*, s.v., 'Mare Nostrum'.

54. Philip C. Jessup and Francis Deak, op. cit., pp. 54 and see pp. 50–103 s.v., 'Contraband of War'.
55. Ibid., p. 44.
56. Ibid., p. 56.
57. Ibid., p. 58.
58. Philip C. Jessup and Francis Deak, *Neutrality, its History, Economics and Law*, vol. i, p. 61.
59. D. J. Llewelyn Davies, 'Enemy Property and Ultimate Destination During the Anglo–Dutch Wars 1664–7 and 1672–4', *British Yearbook of International Law*, 1931, p. 21.
60. Carl J. Kulsrud, op. cit., pp. 244–94.
61. G. N. Clark, *The Dutch Alliance and the War Against French Trade*, p. 108; and Carl J. Kulsrud, op. cit., pp. 206–16.
62. Article 17 of the Commercial Treaty.
63. G. N. Clark, 'Neutral Commerce in the War of the Spanish Succession and the Treaty of Utrecht', *British Yearbook of International Law*, 1928, p. 69.
64. See Sir Herbert Richmond, *The Navy as an Instrument of Policy*, pp. 50–60.
65. R. G. Albion, *Forests and Sea Power*, ch. v.
66. See W. R. Mayer, 'English Privateering in the War of 1688 to 1697', *The Mariners Mirror*, vol. 67 (1981), no. 3, p. 259.
67. G. N. Clark, op. cit., pp. 32, and 65–9.
68. Sir Herbert Richmond, *The Navy as an Instrument of Policy*, pp. 301–10, 319–20; see also John B. Hattendorf, op. cit., ms., pp. 208–35; and John Ehrman, *The Navy in the War of William III 1689–1697*, pp. 517–18.
69. David Aldridge, 'Swedish Privateering, 1710–1718 and the Reactions of Great Britain and the United Provinces', in *Commission Internationale d'Histoire Maritime. Course et Piraterie*.
70. James Pritchard, *Louis XV's Navy 1748–1762, A Study of Organization and Administration*, p. 183.
71. James S. Pritchard, 'The Pattern of French Colonial Shipping to Canada before 1760', *Revue Française d'Histoire d'Outre-Mer*, vol. 63, no. 231, 1976.
72. P. W. Bamford, *Forests and French Sea Power, 1660–1789*, pp. 65–6.
73. Robert Greenhalgh Albion, *Sea Lanes in Wartime*, pp. 34–64; O. W. Stephenson, 'The Supply of Gunpower in 1776', *American Historical Review*, XXX, pp. 271–81, 1925; and Nicholas Tracy, *Navies, Deterrence and American Independence*, pp. 118–58.
74. David Syrett, *Shipping and the American War, 1775–83, A Study of British Transport Organization*, pp. 243–8. See also R. Arthur Bowler, *Logistics and the Failure of the British Army in America, 1775–1783*.
75. Quoted in G. N. Clark, op. cit., p. 90.
76. Eli F. Heckscher, *Mercantilism*, vol. ii, p. 29. See Robert Livingston Schuyler, *Fall of the Old Colonial System*.
77. James Frederick Chance (ed.), *British Diplomatic Instructions, 1689–1789*, vol. i (Sweden), pp. 50 at 52. Quoted in Jessup and Deak, op. cit., p. 118.
78. See Carl J. Kulsrud, op. cit., pp. 202–43.

79. Jonathan I. Israel, 'A Conflict of Empire: Spain and the Netherlands 1618–1648', *Past and Present*, Aug. 1977; and *The Dutch Republic and the Hispanic World, 1606–1661*, *passim*. See also N. G. Parker, *The Army of Flanders and the Spanish Road, 1567–1659*.
80. See James F. McNulty, 'Blockade: Evolution and Expectation', *United States Naval War College International Law Studies Vol. 62, The Use of Force, Human Rights and General International Legal Issues*, p. 172.
81. T. S. Bindoff, *The Schelt Question*, *passim*.
82. Charles R. Boxer, *The Dutch Seaborne Empire 1600–1800*, pp. 84–112.
83. Quoted in Geoffrey Till, *Maritime Strategy in the Nuclear Age*, p. 150.
84. See Sir Herbert Richmond, op. cit., p. 116.
85. Ralph Davis, *The Rise of the English Shipping Industry*, pp. 12–15.
86. *State Papers, Venice*, vol. 34, nos. 379 and 398.
87. W. J. Ecles, *Canada under Louis XIV, 1663–1701*, chs 4 and 5. See also Paul Walden Bamford, 'French Shipping in Northern European Trade, 1660–1789', *The Journal of Modern History*, vol. 26, pp. 201–19 (1954).
88. Alice Clare Carter, *Neutrality or Commitment: The Evaluation of Dutch Foreign Policy, 1667–1795*, pp. 14–15; and Ralph Davis, op. cit., pp. 224–5.
89. Ralph Davis, 'English Foreign Trade, 1660–1700', in *The Growth of English Overseas Trade*, and *Ec H R*, 2nd Series, VI (1954).
90. Carl Marie von Clausewitz, *On War* (Paret & Howard edn), p. 605.
91. Quoted in R. Pares, *Colonial Blockade*, p. 172.
92. Alice Clare Carter, op. cit.
93. Geoffrey Symcox, *The Crisis of French Sea Power 1688–1697*, pp. 177–87. Marshal Vauban, *Mémoire sur la Caprerie*, 30 Nov. 1695, in Rochas d'Aiglun, *Vauban. Sa Famille et ses écrits. Ses oisivets et sa correspondance: analyse et extracts*, vol. i, 454–61.
94. Geoffrey Sumcox, op. cit, pp. 187–220.
95. G. N. Clark, op. cit., p. 127.
96. J. A. Johnson, 'Parliament and the Protection of Trade 1689–1694', *The Mariners Mirror*, Vol. 57, 1971, pp. 399–413.
97. Ralph Davis, *The Rise of the English Shipping Industry*, p. 316; and Sir H. W. Richmond, op. cit., pp. 237–46.
98. See W. R. Mayer, loc. cit.
99. Geoffrey Symcox, op. cit., pp. 187–220.
100. G. N. Clark, op. cit., p. 139.
101. Ralph Davis, op. cit., p. 317; and J. S. Bromley, 'The French Privateering War, 1702–13', in: *Historical Essays 1600–1750 presented to David Ogg*.
102. Jonathan Swift, *Political Tracts 1711–1713*, Herbert Davis (ed.), s.v., 'The Conduct of the Allies' November 1711, p. 22.
103. Patrick Crowhurst, *The Defence of British Trade 1689–1815*, s.v., 'Marine Insurance'. See also A. H. John, 'The London Assurance Company and the Marine Insurance Market of the Eighteenth Century', *Economica*, XXV (1958) pp. 126–41.
104. The symbiotic relationship amongst the insurance, shipping, and privateering businesses is parallel to what appears to have been the

symbiosis between Latin Christian traders and corsairs in the twelfth and thirteenth centuries. John Pryor suggests that the former were able to capture from Moslem and Byzantine merchants the lion's share of the long-distance trades of the Mediterranean because geography favoured the predatory activities of Christian raiders. John H. Pryor, *Geography, technology, and war. Studies in the maritime history of the Mediterranean, 649–1571*, p. 162.

105. George Louis Beer, *British Colonial Policy, 1754–1765*, pp. 72–131.
106. R. Pares, *War and Trade in the West Indies 1739–63*, p. 351.
107. Lucy S. Sutherland, *A London Merchant, 1695–1774*; *passim*.
108. C. P. Crowhurst, 'The Admiralty and the Convoy System in the Seven Years War', *The Mariners Mirror*, Vol. 57 (1971), pp. 163–73.
109. Ralph Davis, op. cit., pp. 317–18. See C. Wright and C. E. Fayle, *History of Lloyds*, p. 156.
110. Michael Howard, *War and the Liberal Conscience*, p. 24.
111. Richard D. Bourland Jr., 'Maurepas and his Administration of the French Navy on the Eve of the War of the Austrian Succession (1737–1742)', PhD, pp. 146 and 434–5. See Chanoine Victor Verlaque, *Histoire du Cardinal de Fleury et de son Administration*, p. 132.
112. Carl E. Swanson, loc. cit., pp. 275–6.
113. James C. Riley, *The Seven Years War and the Old Regime in France, The Economic and Financial Toll*, pp. 104–7, 111, 114–17, 128–9.
114. Pp. 319–20.
115. R. Pares, *War and Trade*, p. 390.
116. See Nicholas Tracy, *Navies, Deterrence and American Independence*, pp. 2–4, 14–22 and *passim*, and Piers Mackesy, *The War for America, 1775–1783*, *passim*.
117. See Daniel A. Baugh, *British Naval Administration in the Age of Walpole*, s.v., 'Cash and Debt', pp. 470–81; and J. A. Johnson, loc. cit.
118. See Nicholas Tracy, *Manila Ransomed*, forthcoming.
119. Ralph Davis, 'English Foreign Trade, 1700–1774', *The Growth of English Overseas Trade in the Seventeenth and Eighteenth Centuries*, and *Ec H R* Second Series XV (1962).
120. A. H. John, 'War and the English Economy, 1700–1763', *The Economic History Review*, VII (1954–55), pp. 329–44.
121. Ralph Davis, loc. cit.
122. James C. Riley, op. cit., p. 192. See also François Crouzet, review of Riley's work in *English Historical Review*, October 1988, pp. 987–90.
123. Carl J. Kulsrud, op. cit., pp. 107–55.
124. Ibid., pp. 61–106.
125. Alice Clare Carter, op. cit., pp. 85–9. See also her 'How to revise treaties without negotiating: common sense, mutual fears and the Anglo–Dutch trade disputes of 1759', in *Studies in Diplomatic History*, 1970; and *The Dutch Republic in Europe in the Seven Years War*, pp. 84–128. See also Francis R. Stark, op. cit., pp. 72–5.
126. O. H. Mootham, 'The Doctrine of Continuous Voyage, 1756–1815', *British Yearbook of International Law*, 1927, p. 62.
127. Public Record Office, London, State Papers 94/175, no. 26, 26 Sept. 1766.

128. O. W. Stephenson, 'The Supply of Gunpowder in 1776', *American Historical Review*, XXX, pp. 271–81, 1925.
129. David Starkey, loc. cit.
130. Gaston Martin, 'Commercial Relations between Nantes and the American Colonies during the War of Independence', *Journal of Economic and Business History*, IV (1932), pp. 812–29.
131. Quoted in R. Pares, *Colonial Blockade*, p. 172.
132. Public Record Office, London, State Papers 84/561, no. 6; Suffolk to Yorke.
133. Alice Clare Carter, op. cit., pp. 97–106.
134. Isabela de Madariaga, *Britain, Russia and the Armed Neutrality of 1780*, pp. 377–86; Alice Clare Carter, op. cit., pp. 97–103; and Bernard Semmel, *Liberalism and Naval Strategy*, pp. 14–20.
135. Robert Livingston Schuyler, *The Fall of the Old Colonial System*, Introduction and ch 1.
136. E. F. Heckscher, *The Continental System*, p. 61.
137. Alexander De Conde, *The Quasi-War*, *passim.*; James Scott Brown (ed.), *The Controversy Over Neutral Rights Between the United States and France, 1797–1800, A Collection of American State Papers and Judicial Decisions*, *passim*; W. Alison Phillips, op. cit., pp. 86–90; Anna Cornelia Clauder, *American Commerce as Affected By the Wars of the French Revoultion and Napoleon, 1793–1812*, pp. 38–47; and Robert Greenhalgh Albion, op. cit., pp. 78–85.
138. A. N. Ryan, 'The Defence of British Trade with the Baltic, 1808–1813', *English Historical Review*, 74 (1959), p. 443.
139. C. Ernest Fayle, 'Shipowning and Marine Insurance', *The Trade Winds*. See also Charles Wright and C. Ernest Fayle, *A History of Lloyds*.
140. W. Freeman Gilpin, *The Grain Supply of England During the Napoleonic Period*, pp. viii, 13, 20, 23, 31, 45, 80, 85, 94, 108, 145, 194, and Mancur Olson, Jr., *The Economics of the Wartime Shortage*, pp. 49–72.
141. Geoffrey Ellis, *Napoleon's Continental Blockade*, pp. 1–26.
142. Eli F. Heckscher, op. cit., pp. 41 and 205; and W. Allison Phillips, op. cit., pp. 158–66.
143. A. N. Ryan, 'Trade with the Enemy in the Scandinavian and Baltic Ports during the Napoleonic War: for and against'; *Transactions of the Royal Historical Society*, V series, vol. 12 (1962), p. 123.
144. Carlton Savage, *Policy of the United States Toward Maritime Commerce in War*, vol. i, document 56, p. 279.
145. House of Lords, 28 February 1812, *Hansard* XXI, p. 1053 (quoted in Heckscher, p. 120).
146. W. Alison Phillips and Arthur H. Reede, *Neutrality*, ii, 'The Napoleonic Period', pp. 91–125; Anna Cornelia Clauder, *American Commerce as Affected by the Wars of the French Revolution and Napoleon, 1793–1812*, pp. 27–38; and Robert Greenhalgh Albion with Jennie Barnes Pope, *Sea Lanes in Wartime*, p. 75.
147. W. Allison Phillips, op. cit., pp. 119–25; Anna Cornelia Clauder, op. cit., pp. 67–119 and 134; and Robert Greenhalgh Albion, op. cit., pp. 85–94.
148. Ibid., pp. 105–9; Louis Martin Sears, *Jefferson and the Embargo*,

passim.; Walter Wilson Jennings, *The American Embargo, 1807–1809*, pp. 70–93; and W. F. Gilpin, 'The American Grain Trade to the Spanish Peninsula 1810–14', *American Historical Review*, XXVIII, pp. 22–44, 1922.

149. See Richard Glover, 'The French Fleet, 1807–1814; Britain's Problem; and Madison's Opportunity', *The Journal of Modern History*, vol. 33, pp. 407–22 (1961); and Bernard Semmel, op. cit., pp. 26–30.
150. Quoted in Albion, op. cit., p. 116.
151. W. F. Gilpin, loc. cit.
152. A. T. Mahan, *Sea Power in its Relations to the War of 1812*, p. 184.
153. Carlton Savage, *Policy of the United States Toward Maritime Commerce in War*, vol. i, document 60, p. 287.
154. W. K. Hancock and M. M. Gowing, *British War Economy*, p. 4.
155. See John M. Sherwig, *Guineas and Gunpowder, British Foreign Aid in the Wars with France 1793–1815, passim.*
156. Geoffrey Ellis, op. cit., ch. 6.
157. François Crouzet, 'Wars, Blockade, and Economic Change in Europe, 1792–1815', *Journal of Economic History*, 24, pp. 567–88, 1964.
158. Francis R. Stark, op. cit., pp. 19–22.
159. Carlton Savage, op. cit., vol. i, pp. 42–54.
160. Bernard Semmel, op. cit., pp. 31–50.
161. 'An Essay on the Influence of a Low Price of Corn on the Profits of Stock, etc'; see William D. Grampp, *The Manchester School of Economics*, p. 23.
162. Robert Livingston Schuyler, *The Fall of the Old Colonial System*, ch. 5.
163. Olive Anderson, 'Economic Warfare in the Crimean War', *Economic History Review* XIV (1961), pp. 34–47; Sir Francis Piggott, *The Declaration of Paris 1856*; and Warren F. Spencer, 'The Mason Memorandum and the Diplomatic Origins of The Declaration of Paris', in Nancy N. Barker and Marvin L. Brown, *Diplomacy in An Age of Nationalism*, The Hague, 1971.
164. W. H. Malkin, 'The Inner History of the Declaration of Paris', *British Yearbook of International Law*, 1927, pp. 1–44.
165. C. I. Hamilton, Anglo–French Seapower and the Declaration of Paris', *The International History Review*, vol. iv, no. 1, Feb. 1982, pp. 166–90.
166. Carlton Savage, op. cit., vol. i, p. 68.
167. Sir Francis Piggott, op. cit.
168. C. I. Hamilton, loc. cit.
169. 'The War Policy of Commerce', quoted in Piggott, op. cit., p. 110.
170. Olive Anderson, *A Liberal State at War*, pp. 261–8.
171. Ibid., p. 274.
172. W. H. Malkin, loc. cit., and D. Schindler and J. Toman (eds), *The Laws of Armed Conflicts*, no. 56.
173. Francis R. Stark, op. cit., pp. 156–9.
174. W. H. Malkin, loc. cit.
175. Quoted in Sir Francis Piggott, op. cit., p. 126.
176. C. H. Stockton, 'Would Immunity from Capture, During War, of Non-Offending Private Property Upon the High Seas be in the Interest of Civilization?', *The American Journal of International Law*, 1 (1907), p. 930.
177. Bernard Semmel, op. cit., pp. 56–66.

178. *Hansard*, 6 March 1871, p. 1364; quoted by Sir Herbert Richmond, *Sea Power in the Modern World*, pp. 63–8.
179. Sir Francis Piggott, op. cit.
180. C. I. Hamilton, loc. cit.
181. M. R. Pitt, 'Great Britain and Belligerent Maritime Rights from the Declaration of Paris, 1856, to the Declaration of London, 1909', University of London PhD, 1964.
182. Jacob W. Kipp, 'Russian Naval Reforms and Imperial Expansion, 1856–1863', in *Soviet Armed Forces Review*, vol. 1 (1977), p. 118; and John E. Jessup, 'Alliance or Deterrence: The Case of the Russian Fleet Visit to America', in Craig L. Symonds (ed.), *New Aspects of Naval History*, pp. 238–52. See also Norman A. Graebner, loc. cit.
183. Sir Herbert W. Richmond, *Imperial Defence and Capture at Sea in War*, pp. 260–1; and see Richmond, *Economy and Naval Security*, pp. 61–72, s.v., 'Defence Against Investment (b) In the Form of Sporadic Attack', London, 1931.
184. See J. I. de Lanessan, *Le Programme Maritime de 1900–1906* (Paris, 1905), quoted by Geoffrey Till, *Maritime Strategy and the Nuclear Age*, p. 155.
185. Ephraim Douglass Adams, *Great Britain and the American Civil War*, pp. 137–71.
186. George Dalzell, *The Flight From the Flag*, pp. 237–48; Frank J. Merli, 'The Confederate Navy, 1861–1865', in Kenneth J. Hagan (ed.), *In Peace and War*; and Robert Greenhalgh Albion, op. cit., pp. 168–70.
187. F. L. Owsley, *King Cotton Diplomacy*, pp. 1–50.
188. Ibid., pp. 134–42.
189. Philip S. Foner, *British Labour and The American Civil War*, pp. 4–5, 11–24 *et passim*.
190. Carlton Savage, op. cit., pp. 87–97.
191. Stuart L. Bernath, *Squall Across the Atlantic*, pp. 33–62.
192. Norman A. Graebner, 'Northern Diplomacy and European Neutrality', in *Why the North Won the Civil War*, David Donald (ed.); Stuart L. Bernath, op. cit., *passim*; Dudley W. Knox, *A History of the United States Navy*, chs 25 and 26; and Frank J. Merli, op. cit., pp. 235–49.
193. Alfred Thayer Mahan, *From Sail to Steam*, 'Incidents of War and Blockade Service', pp. 156–95.
194. David Donald, 'Died of Democracy'; Richard N. Current, 'God and the Strongest Battalions'; T. Harry Williams, 'The Military Leadership of North and South'; and David M. Potter, 'Jefferson Davis and the Political Factors in Confederate Defeat', all in *Why the North Won the Civil War*.
195. Stanley Lebergott, 'Through the Blockade: The Profitability and Extent of Cotton Smuggling, 1861–1865', *Journal of Economic History*, vol. 41, pp. 867–88, 1981; and see Marcus Price, 'Ships that Tested the Blockade . . .', *The American Neptune*, vols 8 (pp. 196–241), 11 (pp. 262–90) and 15 (pp. 97–132).
196. F. L. Owsley, op. cit., pp. 261–2 and 266–7. See pp. 229–67 *passim*.
197. L. H. Johnson, 'Commerce between Northeastern ports and the Confederacy', *Journal of American History*, vol. 54, pp. 30–42, 1967.
198. Frank E. Vadiver, *Confederate Blockade Running Through Bermuda*

1851–1865, Letters and Cargo Manifests, p. xli.
199. F. L. Owsley, op. cit., p. 267.
200. A. J. Marder, *The Anatomy of British Sea Power: a history of British Naval Policy in the Pre-Dreadnought Era, 1880–1905*, pp. 84–105; and Brian Ranft, 'Restraints on War at Sea before 1945', in Michael Howard (ed.), *Restraints on War*.
201. Theodore Ropp (ed. by Stephen S. Roberts), *The Development of a Modern Navy, French Naval Policy 1871–1904*; pp. 162–80, 206–15; and Donald M. Schurman, *The Education of a Navy*, ch. 2.
202. Archibald Hurd, *The Merchant Navy*, vol. I, p. 210.
203. A. T. Mahan, *The Influence of Sea Power Upon History*, pp. 138 and 209.
204. Geoffrey Symcox, 'Admiral Mahan, the *Jeune Ecole*, and the *Guerre de Course*', in *Commission Internationale d'Histoire Maritime. Course et Piraterie*.
205. Archibald Hurd, op. cit., pp. 212 and 218.
206. Mancur Olson, op. cit., pp. 74–5.
207. Georg Schwarzenburger and E. A. Brown, *A Manual of International Law*, 6th edn, pp. 109 and 150.
208. See Albert E. Hogan, *Pacific Blockade*, *passim*; and Neil H. Alford, *Naval War College International Law Studies, 1963, Modern Economic Warfare (Law and the Naval Participant)*, Washington, 1967; s.v., 'Pacific Blockade', pp. 273–79.
209. Quoted in Albert E. Hogan, op. cit., p. 124.
210. Thomas F. Power Jr., *Jules Ferry and the Renaissance of French Imperialism*, p. 172, s.v., 'Undeclared War with China', *et seq*.; A. Thomazi, *La Conquête de L'Indochine*, s.v., 'La Guerra Navale (1884–1885)'. See also Ralph A. Leitner Jr., 'International Considerations in the French Blockade of Formosa (1884–1885)', PhD, 1979.
211. See Holger H. Herwig, *Germany's Vision of Empire in Venezuela, 1871–1914*, *passim*.
212. E. B. Parsons, 'German–American Crisis of 1902–1903', *The Historian*, vol. 33, pp. 436–52, May 1971; P. S. Holbo, 'Perilous Obscurity: Public Diplomacy and the Press in the Venezuelan Crisis, 1902–1903', *The Historian*, vol. 32, pp. 428–48, May 1970; Ronald Spector, 'Roosevelt, the Navy and the Venezuelan Controversy: 1902–1903', *The American Neptune*, 32 (Oct. 1972), pp. 257–63; and Holger H. Herwig, op. cit., pp. 205–7, 220–35.
213. See C. J. Bartlett, *Great Britain and Sea Power*, p. 87.
214. James Cable, *Gunboat Diplomacy, Political Applications of Limited Naval Force*, pp. 20 and 39–40.
215. Albert Hogan, op. cit., p. 3.
216. Leon Friedman (ed.), *The Law of War*, vol. ii, p. 298.
217. Carlton Savage, op. cit., Document 152, p. 494.
218. Carlton Savage, op. cit., p. 106.
219. A. C. Bell, op. cit., p. 9; see also CAB 21/307. Memorandum by Sir C. Hurst on Sir Maurice Hankey's Paper on 'Blockade and the Laws of War', 16 November 1927.
220. G. P. Gooch and H. Temperley (eds), *British Documents on the Origins of the War*, iii, pp. 402–3, and viii, p. 392.

221. M. R. Pitt, loc. cit., p. 447.
222. Ibid., pp. 295–371.
223. Bernard Semmel, op. cit., pp. 154–8.
224. See Marion C. Siney, *The Allied Blockade of Germany 1914–1916*, p. 8.
225. See Brian Ranft, 'The Protection of British Seaborne Trade and the Development of Systematic Planning for War, 1860–1906', in *Technical Change and British Naval Policy*.
226. Bernard Semmel, op. cit., p. 94.
227. ADM 116/1079 and 1087, International Naval Conference held in London, 1908–9, papers relating to the preparation of Britain's position, and cmd 4554 and 4555, March 1909, Correspondence and Proceedings. See the official communiqué, general report, and final protocol in *United States Naval War College International Law Topics; The Declaration of London of February 26, 1909*, Washington, 1910; James Brown Scott (ed.), *The Declaration of London February 26, 1909, A Collection of Official Papers* . . .; C. H. Stockton, 'The International Naval Conference of London, 1908–1909', *The American Journal of International Law*, 3 (1909), p. 596; Marion C. Siney, op. cit., pp. 8–13; and see Dietrich Schindler and Jiri Toman (eds), *The Laws of Armed Conflicts*, 64, Naval Conference of London, 1909.
228. *The Nineteenth Century*, June 1907 (and reprinted in Admiral A. T. Mahan (ed.)), *Some Neglected Aspects of War*, Boston, 1907. See Donald M. Schurman, *Julian S. Corbett, 1854–1922*, pp. 26 and 71.
229. Donald M. Schurman, op. cit., s.v., Corbett. Sir Julian S. Corbett, *Some Principles of Maritime Strategy*, pp. 235–65.
230. Quoted in CAB 21/307 Memorandum by Sir M. Hankey on Blockade and the Laws of War, 31 October 1927.
231. Louis Guichard, *The Naval Blockade 1914–1918*, p. 19; and Bernard Semmel, op. cit., pp. 89–119.
232. ADM 116/1236, Secret, The Declaration of London from the point of view of war with Germany, MPA Hankey, Naval Assistant Secretary CID, 15 February 1911, and Remarks by Sir Charles Ottley on Captain Hankey's Paper, 17 February 1911. See also Marion C. Siney, op. cit., pp. 8–13.
233. Bernard Semmel, op. cit., p. 114.
234. Quoted in CAB 21/307, loc. cit. See also Lord Hankey, *The Supreme Command*, i, pp. 94–101.
235. Quoted in A. J. Marder, *From the Dreadnaught to Scapa Flow: the Royal Navy in the Fisher Era, 1904–19*, vol. i, p. 36.
236. Archibald Hurd, op. cit., p. 225.

Part II
The Twentieth Century

The history of naval action against maritime trade in the twentieth century repeats in many respects the experience of earlier centuries. Britain began World War I with a double strategic purpose, to block German access to contraband, and to continue its own prosperous trade in order to pay the cost of war. Naval force, however, was not used to channel trade as it had been in earlier centuries. To the contrary, from 1915 the growing determination to deny Germany access to all foreign supplies transformed Britain's use of trade control into a system injurious to its own direct economic interests. The blockade of Germany, however, had limited economic impact on the enemy, except possibly after the 1918 armistice. Its psychological effect was greater, and contributed to the German decision to embark on unrestricted U-boat warfare, and, later, to Hitler's conviction that Germany must seek autarchy through control of Eastern Europe. Its effect on Anglo–American relations was also difficult, and led to the inter-war naval arms limitation treaties.

The truth re-established during the war, and eventually learnt, was that in the twentieth century no less than the eighteenth, belligerents could not afford to maximise the economic pressure they could put on an enemy, at the expense of their own military potential. In World War II British economic war policy returned to a quasi-mercantilism in which measures of blockade against Germany were not allowed to impede the development of Britain's own war economy. In any case, Britain's blockade of Germany in World War II was made less effective by the neutrality of the United States and Russia in the first years, and later by the German military occupation of most of the European mainland. All the same, it served to deny Germany access to American sources of supply in the period 1939–41.

German U-boat operations against Britain in World War I also had greater psychological effects than economic ones, not all of them to Germany's advantage. They contributed to the American entry into the war. The British navy was able to deny Germany victory by establishing comprehensive controls on shipping, and by organising convoys. The same means served to keep the much better directed U-boat assault on shipping in World War II from ever really threatening Britain's ability to sustain an effective defensive. In theory, Britain could have been defeated, but in practice the British Commonwealth, supported by the resources of the United States, was too strong. It is not even certain that the cost to Germany of mounting the offensive was less than was the cost of the defensive. However, the U-boat war did create difficulties for the mobilisation of Allied resources for offensive operations. Shortage of shipping ensured that, once Allied resources were deployed to the Mediterranean in 1942, they had to be used there in 1943. The assault on northern Europe had to wait until 1944. The U-boat war also served German strategic needs by compelling Britain and its allies to devote a large part of their naval resources to defensive efforts.

The American blockade of Japan in World War II produced dramatic economic results, despite the relatively small amount of effort that was put into imposing it. Its effects were multiplied by the failure of the Japanese to develop efficient means of trade defence, or the capacity to improvise administrative compensations for shortages. The terrible hardships produced by the blockade, however, did not have such powerful, time-urgent, political effects that the Japanese government could be brought to surrender before the atomic bombs were used, and Russia invaded Manchuria.

Perhaps the only way in which war on trade in the twentieth century has differed fundamentally from that of earlier centuries is that it was no longer a technically necessary part of war strategy, required to ensure private investment in warships, and to stimulate recruitment. Possibly, however, Britain's blockade of Germany in World War I can be said to have served a comparable purpose by sustaining naval morale in a long war which contained frustratingly few battles.

Belief in 1918 that the British blockade of Germany in World War I had alone eclipsed German power, which otherwise had been triumphant in Russia and France, vastly enhanced the prestige of maritime strategy in the period following World War I. American fears at the time of the formation of the League of Nations, that it could not function if Britain's naval strength were not matched by American seapower, reflected the belief at the end of World War I that naval blockade had the power to determine international politics. Illogically, it was also believed that it could do so in a way which was more acceptable to national and humanitarian feeling. The loss of life on the Western Front in 1914–18 inspired more revulsion than did the privation, disease, and death of civilian populations. The dogged defence of belligerent rights by the British government in the 1920s, and American attempts to promote neutral rights, were the results of that unrealistically high estimation of the capacity of blockade. Even before the outbreak of World War II, however, a more sober view had begun to be taken of the value of blockade, perhaps as a result of its limitations as an instrument of the League of Nations. The potential which was demonstrated in 1945 by the American blockade of Japan has not reversed the transformation of expectations.

Naval attack on trade has played only a small role in the wars of the great powers in the period following World War II. The North Atlantic Treaty Organisation takes seriously the possibility that the Soviet Union might conduct operations against shipping as part of a European war, but in practice the Soviets have exhibited a keen awareness of the potential for escalation intrinsic to attack on maritime trade, and their strategic literature does not express any great belief in its utility. There are several examples, however, of wartime use of contraband control by the United States Navy, and the Korean and Vietnam campaigns have established new norms in state behaviour. The Cuban missile crisis is a further example of naval action against shipping, but its didactic importance is limited because it was closer to an act of coercive diplomacy than it was to established ideas of contraband control. Naval blockade has been employed as part of the United Nations sanctions against Rhodesia. Smaller powers have made more use of attack on trade, for a number of strategic purposes. The Iran–Iraq war has produced more violence against shipping than anything else since 1945. British and American reactions to it have been in keeping with the traditional policies of each. The imposition of a total trade embargo on Iraq by the United Nations in 1990, and enforced by a multi-national force, indicates that blockade continues to be an important strategy for the exploitation of seapower.

2 World War I

THE BLOCKADE OF THE CENTRAL POWERS

In 1906–7 an Admiralty committee under Captain G. A. Ballard prepared for the First Sea Lord, Sir John Fisher, war plans which called for blocking German trade, but David French has shown that little attempt was made to discover what would be the economic impact on Germany of an effective blockade, should it indeed be possible.[1] The Liberal administration was more concerned to sustain a prosperous British trade in wartime to pay for its cost, and a subcommittee of the Committee of Imperial Defence under Lord Desard attempted in 1911–12 to address the problem that complete severance of trade with Germany would injure Britain almost as much as it did Germany. It concluded that the Crimean War experiment in free-trade in wartime had gone too far by including trade with the enemy, but Captain Maurice Hankey, who had been secretary of the Ballard committee, wrote a defence of maritime strategy in 1913 in which he asserted that the positive dimension of economic warfare was the fundamental strength Britain enjoyed. As in the Napoleonic war, Britain's strategy should be to protect its own trade, while eroding that of Germany. Britain would be the paymaster of the *Entente*, which would be able to outlast the Germans in the field because of its stronger financial resources. The cabinet did not agree that Britain could take the risk of leaving the French army alone to face a German attack, and the continentalists gained approval for a British expeditionary force large enough to reinforce the French left wing. Its size was to be restricted, however, so that British industry would not lack the manpower to sustain the City of London as a paymaster of liberal democracy at war.

Britain's strategy was not to be actively mercantilist. Wartime commercial prosperity was to be left to the liberal principle of 'business as usual', although in the July 1914 crisis the government did intervene in the marine insurance and banking markets to avert a panic. The use of naval forces to enhance the profitability of British trade was repugnant to liberal ideas, and in fact it was impossible under the prevailing conditions to do so without violating the international conventions on the laws of war at sea. After the appointment of Winston Churchill to the Admiralty in 1911, naval planners had at least faced the fact that technical conditions would no longer permit close blockade of German ports, which was the only legal means of conducting a general war on trade unaffected by the Declarations of Paris and London.[2]

The official historian of the blockade, A. C. Bell, writes that by 1914, despite the technical difficulties, the Admiralty had definitely decided that economic pressure was its first weapon, and concluded that a long-distance blockade at the entrances to the North Sea which eliminated the German merchant marine would have a significant effect on the German war effort. However, Bell also admitted to the readers of the confidential document that

> Nobody operating the campaign ever hoped that a particular object would be gained by it: the economic campaign was simply regarded as an operation valuable enough to be persisted in, providing always, that it did not provoke the American government to an open breach.

He contrasted this *ad hoc* policy favourably with the German gamble of unrestricted U-boat warfare.

> If the German authorities had conducted their own campaign on these two simple axioms, they would probably have subjected Great Britain to pressure nearly equivalent to the pressure exerted upon Germany, and they would not have involved their countrymen in one of the most terrible disasters that has overtaken a proud nation.[3]

On the outbreak of war the British fleet was directed to seize German shipping, and to intercept the supplies upon which the German army depended. It was recognised that the legal definition of blockade could not be stretched to include interception of neutral ships carrying goods on the Free List of the Declaration of London in the waters north of Scotland.[4] Formal blockades in the technically correct usage of the word were eventually declared on the East Coast of Africa, in Asia Minor, Greece, Salonica and Tsingtao, but in waters threatened by the German High Seas Fleet British tactics were directed to the exploitation of the long contraband list of the Declaration of London which was now seen to be useful. The Foreign Minister, Sir Edward Grey, made it clear

> that We have only two objects in our proclamations: to restrict supplies for the German army and to restrict the supply to

> Germany of materials essential for the making of munitions of war. We intend to attain these objects with the minimum of interference with the United States and other neutral countries.[5]

To the British ambassador in Paris, he insisted that

> we have always contended that foodstuffs and raw materials destined for the civil population are not contraband of war . . . Over and over again, we have laid this down as a doctrine of international law; and our Prize Courts would not act on any other.

This limited goal, however, was soon left behind. Rapidly the allied governments became dissatisfied with the limitations on their power and began to expand the contraband list. There was no concrete strategic reasoning behind the reversal of policy. It simply reflected the brutalising impact of war, and the need to impress the French that the British navy was making a contribution to *Entente* defence. Neutral shipping was obliged to submit to search, and contraband manifested to Germany was seized. Despite pressure from the United States government, Britain deviated from the Declaration of London to the extent of applying the doctrine of continuous voyage to conditional contraband.[6] As a result, Washington declared that the United States would expect its commerce to be protected by the legal regime in force before 1909.[7] At first, however, few seizures were made, because the Foreign Office had not yet developed its sources of information about neutral consignees who might or might not be acting as forwarding agents for the enemy.

Cotton was figuratively and technically the most explosive issue. It was the primary crop of an important part of the United States which must not be offended, for which reason it had been put on the Declaration of London's 'free list' of non-contraband, but it was also the basis for the manufacture of modern explosives. The problem was temporarily shelved because experts calculated, incorrectly, that the quantity of cotton needed for the manufacture of explosives was so small that it could not be blocked. It was later to return to trouble relations with the United States.[8] Copper and magnetic iron ore were declared contraband despite the fact that copper was politically important in the mid-western American states and iron was a principal export of Spain and Sweden, but arrangements were secretly made to purchase 95 per cent of the American export supply of copper.[9]

When it was learnt that Germany was not controlling food supplies, and because of the difficulty of checking neutral consignees, it was decided not to make an issue initially of continuous voyage. This policy was embodied in an order-in-council on 29 October 1914 which also contained a proviso that was later used to open a way for large-scale prosecution of economic war, including an attack on food supplies. It permitted a gradual abandonment of international law as the governing factor in belligerent rights at sea. The order-in-council stated that, if it became apparent that any neutral port had become an *entrepôt* of conditional contraband destined for the enemy, all ships sailing to it would be seized. This principle, which had no foundation in law, had actually been suggested to London unofficially by Acting Secretary of State Lansing.[10] The effect of neutral quiescence to this declaration was that the governing factor in the enforcement of the blockade increasingly became the ability of the belligerents to reach political settlement with the neutrals. One of the principal targets of Britain's new policy was food sales by Chicago meat packers to intermediaries in Denmark, either for resale to Germany, or to replace on the Danish market Danish produce sold to German markets.

A contraband committee was formed at the Foreign Office under Sir Eyre Crowe.[11] It immediately began negotiations with the neutrals, beginning with the Netherlands. All Dutch sales of food and forage to Germany were blocked, and a 'Netherlands Overseas Trust' was established to act as consignee of all imports, and guarantor that contraband would not be re-exported to Germany. Bell writes:

> As an instrument of control the agreement was found faulty and elaborated later on; nevertheless it would be difficult to exaggerate the importance of the settlement provisionally concluded. Without provoking political controversy, the agreement transmuted the rule of continuous voyage from a disputed legal doctrine into a workable contract between business men.[12]

The Foreign Office did not want to carry out the threat of declaring Copenhagen to be an enemy port as it would have embarrassed relations with other neutrals, and been difficult to reverse. In the end, the Danes agreed to forbid re-export of contraband except to the other Scandinavian countries, in return for which Britain abandoned efforts to control the export of Danish food to Germany. The Norwegians, Italians and Swiss came to similar agreements. The Swedes, on the other hand, were at once too vulnerable to Germany, and in too strong a position *vis-à-vis* the *Entente* powers, to be so easily dealt with. Sweden was supplying Britain with pit-props and ball-bearings, and controlled vital rail links to Russia. An agreement was reached with the Swedes not to re-export contraband, but it was soon evident that the Swedish government was conniving at violations of the regulations to which it had agreed.[13]

The only really important neutral state was the United States. All sections of the American economy were worried about Britain's settlements with European neutrals which in effect eliminated the difference between contraband and conditional contraband. The fall in cotton exports was blamed on the British blockade, and the copper mining states forcefully expressed their grievances. Shippers were exasperated by the delays which occurred when a ship was detained for inspection. The Chicago meat packers, who hoped to make vast profits out of using Copenhagen as a gateway into Germany, were especially irate. However, although the American government sent Britain a strongly worded note, to which was answered an equally firm reply, it refused to act in consort with other neutrals, and belied its strong language with an evident disposition to give Britain the benefit of the doubt.[14] In January 1915 Secretary Bryan advised the Senate Committee on Foreign Relations that British practice with respect to continuous voyage was one which had been enforced by American courts when the United States was a belligerent. London and Washington reached a 'working arrangement' by which the American government itself tightened up shipping manifests of American merchant shipping to prevent evasion of the blockade.[15]

One of the American complaints was that Britain's attitude to its own export trade was not entirely free from the old mercantilist concept. There was a basis of truth in that belief. In keeping with the incoherent strategy of the liberal government in 1914, that the British economy could become the arsenal of the *Entente*, British businessmen were urged to 'capture' Germany's former markets. The British proclamation of 5 August 1914 prohibiting all new trade with residents of the German and Austrian empires was a clear departure from the mercantilism of British policy in the Napoleonic war.[16] Nevertheless, common sense modified in practice the 'purity' of British strategy. In 1911 the Board of Trade had recognised the need for new legislation on trading with the enemy, but throughout the war it continued to maintain that severity in the curbs on exports to the neutral neighbours of Germany would hurt Britain more than it would Germany. It felt that it would be impossible to stop leaks, but in any case it did not want to oblige British traders to watch Americans supplying the inflated demands of the border neutrals.

The initial legislation controlling British exports was inadequate to deny Germany access to British commodities, or to answer the American charge that the British blockade was being used to support the British economy. The fear of mercantilism was exacerbated by British interception of mails and cables, which led American businessmen to charge that the British censors were deliberately passing on trade secrets to British firms.[17] In 1916 there were discussions between Italy, France and Britain about economic integration to strengthen their position in post-war economic competition with the Central Powers, but Lord Grey was not interested in the idea.[18]

The alarm of American business interests may have been justifiable, but, even if Britain's blockade could not be conducted without some regard for the needs of positive economic warfare, other priorities precluded a successful mercantilist strategy. Lord Kitchener's vast expansion of the British army, undertaken by the cabinet 'in a fit of absence of mind' and without consideration to its significance in economic strategy, so severely affected manpower available for industry that competition with neutral traders became ever more difficult. The requirements of the negative objective of the blockade, the strangulation of German trade, were allowed to frustrate any hope of trade expansion. When in 1915 the coalition government undertook a massive expansion of the armaments industry, all hope of financial survival came to depend upon an unprecedented degree of state management. Offensive trade strategy became impossible.[19]

The financial outcome of World War I makes it clear that mercantilism was not a dominant aspect of British policy. The financial burden for all the participants was enormous. When it became evident in 1915 that the war would be protracted and dreadfully expensive the British Treasury had to move beyond the norms of peacetime finance. In the September 1915 budget the income tax was raised from 1*s* 3*d* to 6*s* in the pound, with a heavy surtax on top, but during the course of the war only one quarter of expenditure was paid for out of the tax and customs revenue which also had to meet interest and sinking fund payments on war loans. Inflation reduced the value of the pound by 66 per cent in six years. In 1915 the Treasury began to resort to the New York money market, but the cost of war remained a serious problem for Britain. Kathleen Burk believes that there is a strong possibility that Britain's finances would have collapsed in 1917 had the United States not became a belligerent, when loans were obtained from the American Treasury of more than $2 billion which were used to offset the loans Britain had made to its allies.[20] Critics of the British Treasury pointed out that 47 per cent of the expense of the war against Napoleon had been paid out of taxes. Treasury expenditure in the earlier war had led to a 50 per cent devaluation of the pound over 20 years, which had occasioned vehement protests from David Ricardo and other advocates of the gold standard, but that rate compared well with the inflation of World War I. Conditions are too different for the economic strategies of the two wars to be closely contrasted, but a rather obvious inference can be made that a mercantilist strategy was less destructive to the belligerent than was Britain's blockade policy of World War I.

Germany suffered an even greater loss of spending power. Once the 'war chest' had been consumed, the war was financed on inflation, which reduced the ratio of gold to notes from the 1914 level of 76.2 per cent to 29.9 per cent in 1917, and raised the cost of living in the first year of war by 48.7 per cent.

Limited as the British economic campaign was in 1914 it did cause the German government concern, and led them to undertake their own campaign. The German war plan had been predicated on the assumption that Germany could not win a long war. When the sweep into France failed to bring a rapid end to the fighting, concern was immediately felt about Britain's efforts to cut supplies of foreign commodities. Attempts were made to encourage the Americans to resist the British blockade, but the effort was balanced and ultimately cancelled by retaliatory action against British trade. Admiral Tirpitz and the German Admiralty had firmly rejected in pre-war planning any concept of trade war against Britain because of Germany's geographical disadvantages. In 1914 the German High Seas Fleet had not been able to erode British naval power to a point where the geographic difficulties could be overcome and a surface blockade of British trade attempted, but the few U-boats Germany had were finding it too difficult to operate against warships and wished to undertake a campaign against trade. Eventually the German navy overcame the objection of Chancellor Bethman-Hollweg, that attacks on trade would exasperate America, by saying the targets could be confined to British ships. The Kaiser was rushed into signing the order. On 4 February 1915 a 'war zone' was declared to exist around the British Isles, within which all merchant ships were liable to be sunk 'without it always being possible to avoid danger to the crews and passangers'.[21] The declaration was justified on the quite correct grounds that Britain's blockade of food supplies was illegal.

The German navy was only able to keep four to six U-boats continuously at sea. The success of the strategy depended on the hope that they could create a panic that would confine British merchantmen to port. In July 1914 London had been obliged to avert the danger of famine, food riots and revolution by ordering all British merchant ships carrying food cargoes to Germany to divert to British ports. The threat that American grain dealers would cut off supplies to Britain had put an end to that practice, but by 1915 more sophisticated machinery of state management of maritime shipping had been created. In August 1914 the Trade Branch of the Operations Division had been expanded into a separate division of the War Staff, known as the Trade Division. British government war risk insurance, and the strength of Lloyds Marine Insurance, ensured that there was no shipping panic until the crisis of 1917.[22]

Neutral reaction to the German U-boat campaign, which in the early stages was largely conducted according to the Hague rules on search and sinking, was not at once a problem to Germany. More dangerous to it was the use to which the British government was able to put the German violation of the principle of the Hague convention. In 'reprisal', Britain expanded the scope of its 'contraband control' to include all cargoes destined for Germany.[23] Unlike the use of reprisal in land warfare, its use in naval warfare inevitably injures neutrals as well as the enemy. In effect, the two controls on violation of international law, reprisal and neutral reaction, may cancel each other.[24] However, the northern neutrals had no choice but to accept the order, and the American reaction was ambiguous.[25] Britain continued to be supplied throughout the rest of the war with excuses for intensifying the blockade. By an Order-in-Council of 7 July 1916 the British government finally abrogated the Declaration of London, impelled by the *Zamora* judgment which made it imperative to ensure that British prize courts would not hold the Declaration of London to be established law. French prize courts felt no comparable restraint upon their enforcement of municipal jurisdiction, but the French, somewhat unwillingly, followed the British lead.[26] The recommendation made by an Admiralty International Law Committee on 30 April 1918, that the Declaration of Paris should also be abrogated, was not acted upon.[27] The principle of reprisal, however, had already justified setting it aside. Prize Law returned to the older practices of admiralty, and even those legal forms were sometimes entirely disregarded by the Foreign Office.

In 1915 the *Entente* were desperate to find ways of by-passing the deadlock on the Western Front. The British in particular hoped they could find means of using their naval power to reduce the slaughter in France. The abortive campaign to turn the German flank by an attack on Turkey was one means tried, and the other was intensification of the blockade. Germany had survived the winter of 1914–15 despite the blockade of imported foodstuffs upon which the industrial north and the Rhineland usually depended. It was believed, correctly, that there was a steady leakage through the neighbouring neutral states. Accordingly, London in effect made war against those neutrals, for the limited purpose of stopping their *entrepôt* trade. The situation, though undeclared, was similar to that of the Napoleonic war when Napoleon declared there were no neutral states in the struggle to destroy the British economy. The 11 March 1915 Reprisal Order to the fleet instructed it to bring in and hold indefinitely cargoes suspected of being destined for the enemy. If the cargo manifest showed a neutral destination, the release of the ship depended on the Foreign Office's being persuaded that the neutral was enforcing a ban on re-export of contraband. If the ship were suspected, it was to be held long enough to ensure that its owners did not make a profit from the voyage. In the first five months of the new policy 708 ships were detained.

TOTAL ARRIVALS FROM OVERSEAS (those detained).

	Netherlands	Denmark	Norway	Sweden
March	140 (26)	95 (19)	78 (10)	71 (35)
April	176 (37)	105 (31)	43 (18)	64 (51)
May	199 (48)	91 (35)	43 (26)	79 (38)
June	156 (65)	73 (43)	48 (27)	46 (41)
July	186 (51)	59 (44)	38 (34)	46 (39)
	(227)	(172)	(115)	(204)
				= 708

Only the ships with cargoes manifested to the Netherlands Overseas Trust were exempt from detentions, because the Trust was held to be reliable. Indeed it had a Foreign Office negotiator as its 'English Secretary'. The hostility of the Swedish government prevented the Scandinavian governments agreeing to similar settlements. Other arrangements began to be made, however, directly with the neutral shippers. Ultimately they were to prove more satisfactory. Neutral governments were vulnerable to countervailing pressures from Germany, backed possibly even by the threat of invasion. Neutral shippers, on the other hand, were only exposed to coercion by the British government. They suffered financially from the detentions, because the Foreign Office always insisted on the shipper formally signing away his right to demurrage before ships were released. Consequently, they began to approach the Foreign Office with the age-old request that it make clear what were the grounds it used for ordering a detention. According to Bell, no complaint was made about the determination to prevent cargoes going to Germany; the shippers only wished to be told what they were allowed to do so that they could stay in business. Gradually, the larger and respected shippers came to agreements with the Foreign Office to guarantee the ultimate destination of the cargo. For this purpose, they ran their own intelligence services. In effect, the blockade was imposed by diplomacy backed by coercive force arbitrarily applied against neutrals, and administered by the neutral businessmen themselves under supervision.[28] The Admiralty drew the lesson after the war that blockade agreements worked

> moderately well whenever we were able to make them directly with individuals or associations, as in Norway. A large organization, such as the N.O.T., necessarily suffered from leakage, while no Government agreement was satisfactory.[29]

Except when there happened to turn up evidence that a particular consignment of cargo was destined for known agents of the enemy, the supervision of neutral shippers had to depend largely upon statistical evidence. The amount of imports into neutral harbours was compared to pre-war requirements. The ultimate realisation of this control was a system of rationing of neutral imports which was suggested by the French, largely because of their concern at the quantity of British exports which were reaching Germany. The Prize Courts could not be used to enforce the quotas because statistical evidence is not admissible in law. Although the British Prize Court did not let conceptions of international law obstruct its enforcement of British municipal law, the Judicial Committee of the Privy Council insisted that it could not take instructions from the Crown, which, as it observed in the judgment on the *Zamora* case quoted above, 'is a party to the proceedings'.[30] The result was that the Foreign Office only rarely sent cargo cases to the prize courts for adjudication. The coercion it relied upon was almost entirely outside the law, which did not sanction arbitrary detentions or the extortion of agreements not to claim damages. Eventually, in April 1916 in the case of the *Baron Sternblad*, the prize court ruled that the *prima facie* case presented by statistical evidence justified seizure of the cargo, but not the ship.[31]

The Declaration of Paris clearly prevented any British action against Germany's export trade, but that restraint was soon set aside. It had been assumed in Britain before the war that Germany's export trade would automatically disappear if imports to Germany were blocked, because neutral states would not buy German goods if the blockade prevented redress of their balance of trade by selling on the German market. The Germans, however, had been as successful in sustaining their export trade as were the British. London could not tolerate that. As Bell wrote:

> The *Rotterdam* was therefore ordered to discharge the suspicious consignments at Avonmouth, and this was done, not to assert a legal right, but as an act of power, ordered *in terrorem*.[32]

The impact of the order was all the greater because the *Rotterdam* had been freighted by the Netherlands Overseas Trust. Writing after the war, H. W. Malkin argued that the law of continuous voyage must be applied to general economic blockade as well as to contraband control. He believed that international law must accommodate change in detail so as to permit continuity in principle. This was a case of special pleading to cover the violation of the clearly stated principles of the Declaration of Paris.[33]

A crisis in Anglo–American relations appeared unavoidable when it became evident that cotton was too important to German armaments and armies to continue on a free list. The French government and the British public demanded that something be done to deny it them. The March 1915 order-in-council had meant that cotton cargoes were detained along with everything else until satisfactory guarantees were received that they would not be re-exported to Germany, but because of the political importance of cotton in the United States it had been felt necessary to purchase the detained cargoes. Sir Edward Grey reacted strongly to the danger, and was even prepared to contemplate agreement with President Wilson's demand that states recognise the 'Freedom of the Seas', if doing so would eliminate the danger from the U-boats. Sir Eyre Crowe suggested that Britain might give up the food blockade if Germany gave up submarines. Sir Julian Corbett, who was working for the Committee of Imperial Defence, appears to have supplied Sir

Maurice Hankey, who was now the Secretary of the War Committee, with a memorandum for cabinet opposing the idea.[34] Grey did not pursue it, however, and the American State Department itself suggested a way out of the dilemma. On 20 August London declared that cotton was contraband. By then American cotton growers had evidently decided that the *Entente* powers were the better market, and did not raise strong objections.[35]

Even within Europe, the blockade was never completely effective. There were limits to the reach of Britain's coercion, even with the assistance of France and Italy. Switzerland posed a perplexing problem because the German cantons were virtually part of the industrial system of Germany. It was undesirable to treat Switzerland as a virtual enemy because Swiss industry was also supplying the *Entente* armies. The French government was most directly involved in negotiations with the Swiss, who agreed in the end to police themselves and restrict to the *Entente* powers the sale of items manufactured from raw materials supplied by the *Entente*.[36] Sweden refused to co-operate. The Swedish Court, nobility and army were openly pro-German and were only restrained by the middle class. Anti-Russian sentiment was great, and only the frightening scale of the German defeat of Russia was ultimately to reduce Swedish hostility to the other *Entente* powers. In the meantime, Britain preferred to avoid any formal agreement with the suspect Swedish government, and relied upon day-to-day arrangements.

In the light of the tremendous prestige the German armies had acquired during the course of 1915, it was fortunate for the *Entente* that the blockade no longer depended upon the contraband agreements of 1914 but had been transformed into a business arrangement with private citizens. It had to be accepted that Denmark would not ban export of home-grown foodstuffs when they feared a German invasion that the *Entente* would be powerless to stop. British coercion of Norway, to reduce Norwegian fish and pyrites sales to Germany, was followed so closely by U-boat attacks on Norwegian shipping in the Arctic that it appeared to be deliberate reprisal action. It even appeared possible that Germany would declare war on Norway.[37]

The economic effect of the blockade on Germany in 1915 was not great. Food prices in Berlin rose, but not so much as to produce important strategic or political results, and perhaps more as a result of inflation produced by the cost of war than because of the blockade. A few examples will suffice.

	Dec. 1914	Dec. 1915	% Increase
Beef	1m per lb	1.5m per lb	50%
Potatoes	9.7 pfgs p/k	8.5 pfgs p/k	−12%
W Bread	61.2 pfgs p/k	67.6 pfgs p/k	10.4%
Rice	74.3 pfgs p/k	171.1 pfgs p/k	130.2%
Pig Lard	199 pfgs p/k	499.8 pfgs p/k	151.1%

Cotton yarn rose in price from 159–171 pfgs per English pound in July 1915 to 238–257 pfgs in December, forcing textile factories making cloth for civilians to close down. The German government, however, made inroads into civilian supplies to ensure that the armed forces did not suffer. The belated campaign against German exports was more successful. An example is the fall in German exports to the United States from the 1913 level of US$188.9 million, and 1914 level of US$189.9 million, to the 1915 level of US$91.3 million.

In 1916 the British government cautiously tightened the blockade, taking care to avoid a crisis with the United States. American dislike of 'British Navalism' nearly equalled the detestation of 'Prussian Militarism'. Interception of neutral shipping was a major grievance, and Americans were especially irate at the deployment of British cruisers close outside American harbours.[38] However, London was largely able to avoid the sort of incidents which stir public indignation. The privateers which had caused so much trouble in earlier wars were a thing of the past, lamented by none. Even the highly disciplined but dangerously high-handed regular naval officers were employed only in carrying out Foreign Office instructions. Great care was taken in the timing of seizures to avoid friction at inopportune moments. The policy of control by a diplomatically sensitive civilian agency did not change when popular clamour in Britain against the Foreign Office's restraint, and a House of Commons debate on trading with the enemy, made it politically necessary to create a separate Ministry of Blockade (23 February 1916). A senior member of the Foreign Office, Lord Robert Cecil, was appointed as its minister. In consequence, the new department actually increased the degree of Foreign Office control over blockade and war trading strategy, because it superseded the functions of nearly a dozen committees and departments.[39]

The bureaucratic apparatus of the Blockade Department minimised the occasions when neutrals were confronted by raw military force. British control of neutral shipping was largely effected by controlling access to British coaling stations around the world, and by controlling the supplies of vital commodities available in quantity only from the British and French empires – jute sacking and tin plate needed for containing raw products, and oil seeds. One of the first duties of the new Ministry of Blockade was to draw up a 'statutory list', referred to generally as the 'Black List', of firms known to be trading with the enemy. The French established their own Black List. The effect was that neutral businessmen were obliged to chose between trading exclusively with the *Entente* and with neutrals, or trading with the Central Powers. If they chose the latter course, no citizen of an *Entente* state could do business with them, no coal could be supplied to any of their ships except in the very few neutral ports, and other vital commodities would be unavailable. Bunker control was also used to oblige neutral shippers to serve British trades. Eventually even the Swedes decided to negotiate about the rationing system.[40]

Although control over the commercial activity by Britain and France of their subjects violated no principle of international law, the Black List was a most severe and entirely arbitrary attack upon the livelihood of neutral citizens who could be forced into bankruptcy. In effect, it favoured British and French commercial enterprises abroad, and for that reason it was subjected to especially bitter attack by the United States. The Black List was not mercantilist in intention, but its effect on neutral traders was no different than if it had been unashamedly mercantilist. Because of the diplomatic repercussions of placing a neutral firm upon the list, a separate and secret Black List had to be kept listing those firms against which the evidence was not great enough to defend in court, but with which the British government were nonetheless not prepared to permit trade.

The tactically drawn battle of Jutland on 31 May 1916 sustained Britain's ability to enforce the blockade, but, perhaps as a result, the American government came closest to attempting interference in the blockade in the following months. President Wilson was converted to a big-navy policy by the sinking of the *Lusitania* by a German U-boat in 1915, but his motive for seeking a navy on 'an equality with the most efficient and practicably serviceable' foreign navy was the need to protect American trade as much from a post-war Anglo–Japanese alliance as from a Germano–Japanese one. The American Naval Act of 1916 authorised the construction of 160 ships, including 16 battleships and battlecruisers.[41] The Foreign Office was convinced that the United States would have to be confronted. A letter from the

Ambassador in Washington, Sir Cecil Spring-Rice, was minuted

> Nothing so much impresses the people of the United States as the certainty that we will not stoop either to cajolery or irritation; but will proceed calmly with the destruction of modern Germany by blockade.[42]

The hanging of Sir Roger Casement and the other 1916 Irish rebels added to the image of British arrogance, which encouraged the feeling that there was little to choose between the sides. During the 1916 presidential campaign the Black List created great strain in Anglo–American relations, although the candidates were careful to distance themselves from an issue which might backfire.[43] A crisis was avoided, however, because Sir Edward Grey was prepared to compromise with the blockade in the interest of Anglo–American relations.[44]

London was able to meet some American needs in a manner which in fact was greatly to the British interest. Strong protest from American shippers at delays caused by British inspections of neutral ships led the American Consul-General in London, Mr Skinner, to suggest a system of cargo passports. London welcomed the suggestion, and in March 1916 the 'navicert' system was established. It proved to be a highly effective way of administering the rationing system.[45]

The depredations of the German U-boats created much stronger feeling in the United States. Secretary of State Bryan had resigned in June 1915 when Wilson agreed with Robert Lansing's insistence on vigorous protest at the sinking of the *Lusitania* with heavy loss of American lives. Lansing was put in charge at the State Department, in effect committing the United States to the pro-British policy that eventually led to the American declaration of war against Germany.[46] The civilians in Berlin reasserted themselves in October 1915 and ordered that passenger steamers should not be attacked. Their policy was not at first consistent and neither did the German navy carry it out consistently. In April 1916, however, fear of American resentment persuaded Berlin to order the U-boats to conform to the Hague rules on search of merchant ships, and care for their crew's safety. Rather than accept the dangers involved, the new C-in-C, Admiral Scheer, recalled all the U-boats from trade warfare. The *volte face*, however, did not bring a return of public goodwill in the United States.

The economic impact of the British blockade in 1916 is hard to assess. H. W. Carless Davis, in his official monograph history of the administrative machinery of the blockade, wrote that assessment of intelligence in Britain about the impact of the blockade was unsatisfactory. Not only was it impossible to assess the amount of food available in the German black market, but more important

> there was the insoluable problem how long the German people would resign themselves to existing upon a diet which, so far as the masses were concerned, was certainly insufficient to maintain the vital forces at their normal level. There were always experts who professed to know how many calories per diem were necessary to existence, and who would prove that the diet of the average German fell below this minimum by this or that appalling figure. But the most precise of these statisticians could never say how long the Germans would continue to endure the unendurable.[47]

A. C. Bell states that there were over sixty food riots in German cities.[48] The shortages, however, were at most only an indirect product of the blockade. There was ample food in the German countryside, but not the administrative control needed to get it to the cities. Nor was there the bureaucratic insight needed to obtain supplies from captured territories. Typically short-sighted was the requisitioning of draft animals for the German and Austrian armies, which left conquered territories without the means of producing food. The German administration of Belgium accepted a convention with the United States that it would not permit the export of foodstuffs, in order to secure American relief supplies for starving Belgians.[49]

The political effect of the blockade was more important, although they were not those hoped for by the British government. The economic campaign produced a sense of desperation in the German high command, and a thirst for revenge in kind. The successful French counterattack at Verdun added to the worry of the army command, and to the determination of the navy to show that it was earning its keep, despite the failure at Jutland. The Chancellor, Bethman-Hollweg, was convinced that a return to unrestricted U-boat operations would lead to war with the United States, but he was overwhelmed by the shrill demand of the military that the 'last gambler's throw' be attempted. A memorandum produced by the German navy asserted that the U-boats could sink 600 000 tons of shipping a month. In five months losses at that rate, and the additional loss of neutral shipping diverted from British ports, would reduce British tonnage available for imports by 40 per cent. The expected failure of the American 1917 grain harvest supported the belief that Britain would be unable with that shipping to import the necessary food from Australia and would have to seek peace.[50] The decision was taken to resume all-out U-boat warfare on 1 February 1917. It was justified, in a note delivered to the American government on 31 January, by the insistence of the English government 'upon continuing its war of starvation, which does not at all affect the military power of its opponents but compels women and children, the sick and the aged to suffer for their country . . .[51]

THE 1917 U-BOAT CAMPAIGN

The 1917 U-boat campaign was spectacular, especially in its impact upon neutral trade. The inadequacy of shipping available to the *Entente* even before the recommencement of unrestricted U-boat operations, and the necessity to anticipate the failure of the North American grain harvest by contracting to bring 3 500 000 tons of wheat the long way from Australia, had already led Lloyd George in December 1916 to announce the appointment of a Shipping Controller to ensure the efficient use of available tonnage.[52] The panic produced by the U-boat attacks brought British trade virtually to a standstill. The only way the newly formed Ministry of Blockade could get neutral ships moving again in British trades was to refuse to grant clearances to sail neutral ships which were already in British ports, until satisfactory evidence was received that an equivalent number of ships of the same registry had cleared for Britain from foreign ports.[53]

An unintended result of the U-boat campaign was that it very effectively enforced the British rationing system by putting all shipping in the North Sea area at risk. In the first three months of the campaign imports into the United States from Denmark, the Netherlands, Norway and Sweden fell from 725 670 tons, for the same period in 1915, to 330 524 tons. The greatest reduction took place in March when imports were one quarter the 1915 level. Exports clearing US ports for those countries suffered the same cuts, falling from the 1915 level of 1 203 920 tons for February to April, to 479 439 tons.[54] Only 313 ships arrived in the four northern neutral countries during February to April 1917, compared to the 1070 which had arrived during those months in 1915. Nowhere near that number of ships had been sunk. Enough were, however, to persuade neutrals to keep their ships in port.

The effect of the U-boat campaign on the *Entente* war effort was for a time highly alarming to British leaders. In January 1917 171 ships had been lost due to enemy attack of all sorts. In February the number rose to 234, March 281, and the peak occurred in April when 373 ships were sunk totalling 869 103 tons. On 21 February the First Sea Lord, Earl Jellicoe, issued a warning to the Imperial War Cabinet that forces should be withdrawn from the eastern theatres, to conserve shipping, and before shipping losses made it difficult to find the tonnage with which to do it. On 12 April a War Staff paper advised against a French plan to invade Greece as it would require too much shipping. On 1 May Jellicoe renewed his demand that reductions be made in shipping commitments, urging especially that the army in Salonica be withdrawn.[55] Efforts to out-build the shipping losses were falling very short, although the monthly average of new construction in the British Empire and the United States increased from 1 134 000 gross tons in 1916 to 2 227 000 in 1917 and to 4 612 000 in 1918.[56] War risk insurance rates on fast liners remained constant at 8 per cent but the top rate for slower vessels was 10 per cent in February, and 12 per cent in March. In May neutral shippers were paying up to 15 per cent, and 20 per cent in August.[57]

Only limited withdrawal was ordered from Salonica, but a major economy of shipping was achieved when the North American grain harvest proved to be better than had been expected. It was directed that all supplies be purchased in North America so that ships could be withdrawn from the longer trades.[58] At the end of April the Admiralty at last was brought to attempt organisation of convoys for the ocean trades, and the result was that shipping losses for May and June fell slightly to 287 and 290 ships respectively.[59] In September war risk insurance rates began to fall.[60] Due to the additional number of ships out of service from damage, the amount of shipping available at the end of June was down 10 per cent from February. The organisation of merchant shipping into convoys may also have reduced their commercial efficiency by as much as a notional 30 per cent, but the delays experienced by ships sailing independently and forced to shelter in harbour when U-boats were operating nearby may have exceeded that figure, and certainly were less predictable. Jellicoe continued to be extremely pessimistic, and urged that the army attempt to capture the Flanders U-boat bases. The War Cabinet did not share his view, but his pessimism certainly contributed to the decision to mount the disastrous third Ypres campaign.

Administrative measures were more successful.[61] Coercion of neutral and *Entente* shipowners was just one of the many ways in which the economic war led to state planning taking the place of nineteenth-century *laissez-faire* doctrine. The British government continued to rely on private enterprise to provide management for shipping, but the introduction of convoy, and state control of purchasing and distribution, all violated the idea that efficiency depended upon the collectivity of individual decisions governed only by a profit motive. The Black List was a clear infringement of liberty. The British democracy proved to be more adroit at devising such instruments of central control than was the German Imperial government.[62] In the opinion of P. E. Dewey, the solution to the potential problem of food shortage was neither convoy, which came too late, nor the farm production policy which was so mismanaged as actually to be counterproductive. The rationing system to ensure equitable distribution, on the other hand, was a great success.[63] Mancur Olson's earlier work gives greater credit to the farm production policy, but agrees with the importance of consumption control in defeating the German U-boat campaign. The German navy sank as much tonnage in the first six months of the U-boat campaign as they had anticipated, despite the British introduction of trade convoys, but the results were not what had been hoped. It reached its operational goal but found that it had ceased to represent a politico-economic milestone.[64]

The political effects of the decision to renew the U-boat war made it counterproductive for Germany, as Bethman-Hollweg had predicted would be the case. The ineptitude of German timing, while negotiations were in progress to obtain American mediation in the war, and within days of Wilson's address to Congress describing in optimistic terms the results of negotiations with the belligerents, made a breach with Washington virtually inevitable. Wilson initially confined the American reaction to severance of diplomatic relations, and a policy of armed neutrality. Despite obstruction in the Senate, Wilson ordered the arming of American merchant ships sailing in the war zone, but convoy was not provided. American opinion was dramatically settled in favour of intervention in the war when British intelligence deciphered a telegram from the German Secretary of State, Emil Zimmerman, to the German ambassador in Mexico suggesting a Mexican invasion of the United States in the event of an American declaration of war. American neutrality suddenly became very benevolent towards the *Entente*. American bankers were encouraged to provide credit, and no more objections were made to the ever-tightening British blockade regulations. Nevertheless it was not until 2 April that the United States declared war on Germany, in somewhat reluctant association with the *Entente* powers.

The decision to do so was directly linked to the beginning of German attacks on American merchant ships, although President Wilson and his administration were not impelled into the war simply for the purpose of defending neutral trading rights, or the lives of American seamen and travellers. Wilson's every instinct was against war, but when American merchantmen began to be sunk he felt he had no choice. He believed that international law prevented the United States taking effective action against the U-boats unless a state of war were declared. He was also concerned to preserve the influence of the United States which could be used to find a peace settlement that would be stable and just. Tolerance of attacks on US shipping would have gravely undermined American prestige. Lansing had long ago decided that Prussian militarism would have to be crushed, and Wilson's confidant, 'Colonel' Edward M. House, firmly believed that American security depended upon the military power of Britain. Wilson, however, does not appear to have thought the *Entente* was in danger of losing the war. The effect on American public opinion of the German attacks on US ships was an additional reason for Washington to go to war, and a development which facilitated that policy.[65]

The American entry into the war would not have effected its outcome had the predictions of the German military about the economic effect of unrestricted U-boat war been fulfilled. Although the German Navy could maintain continuously at sea no more than 36 operational U-boats, the confident assertion had been made publicly that Britain could be defeated in six months. As British convoy operations got into full routine, however, shipping losses to all causes fell in each of the last six months of 1917 to 227, 188, 160, 169, 128 and 168 ships respectively. Great pressure was put on Washington through Admiral Sims who had been sent to London for liaison with the Admiralty, and through diplomatic channels, to provide naval support as quickly as possible for defence of trade.[66] The tide had turned, however, before the US Navy could provide more than token assistance. By July it was evident in Germany that the campaign was not reaching expectations. The effect was politically demoralising. The government was upbraided in the Reichstag for misleading the nation. Before the winter the Army High Command had decided that it would have to depend upon its own resources if the *Entente* were to be defeated before the United States could deploy its full weight.[67]

ASSESSMENT OF THE UTILITY OF THE *ENTENTE* BLOCKADE

The American declaration of war made possible the near perfection of the blockade, despite the insistence of the American government that they were co-belligerents rather than allies and that they could not go against their own declared principles of free trade. The American navy did not participate in the blockade, but there was no need for it to do so and the American government used its control over commodities produced in the United States to coerce the neutral European states into making formal agreements not to re-export to the Central Powers. In doing so it was conforming with the extreme views urged by the French about the treatment to be accorded to neutrals.[68] The United States had mercantilist concerns of its own, and was reluctant to impose a Black List which might make it difficult to trade in South America. Eventually, however, American practice was brought into line with that of the *Entente*. The American government brought in and censored mail, instituted bunker control to oblige neutral shipping to sail on routes useful to the war effort of the 'Associated' powers, and even went so far as to use embargo of food supplies and other commodities to coerce neutral states into employing their merchant shipping within the danger zone. The final treaty imposed by the coercive efforts of the United States and its associates was concluded with Sweden on 29 May 1918.[69]

The significance of the blockade in the eventual defeat of the Central Powers is hard to assess. In their memoirs Marshal von Hindenburg, General Ludendorff, and Grand Admiral von Tirpitz all emphasised the importance of the blockade on the domestic political scene. In 1927 Maurice Hankey, Secretary to the Cabinet, used their assertions to support his belief that

> In the long run the blockade proved to be one of the most essential means for supplementing the actions of the military forces in bringing the war to an end. It was the home front in Germany which broke first.[70]

After the war the German government published detailed statistics of dietary deficiencies and deaths attributable to the blockade. The death rate amongst those groups most exposed to shortages rose steadily throughout the war until in 1918 it was 37 per cent above the 1913 level.[71] The value of this evidence, however, is uncertain. It was published as vindication of the Germany army, which supposedly remained 'undefeated in the field'. There is no question that the blockade, the effect of which was compounded by German maladministration, caused privation.[72] The question is whether that privation generated useful and powerful political effects. Admiral Jellicoe was convinced, as early as February 1917, that it could not do so. He firmly told Admiral Beatty that Germany would not be defeated by the blockade:

> We may cause them a great deal of suffering and discomfort by the blockade, but we shall not win the war by it. The war will not be won until the enemy's armed forces are defeated – certainly on land and probably on sea . . .[73]

The shortage of food no doubt contributed to the growth of the civilian peace movement in 1917 and 1918, especially in the Austro-Hungarian empire where it encouraged the food-producing areas of Hungary and Croatia to defy central authority, but at best it was a contributory factor. The socialists found a strong case against the Imperial government in their maladministration of the food supply.[74] The disillusionment caused by the failure of the U-boat campaign and the inability of the Army High Command to use their victorious battles to bring peace also produced powerful political forces. Only with victory could the army, the aristocracy, and the Prussian monarchy continue to justify their political power. It is significant that it was the food-producing areas of the two empires, notably Bavaria in Germany, and the capital cities, not the hungry industrial towns of the north, which were most radical. Emperor Karl put the effects of the blockade in perspective in April 1917 when he appealed to the German government to seek peace at almost any price:

> We are fighting a new enemy, who is more dangerous than the entente: our enemy is international revolution, which is finding a powerful ally in the general famine. I do sware to you that I am not forgetting how fateful a moment of the war we have now reached; and do beg you to reflect, that, if we end the war soon – even at a heavy sacrifice – we shall (at least) have an opportunity of checking the upheaval that is now preparing.[75]

In August 1917 there were a number of incidents in the German fleet when sailors refused to eat their disgusting rations, but the poor conditions in the German mess-decks were attributed to misbehaviour of the ships' officers rather than to the blockade. The sailors' experience of collective action, and the repressive measures of their officers, created the potential within the fleet for the October 1918 mutiny which prevented the naval command defying the new democratic government in Berlin. The momentum of the October mutiny brought about the November revolution which drove the Kaiser to abdicate, and brought the end of the war.[76] A. C. Bell's own view was that only the blockade could have raised the new men to leadership in Berlin 'from their previous condition of human vermin, grubbing in the refuse of the workshops'.[77] However, the evidence is inadequate to sustain a thesis that the blockade played the principal role in defeating the Central Powers.

The German economic historian Gerd Hardach has concluded that the blockade posed a number of problems for those directing the wartime economic policy of the Central Powers, and the necessary process of adjustment placed a considerable burden on the economies of those countries – that of Germany in particular. However, the tremendous economic decline of the Central Powers between 1914 and 1918 was caused less by the blockade than by the excessive demands made on their economies by the war. In Hardach's view,

> a fundamental misconception underlying the allied blockade no less than the German U-boat campaign was the over-estimation by both sides of the degree of dependence of industrial countries on foreign trade. The growth of economic interdependence on a worldwide scale, which had been observable prior to 1914, was interpreted as a vital concomitant of industrialization. But in reality the decisive factor was not industrialization per se, but the liberal-capitalist framework in which it took place. One of the lessons learnt from the war and the post-war period is that industrial countries can achieve a measure of self-sufficiency, irrespective of whether their economic systems are based on socialism or state monopoly.[78]

Jellicoe's view that the war would have to be won on land was certainly correct. The collapse of the German army in late 1918, during the last 'Hundred Days' of the war, was brought about by the final success of the British army in overcoming the difficulties of controlling the vast battlefield by developing teams of well-trained men using new machines and new techniques. The soldiers had at last got their act together.[79] Defeat on the battlefield generated revolution. In the immediate aftermath of the war, however, there was little sympathy for the army which had destroyed so many lives. The British public was more than half prepared to believe the assertion of the German Right that the German army had been 'stabbed in the back', and took satisfaction in the idea that the German civilian revolt had been set off by the blockade. The Navy and Foreign Office had perfected the techniques of blockade early in the war, and needed to believe in its efficacy to compensate for the years of toil without battle. The reputation of naval blockade thus erroneously generated, a reputation which had indeed played a part in panicking the German High Command into attempting the U-boat war in 1917 and the Amiens campaign in 1918, was to have great significance in the inter-war years.

Probably the *Entente*'s blockade had most effect in the period between the signing of the Armistice on 11 November 1918 and the conclusion of the Versailles treaty eight months later. With great misgivings the German High Command had accepted Article 26 of the Armistice which stipulated that the blockade should be continued, but that the allies would 'contemplate the provisioning of Germany during the Armistice as shall be found necessary'.[80] Admiral Wemyss, the British First Sea Lord, wrote contemptuously of the German naval representative on the armistice commission, that

> He is afraid of the blockade and seems actually to think that we shall keep it up for the purpose of starving their country during the Armistice! Such is their mentality, so I suppose that is what they would have done had the cases been reversed.

Nonetheless, the blockade during the winter of 1918–19, and the pillaging of occupied countries carried out by the retreating German armies, did bring central Europe closer to famine that it had been at any point during the war. The problems for German food administration were exacerbated by the refusal of the French to permit Germany to use its gold to buy food, and by the refusal of the United States to supply the Germans with food as a gift when Germany had gold in reserve. There was such privation that by the early spring of 1919 there were strong feelings in Britain that the blockade should be lifted. The Weimar government held up the transfer of the German merchant marine to the allies hoping to obtain a deal by which they would guarantee to feed Germany. The French resisted, but Lloyd

George compelled them to compromise by obtaining from General Sir Herbert Plumer, the commander of British forces in Germany, a telegraph asserting that his men were rebelling at the sight of such starvation.[81] Admiral Wemyss promised substantial delivery of grain and meat. The blockade in other respects was not lifted until after German signature of the Versailles Treaty.[82]

Stephen Roskill denies that continuation of the blockade in the winter of 1918–19 was 'brutal', and places the blame on the Weimar government, which failed adequately to control militaristic elements which obstructed the execution of the armistice.[83] On the other hand, the future American president, Herbert Hoover, having been director of American relief operations in Belgium before April 1917, and in 1918–1919 being appointed director of all food-relief, was well placed to observe the effects of blockade. He repeatedly asserted that the blockade of Germany after the conclusion of the armistice added greatly to the forces undermining the very structure of German society, and discredited the republican government which had brought the capitulation of Germany. In his memoirs he wrote that 'the maintenance of the blockade on food during those four months from the Armistice until March was a crime in statesmanship and against civilization as a whole'.[84]

The truth is paradoxical, but typical of the political effects of blockade. The privation caused by the continuation of the blockade after the Armistice probably was more irksome than unhealthy, although it doubtless exacerbated the effects of the influenza epidemic. Because the German people knew so little about conditions at the front, however, they found it hard to believe that Germany had been defeated. The blockade added fuel to the feeling that the eventual German signature of the Versailles Treaty was an extorted submission to an unjust peace. The blockade could be put to political use by German patriots in ways which would have been impossible had the reality of military defeat been made evident by a military occupation of Berlin.[85]

It was Germany's victims, especially Belgium and Poland, which suffered most from food shortages both before and after the Armistice. However, the long-term political effect of the 'hunger blockade' on Germany was important. The highest premium had been placed on the military control of territories containing the most vital raw materials. For Germany that meant control of eastern Europe. Hitler succinctly expressed the philosophy of the *Drag noch Osten* in 1939 when he told a cabinet meeting:

> It is not Danzig that is at stake. For us it is a matter of expanding our living space in the East and making food supplies secure and also solving the problem of the Baltic States. Food supplies can only be obtained from thinly populated areas. . . . Colonies: a warning against gifts of colonial possessions. This is no solution of the food problem. Blockade![86]

Amongst the factors which led to the rise of Hitler must be accounted the post-war blockade which effectively undermined liberal views by making it appear that Germany's only error had been its military weakness. Evidently the British 'liberal democracy' was not to be trusted.

NOTES

1. David French, *British Economic and Strategic Planning 1905–1915*, pp. 22–38, 51–70. See *The Papers of Admiral Sir John Fisher*, P. K. Kemp (ed.), vol. II, pp. 315 *ff*.
2. Marion C. Siney, op. cit., p. 15.
3. A. C. Bell, op. cit., p. 602. See also Paul Haggie, 'The Royal Navy and War Planning in the Fisher Era', *Journal of Contemporary History*, vol. 8, no. 3, pp. 113–31, July 1973.
4. H. W. Carless Davis, *History of the Blockade. Emergency Departments*, pp. 4–5.
5. Ibid., p. 45. See also ADM 116/1233, papers relating to British announcement of intention to put the Declaration of London into force, and Arthur Marsden, 'The Blockade', in F. H. Hinsley, *British Foreign Policy under Sir Edward Grey*.
6. ADM 116/1233, papers relating to the British decision to regard German food imports as conditional contraband.
7. Order-in-Council of 20 August 1914, and US Acting Secretary of State Lansing to Ambassador Page, 22 October 1914, in *Supplement to the American Journal of International Law, Diplomatic Correspondence between the United States and Belligerent Governments Relating to Neutral Rights and Commerce* (hereafter cited as *Supplement to AJIL*), Vol. 9, p. 7; see Carlton Savage, op. cit., Vol. ii, pp. 1–7; and Daniel M. Smith, *Robert Lansing and American Neutrality 1914–1917*, pp. 17–30.
8. Marion C. Siney, op. cit., pp. 126–9.
9. David French, op. cit., p. 117.
10. Carlton Savage, op. cit., II, p. 8; and Daniel M. Smith, op. cit., pp. 27–8.
11. H. W. Carless Davis, op. cit., pp. 6–7.
12. A. C. Bell, op. cit., p. 71.

13. Marion C. Siney, op. cit., pp. 33–59.
14. US Secretary of State Bryon to Ambassador Page, 26 December 1914, and Secretary of State Grey to Ambassador Page, 10 February 1915, in *Supplement to AJIL*, Vol. 9, pp. 55–60 and 65–82; and see A. M. Morrissey, *The American Defense of Neutral Rights, 1914–1917*, *passim*; Nils Ørvik, *The Decline of Neutrality*, pp. 89–107; and Marion C. Siney, 'British Negotiations with American Meat Packers, 1915–1917: A Study of Belligerent Trade Controls', *The Journal of Modern History*, vol. 23, pp. 343–53 (1951).
15. See Secretary of State Grey to Ambassador Page, 7 January 1915, in *Supplement to AJIL*, Vol. 9, pp. 60–5; and Carlton Savage, op. cit., II, pp. 13–15. See also Bernard Semmel, op. cit., pp. 1–4.
16. H. W. Carless Davis, op. cit., pp. 80–124.
17. See *Supplement to AJIL*, Vol. 9, pp. 270–313.
18. A. M. Morrissey, op. cit., pp. 172–88; Marion C. Siney, op. cit., pp. 78, 173–9, 252–5; and Bernard Semmel, op. cit., pp. 162–4.
19. David French, op. cit., pp. 85–97, 109–13.
20. W. K. Hancock and M. M. Gowing, *British War Economy*, pp. 3–12, and Kathleen Burk, *Britain, America and the Sinews of War, 1914–1918*, pp. 6–8 and *passim*. See also Frank L. McVey, *The Financial History of Great Britain 1914–1918*, pp. 59–60; and Ernest L. Bogart, *Direct and Indirect Costs of the Great World War*, pp. 40 and 19–22.
21. See the appraisal of Germany's war zone declaration in: W. T. Mallison, Naval War College International Law Studies 1966, Studies in the Law of Naval Warfare: *Submarines in General and Limited Wars*, pp. 62–74.
22. C. Wright and C. E. Fayle, *History of Lloyds*, pp. 400–19. See also David Kinley, *Influence of the Great War upon Shipping*, pp. 49–73.
23. H. W. Carless Davis, op. cit., pp. 10–11.
24. A. Pearce Higgins, 'Retaliation in Naval Warfare', *British Yearbook of International Law*, 1927, p. 129.
25. Carlton Savage, op. cit., II, pp. 16 *et seq.*; and see Lord Hankey, *The Supreme Command*, pp. 352–75.
26. Marion C. Siney, op. cit., pp. 179–85.
27. CAB 21/307, Report of Lord Cave's Committee of December 1918.
28. A. C. Bell, op. cit., p. 41.
29. CAB 21/307, 'The Freedom of the Seas', Appendix, 21 December 1918.
30. James Wilford Garner, op. cit., section 126; and A. C. Bell, op. cit., p. 463.
31. C. Ernest Fayle, *Seaborne Trade*, iii, pp. 36–7; and see H. W. Carless Davis, op. cit., pp. 13, 23–34 Extracts from Minutes by Mr O. R. A. Simkin, formerly Head of the Blockade Section of the War Trade Intelligence Department, on 'The Evidential Method' and 'Legality of the Rationing Method'.
32. A. C. Bell, op. cit., p. 286; and H. W. Carless Davis, op. cit., pp. 14–15.
33. H. W. Malkin, 'Blockade in Modern Conditions', *British Yearbook of International Law*, 1922–23, p. 87.

34. Donald M. Schurman, *Julian S. Corbett*, pp. 170–2. Corbett was rewarded for his work in support of maritime strategy by his knighthood in the 1917 New Years list.
35. A. C. Bell, op. cit., p. 309; and Marion C. Siney, op. cit., p. 78.
36. See Margarie Milbank Farrar, *Conflict and Compromise*, pp. 95–134.
37. Marion C. Siney, op. cit., pp. 205–12; Olav Riste, *The Neutral Ally*, pp. 126–59; and Nils Orvik, op. cit., pp. 53–6.
38. See *Supplement to AJIL*, Vol. 10, pp. 373–86.
39. Marion C. Siney, op. cit., pp. 129–33, 136–7; see also Z. A. B. Zeman, *A Diplomatic History of the First World War*, p. 180.
40. Marion C. Siney, op. cit., pp. 157–72.
41. David F. Trask, 'The American Navy in a World at War, 1914–1919' in Kenneth J. Hagan (ed.), *In Peace and War*, pp. 207–8.
42. Quoted in A. C. Bell, op. cit., p. 543.
43. Daniel M. Smith, op. cit., pp. 132–44; Marion C. Siney, op. cit., pp. 144–8; and Z. A. B. Zeman, op. cit., pp. 181–2. See *Supplement to AJIL*, Vol. 10, pp. 111–50, and Ambassador Page to US Secretary of State, 12 October 1916, enclosing Secretary of State Grey to Page, 10 October 1916, in Vol. 11, pp. 42–8.
44. ADM 116/2466, subject file on US and other neutral claims arising from the blockade, 1925–26. See Edgar Turlington, *Neutrality*, vol. III, 'The World War Period', for an account of the economic impact the blockade had on neutral states, and the measures they took to protect their interests.
45. H. Ritchie, *The 'Navicert' System During the World War*, pp. 4–7 and *passim*; H. W. Carless Davis, op. cit., pp. 175–98; and Marion C. Siney, op. cit., pp. 139–42.
46. Daniel M. Smith, op. cit., pp. 60–7.
47. H. W. Carless Davis, op. cit., p. 153.
48. A. C. Bell, op. cit., p. 567; and Marion C. Siney, op. cit., pp. 256–7.
49. Ralph Haswell Lutz, *Fall of the German Empire*, ii, pp. 141–86.
50. Admiral von Holtzendorf to Field Marshal von Hindenburg, 22 December 1916. Carnegie Endowment for International Peace, Division of International Law, *Official German Documents Relating to the World War* (2 vols, NY, 1923), II, pp. 1214–77; and see Mancur Olson, op. cit., p. 82.
51. Ralph Haswell Lutz, op. cit., i, p. 227; see also ii, pp. 186–96; C. Ernest Fayle, op. cit., iii, p. 39.
52. Ibid., iii, pp. 1–21; and Archibald Hurd, op. cit., Vol. i, p. 225.
53. Ibid., p. 605.
54. A. C. Bell, op. cit., p. 615.
55. See *The Jellicoe Papers*, A. Temple Patterson (ed.), nos 33 and 45, pp. 144 and 160. See also Lord Hankey, op. cit., ii, 632–40; and Rear Admiral William Sowden Sims, *The Victory at Sea*, pp. 1–19.
56. J. A. Salter, *Allied Shipping Control. An Experiment in International Administration*, p. 361.
57. Robert Greenhalgh Albion, op. cit., p. 247.
58. C. E. Fayle, *The War and the Shipping Industry*, p. 226; and *Seaborne Trade*, vol. III, pp. 20–1 and 477; and Arthur J. Marder, *From the Dreadnought to Scapa Flow*, pp. 63–9.

59. See Peter Gretton, 'The U-boat Campaign in Two World Wars', in *Naval Warfare in the Twentieth Century*, Gerald Jordan (ed.); and Arthur J. Marder, op. cit., vol. iv, ch. vi.
60. Robert Greenhalgh Albion, op. cit., p. 247.
61. Mancur Olson, op. cit., pp. 85–90.
62. See J. A. Salter, op. cit., *passim*; and E. M. H. Lloyd, *Experiments in State Control at the War Office and the Ministry of Food*, *passim*.
63. P. E. Dewey, 'Food Production and Policy in the United Kingdom, 1914–1918', *Transactions of the Royal Historical Society*, V series, vol. 30 (1980), p. 71.
64. Mancur Olson, op. cit., pp. 90–113.
65. See Arthur S. Link, *Wilson Campaigns for Progressivism and Peace 1916–1917*, iii, pp. 296 *et seq.*, 340 *et seq.*, 411–16; Karl E. Birnbaum, *Peace Moves and U-boat Warfare*, pp. 315–39; Z. A. B. Zeman, *A Diplomatic History of the First World War*, pp. 183–206; E. H. Buehrig, op. cit., pp. 135–8 and 189; and Nils Orvik, op. cit., pp. 73–88.
66. See David F. Trask, *Captains & Cabinets*, pp. 61–102.
67. See A. J. Marder, op. cit., vol. IV, pp. 52, 67, 102, 162, 271 and 287; and A. C. Bell, op. cit., pp. 676–9.
68. Marjorie Milbank Farrar, *Conflict and Compromise, The Strategy, Politics and Diplomacy of the French Blockade, 1914–1918*, pp. 157–89, The Hague, 1974.
69. Carlton Savage, op. cit., II, pp. 89–158, *passim*. See Jeffrey J. Safford, *Wilsonian Maritime Diplomacy 1913–1921*, New Brunswick, USA, pp. 117–40, and Thomas A. Bailey, *The Policy of the United States Towards the Neutrals, 1917–1918*, *passim*.
70. CAB 21/307, Maurice Hankey's Memorandum on Blockade and the Laws of War, and Appendix containing abstracts from Marshal von Hindenburg, *Out of my Life*, General Ludendorff, *My War Memories 1914–1918*, and Grand Admiral von Tirpitz, *My Memoirs*.
71. A. C. Bell, op. cit., p. 672.
72. Leo Grebler and Wilhelm Winkler, *The Cost of the World War to Germany and to Austria Hungary*, pp. 73–83.
73. Jellicoe to Beatty, 4 February 1917, in *The Jellicoe Papers*, A. Temple Patterson (ed.), no. 31, p. 142.
74. Ralph Haswell Lutz, op. cit., ii, pp. 193–98.
75. Quoted in A. C. Bell, op. cit., p. 694. See Bernadotte E. Schmitt and Harold C. Vedeler, *The World in the Crucible*, New York, 1984, pp. 376–401.
76. Daniel Horn, *The German Naval Mutinies of World War I*, pp. 94 *et seq.*, 169–97.
77. A. C. Bell, op. cit., p. 689. See ADM 116/3303; Bell's draft monograph was savagely criticised in CID for its violent language and for Bell's assertion that only neutral pressure obliged Britain to restrict the impact of the blockade.
78. Gerd Hardach, *The First World War*, pp. 33 and 52.
79. See Dominic Graham and Shelford Bidwell, *Firepower*, pp. 131–46.
80. Quoted in H. W. V. Temperley, *A History of the Peace Conference of Paris*, i, p. 468.

81. Lord George Alyerdice Riddell quotes Lloyd George as saying: 'Of course I knew that he would tell the truth, whatever it was. He is an honest, truthful man, and would not say anything he did not believe'. *Intimate Diary of the Peace Conference and After 1918–1923*, London, 1933.
82. S. L. Bane and R. H. Lutz (eds), *The Blockade of Germany after the Armistice, 1918–1919, Selected Documents*, *passim*, especially pp. 184–200, 225–9, 519, and 552–3; James A. Huston, 'Allied Blockade of Germany 1918–19', *Journal of Central European Affairs*, vol. 10 (1950), p. 145; and Ralph Haswell Lutz, *The Fall of the German Empire*, ii, pp. 198–201. See also ADM 116/3159, File dated April to June 1919 containing plans for blockade should Germany not sign the Peace Treaty.
83. Stephen Roskill, *Naval Policy Between the Wars*, i, p. 79.
84. H. C. Hoover, *The Memoirs of Herbert Hoover*, vol. I, p. 352.
85. Conversation with Sally Marks at University of New Brunswick, 24 March 1987.
86. W. N. Medlicott, *The Economic Blockade*, ii, p. 641.

3 The Belligerents' Rights Dispute and the 'New Mercantilism'

The resentment British blockade practice had stirred up amongst American businessmen was not erased by the American entry into the war. The trouble came to a head before the Armistice, when the allied and associated powers were meeting in Paris to discuss the terms they should offer. In asking for an armistice, the German government had referred to the 'Fourteen Points' President Wilson had proposed as a basis for a negotiated peace, number two of which was 'The Freedom of the Seas'. Wilson's representative, Colonel House, insisted that the right of belligerents to intercept neutral trade must be given up for wars outside the auspices of the League of Nations, which was to be established. If this demand were not accepted, House warned that the United States would build a greater army and navy than Britain possessed. American distrust of British naval power was enhanced by the Anglo–Japanese alliance, and by the wartime Anglo–French *Entente*. House threatened that the United States would make a separate peace if Britain refused to give up its claim to belligerent rights, and President Wilson warned that Congress would 'have no sympathy whatever with spending American lives for British naval control'.[1]

American distrust of British naval power was not exclusively, or even primarily, directed at its apparent capacity to defeat a great power in a few years of war. The long-term economic effects of naval dominance were thought to be of even greater concern. The most convincing aspect of Mahan's argument to American businessmen, and to British statesmen as well, was that the British commercial empire was a product of years of naval dominance. The success of the British Board of Trade in promoting British exports during the war was taken as evidence that the British blockade in 1914–18 had the same mercantilist objectives that had been paramount during the war against Napoleon. Wartime propaganda films castigating German commercial agents for their penetration of British markets cast sinister implications. Lord Milner's 'New Imperialists' who redirected British strategy in 1917–18 towards acquisition of large parts of the

Turkish Empire, and the British Admiralty's participation in negotiations with the French government during and after the war settling the disposition of Mesapotamian oil, reinforced the image of mercantilist trade war. The US Navy planning section in London had prepared a paper in 1917 in which it warned that

> Four great powers have arisen in the world to compete with Great Britain for commercial supremacy . . . Each one in succession has been defeated by Great Britain and her fugitive allies. A fifth commercial power, the greatest one yet, is now arising to compete for at least commercial equality. Already the signs of jealousy are visible.

The paper was resurrected in 1918 and sent to Admiral Benson who was US Chief of Naval Operations, and naval representative in Paris.[2]

The difficulties of American businessmen attempting to penetrate markets in the sterling area during the post-war recession, and later during the great depression, sustained the inter-war American distrust of British naval power. The First Lord of the Admiralty in 1920, Lord Long, made an extremely ill-judged statement that 'if we secure the supplies of oil now available in the world we can do what we like'.[3] In 1921 the General Board of the US Navy reiterated the view that Britain 'aims at a dominant commercial position, has repeatedly fought for it, and resents its challenge'.[4] Crowe's warning in 1907, that the world would react strongly against British use of sea power to control trade, was being fulfilled.

Lloyd George won the first round of this battle. He declared that Britain would fight on, alone if necessary, to defend the influence of its navy. For the British, the apparent success of the naval blockade of Germany created the hope that future generations could enjoy security based on naval strength. Britain had always found naval power a weak tool of foreign policy, an army having usually been necessary to translate into international influence the economic power generated by sea control, but in 1918 there was a strong conviction that at last the technique had been perfected by which a great empire could be defeated by naval blockade. When agreement on the terms of the Armistice was reached on 5 November, the Americans had temporarily submitted. The German government was advised that the Allied Governments 'reserve to themselves complete freedom on this subject [that is, the Freedom of the Seas] when they enter the Peace Conference'.[5]

In a series of speeches in November and December 1918 Winston Churchill insisted that the British government could not 'lend ourselves in any way to any fettering restrictions which will prevent the British Navy maintaining its well-tried and well-deserved supremacy'.[6] There was no confidence in the British government that a League of Nations would be effective enough to compensate for any reduction in Britain's military capacity. The decision to continue the blockade during the period of the Armistice underlined British disregard for American feelings.

The American government was determined that the British should be denied the power to dominate the world with naval forces. If the manner in which navies were employed could not be controlled by treaty, then Britain had to be denied naval dominance. The big-navy interests in the United States were vociferous in their demand for 'a navy second to none', and they were able to use the argument that the League of Nations could not function if one of its members had exclusive access to a naval weapon of such apparent power. Accordingly, the disposition of the German fleet, and the post-war American naval building programme, became involved in the discussion of belligerent rights. Harold and Margaret Sprout suggest that the antipathy between Britons and Americans was a result of a general recognition that the development of submarines, mines, and aircraft had favoured American aspirations. The difficulty of defending shipping in the confined waters around Britain was increased immeasurably, but the United States could expect to profit from the new naval technologies which would render close attack on the American seaboard hazardous in the extreme.[7] At any rate, the prospect of a strong and invulnerable American navy, which might be used to convoy neutral trade, threatened Britain's new source of power and security.[8] The irony was hard to bear in London.

At the Paris Peace Conference in the spring of 1919 the Americans made a determined effort to limit the strength of the British navy. Wilson and Benson toyed with the idea of leaving Germany with some naval power so as to oblige Britain to retain naval forces in European waters, and House insisted that the German fleet should be sunk rather than divided up. The British also favoured destruction of the German fleet, but exploited the internment in British ports of a major portion of it as a latent threat that it might be taken into the British navy to augment its battle-line. When the German navy scuttled the ships, Britain lost a bargaining asset. Wilson, for his part, put great pressure on Congress to approve funds for a massive naval building programme. He cabled from Paris that failure to pass the bill would be 'fatal' to his negotiations with Britain. Admiral Wemyss and Navy Secretary Josephus Daniels exchanged strong words about who most needed naval defences.

Wilson and Lloyd George agreed on 9 April 1919 to a truce. Wilson withdrew support for a second US Navy construction bill, and Lloyd George undertook to support the establishment of a League of Nations. Sir Edward Grey, now Lord Grey, visited Washington that autumn apparently to negotiate a naval balance, which Wilson's physical collapse precluded. When the American public learnt about the truce it was indignant. Wilson created great concern in London when he attempted to generate support in the United States for the League by threatening that the only alternative was massive American armament. That put him in paradoxical alliance with the big-navy interests. It proved to be inept politics. The majority of Americans could not agree that Great Britain constituted a deadly peril. By the end of 1920 anti-navalism had defeated the American naval building programme.[9]

Public pressure in the United States and in Britain led to President Harding inviting the great naval powers to meet in Washington in 1921 to negotiate a general limitation on naval arms. The impossibility of funding a major naval building programme because of war debts stimulated the willingness of Lloyd George to negotiate. When the Washington conference assembled, however, it proved to be exceptionally difficult to resolve the contradictory strategic needs and aspirations of Britain, the United States, France, Italy and Japan by the crude means of quantitative and qualitative limitation of armaments. Only by ending the Anglo–Japanese alliance and replacing it with a Four-Power Pacific Treaty, and by agreement to limit the construction of fortified naval facilities in the western Pacific, was it possible to proceed with limitations on battleship construction. In the Atlantic area, the unvoiced strategic conflict was clearly the issue of blockade. The American delegation did not risk failure by broaching again the issue of 'Freedom of the Seas', but the power of Britain to blockade the world's commerce was central to all discussion.

Limitations on capital ships produced a somewhat symmetrical effect for Britain and the United States. Britain would be made unable to sustain an operational battle-line in American waters sufficient to support blockade of the American coast, and the United States would be unable to interfere in a British blockade of European states. Limitation on submarines, however, had asymmetrical implications, and no agreement was reached to limit them, or any other ship smaller than a battlecruiser.[10] The British sought to have the submarine abolished altogether. The United States saw the submarine as a means of keeping an enemy blockade force away from American coasts. The French, who had rapidly come to see themselves as threatened by the power of a British blockade, were building up a submarine force capable of destroying British trade, in order to have the means of deterring British coercion. The substantial technical success of the German U-boat war in 1917 had shown that the arguments of the *Jeune Ecole* deserved some respect. Britain was able to extort an agreement that submarines would not be used to attack trade, on the grounds that they could not provide for the safety of merchant seamen. Such attacks were labelled 'piratical'. The French, however, failed to ratify the treaty. Because there were no effective reductions in the submarine threat, Britain refused to agree to any quantitative limitations on cruisers and destroyers which were needed for trade defence. Because those very classes of ships were also the principal instruments of naval blockade, the United States was far from happy with the outcome of the Washington Conference.[11]

Britain's defence of belligerent rights was not, in fact, influenced to any great extent by mercantilist ideas. All the same, American perceptions were not entirely wrong. When the euphoria produced by victory subsided, the cost of the war appeared all the more shattering. Dissenting voices began to be raised in Britain which questioned the concentration of economic war policy on trade-denial to the enemy. One of the important lessons of World War I is that, in the technical conditions of the twentieth century no less than in the eighteenth, economic warfare has to give at least as much importance to enrichment of the belligerent as it does to impoverishment of the enemy. At the Admiralty, this perception was obscured by the fact of victory, but elsewhere it was gradually being recognised.

The new voices, however, did not pose a threat to the United States. It was the dissenters who urged the priority importance of reconciliation. They found their champion in Lord Grey, who had been prepared to abandon Britain's blockade during the war if that was the price which had to be paid for protecting Anglo–American relations. His successors in the Foreign Office continued his policy after his retirement.

As early as May 1923 the Committee of Imperial Defence, in the report of findings by a sub-committee on 'Trade, Blockade and Enemy Shipping', cautioned that

> The cost of economic pressure to the country which applies it, especially to a highly-organized commercial and industrial country like our own, must always be taken into consideration. If it is to be complete, it involves a very minute and extensive control of commercial and financial operations. British interests are bound in any case to suffer from an interference with the free flow of international trade. But the measures required to maintain a system of economic pressure are apt to be particularly detrimental, because every form of control involved is likely to discriminate against British business. Persons within British jurisdiction can be directly and effectively prevented from engaging in the prohibited transactions, whereas the pressure put upon their foreign competitors can at the best only be partial.[12]

The future capacity of Britain to limit an enemy's financial transactions in wartime could not be predicted, and in any case

> The difficulties and risks of interfering with financial operations are so great and the results so far-reaching, that especial care should be taken to balance the advantages against the disadvantages before any machinery for interfering with finance is put in motion.[13]

The sub-committee was evidently impressed by a memorandum drawn up by Sir Normal Hill, a shipping and insurance magnate, warning that Britain's blockade policy in the Great War had been justified exclusively on grounds of reprisal. It could not be guaranteed that a future enemy would provide any excuse for similar British restraints on neutral trade. If neutrals were to be free to trade then it was imperative that British traders should be free to compete. Such was all the more important because a blockade restricted to the seizure of contraband would 'subject an enemy who has neutral land frontiers to a great deal of inconvenience and to some hardship, but it [would] never become a comprehensive blockade'.

Sir Norman Hill clearly agreed with the American critics who regarded Britain's blockade as having had mercantilist overtones, although he did not think Britain had gained greatly thereby.

> The policy underlying prohibitions against trading by British subjects with the enemy went beyond the attainment of military

> objects and the destruction of the *morale* of the people in Germany; it aimed deliberately at the crippling, if not the permanent destruction, of German export trade, and . . . the elimination from the markets of the world, of the German middleman. . . .
>
> Even during the war the wisdom of this policy came in question. In the East it was found impossible to destroy German credit without imperiling, amongst the Asiatics, the whole of European credit. In the East and elsewhere it was found practically impossible to drive out all German middlemen and at the same time to retain the market.
>
> The extent to which British traders and shipowners were able to step into the places of the displaced Germans was limited owing to the heavy demands made by the war on their resources and services. To a considerable extent the opportunities were seized on by the traders and shipowners of the United States and Japan.[14]

Hill concluded that a British refusal to curtail belligerent rights could seriously undermine post-war British prosperity as it would lead neutrals to seek more reliable financial and insurance contacts outside Britain.

The sub-committee did not adopt that aspect of Hill's memorandum, and the Admiralty won its case for the preservation of belligerent rights, although the sub-committee did assert the importance of the Foreign Office's continuing to dominate the conduct of any future exercise of blockade.[15] In 1925, Lord Grey wrote in his memoirs of the war that it was better 'to carry on the war without a blockade, if need be, than to incur a break with the United States about contraband and thereby deprive the Allies of the resources necessary to carry on the war at all, or with any chance of success'.[16] Sir Norman Hill and Lord Grey, however, were as yet a lonely vanguard.

The predominant British position throughout the 1920s and into the 1930s continued to be that Britain needed naval forces and belligerent rights to contain threats from continental military powers, but would not use them to channel trade into British hands. The American reaction continued to be unsympathetic. In June 1925 the virulent anglophobic Rear Admiral Hilary P. Jones, replying on behalf of the General Board of the United States Navy to proposals for further arms limitations, wrote that during the war Britain had

> swept aside the Declaration of Paris and the Declaration of London, nullifying all the efforts of 100 years towards establishing

> neutral rights on the high seas . . . any further limitation of naval armament may increase Great Britain's power to ultimately dictate to the United States what our domestic navigation laws shall be.[17]

Anti-British feeling was strong in the American Navy League, although perhaps only because, as its historian Armin Rappaport suggests, 'a justification for a navy second to none had to be made. Were Britain omitted from the list of potential adversaries the League would have had a weak case'.[18] Perhaps, as M. Vlahos suggests, the real 'enemy' of the US Navy was Congress, which failed to authorise building up to treaty limits so that the British navy retained a qualitative and quantitative superiority throughout the 1920s.[19] The Irish-American feeling against Britain was also strong and could be exploited by shipbuilding and big-navy interests. Nevertheless, it is evident that anti-British feeling was too prevalent at higher levels of government in Washington to be attributed entirely to interest groups, or to domestic politics.

At the Geneva conference on naval arms limitation in 1927, it proved to be impossible to find a compromise between the British demand for 70 light cruisers to protect trade and the American need for heavy cruisers suitable for a war in the Pacific, while retaining the American principle of numerical equality with Britain. The negotiations were conducted by servicemen, and Admiral H. P. Jones dominated the American delegation. It may be exaggerated to assert that the failure to reach any agreement led to the nadir of Anglo–American relations in the post-war period, or even to assert that naval concerns dominated governmental attitudes. There can be no doubt, however, that the naval problem had great potential for discord.

Admiral Jellicoe, who had represented the New Zealand government at the Geneva conference, recorded his belief that the incessant American 'demands for parity had more behind them than prestige, . . . The Americans were probably determined to ensure no interference by the Royal Navy with their trade in a future conflict in which the United States remained neutral'.[20] Major-General Preston Brown, commander of the 1st Corps Area (Boston), remarked to the British defence *attaché*, Colonel Pope-Hennessy, in September 1927 that

> The conference failed because neither side would tell the truth; you (British) want numerous cruisers not only to protect your trade routes – which is obvious – but in order to apply in war your

> historic weapon of blockade. Small cruisers can do that. We (Americans) want a smaller number of big cruisers to ensure that your blockade does not interfere with our commerce as a neutral.

The British Foreign Secretary, Austin Chamberlain, was impressed.

> It cannot be denied that the present difference on this subject between the United States and ourselves is the only matter which makes war betwen our two nations conceivable. But I go further; I believe that General Preston Brown does not exaggerate when he says that any attempt by us to enforce our rights in a future war where the United States were neutral, as we enforced them in the late war, would make war between us 'probable.' The world position has been altered to our disadvantage, and what was possible in the past may have become impossible for the future.

Chamberlain, heir to Lord Grey, was not convinced that blockade was an indispensable instrument of British policy:

> it is extremely unlikely that, if and when we are again engaged in a serious war, the conditions governing the application of blockade will be at all comparable to those of the last great struggle, in which all the great land frontiers of our enemies were closed to trade. The present tendency is to exaggerate the potency of the blockade weapon, even when the attitude of the United States is left out of account.

In any case, he was a realist.

> whatever we contend are our rights, we cannot, in fact, afford to exercise them if it involves war with the United States when the United States possesses a navy equal in combative force to our own. It is not even necessary for the United States to declare war to bring us to destruction. They have only to refuse us supplies and credits in order to deal us a fatal blow.[21]

Early in 1928 the Americans formally raised the issue of belligerent rights when Senator Borah introduced into the Senate a resolution which linked the renewal of the General Arbitration Treaty with Britain to the recodification of maritime law. This diplomatic ploy had been anticipated in Britain. A sub-committee on belligerent rights had been formed in the Committee of Imperial Defence, under the chairmanship of Lord Salisbury.[22] The Foreign Office was in favour of some diminution of belligerent rights if an accord could be reached thereby with the United States which would make it possible to be confident of having a free hand to exercise the remaining controls over trade. Winston Churchill, then Chancellor of the Exchequer, suggested that it would be well to abandon the right to interdict trade because the ability of the British navy to protect trade was in such doubt. The Admiralty, however, firmly supported by the King, stoutly resisted any change.[23] They argued, with some wisdom, that it would be impossible to reach a compromise in the current political climate within the United States.

Sir Maurice Hankey, Secretary to the Cabinet and to the CID, played the major role in defence of Britain's belligerent rights. Admiral Sir Herbert Richmond was brought in as an expert, and the work of the Sub-Committee on Belligerent Rights was drawn out to allow American feelings to cool. The Balfour cabinet was reluctant to make any decisions in the months before the 1929 election, with the result that Ramsay MacDonald and the Labour Party were faced with the problem when they took office.[24]

That same year, the American presidency was taken over by Herbert Hoover. His experience organising the relief of Belgium during the war was the poignant origin of his hatred of blockade as a political instrument, and the post-Armistice blockade had put an end to his sympathy for Britain. After his election to the Presidency, however, Hoover wrote in his memoirs that,

> Believing that elimination of friction with Great Britain must be one of the foundation stones of our foreign policies, I sought ways to end the various gnawing differences between us. The most dangerous of these frictions was of course competitive naval building.

In London MacDonald expressed an intention of taking a personal interest in Anglo–American relations, and the CID Sub-Committee report was immediately brought to his attention. When he travelled to the United States to discuss outstanding problems, Hoover gave him a study paper in which he had written

> We recognize that the most troublesome questions in international relations is that of freedom of the seas. Not only does this subject arouse fear and stimulate naval preparation, but it is one of the pregnant causes of expansion of the area of war once it may have broken out, by dragging other nations in as the result of controversies with belligerents. . . . The President proposes, and he

> hopes the American people will support the proposal, that food ships should be declared free from interference during times of war and thus remove starvation of women and children from the weapons of warfare.[25]

At Hoover's summer 'camp' on the Rapidan River it was agreed that a conference should be held in London in 1930 at which no naval officers should be present. The delegations should be made up of political leaders who could be trusted to prevent technical arguments obstructing a settlement. Hoover and MacDonald reached tentative agreements about further limitations on naval arms. The most important was that a formula should be devised by which the British need for a large number of light cruisers, and the American for a smaller number of heavy ones, could be reconciled while sustaining the appearance of parity. Hankey, however, succeeded in keeping belligerent rights from becoming part of the agenda of the London Naval Conference.[26]

When MacDonald returned to London he found general opposition to any concession on belligerent rights. Hoover's hope that food ships could be declared immune from seizure was baffled. The Admiralty was insistent. MacDonald felt constrained to reassure Lloyd George in the Commons that, whilst he was in the United States, he had made no concessions on belligerent rights. He warned the President that 'our people have a deep sentimental regard for their historical position on the sea and . . . the simple fact of a re-examination is apt to unsettle and stampede them'.[27] Hankey exceeded norms of behaviour for a civil servant in defence of belligerent rights, and in opposition to further, and in his view futile, appeasement of the United States.[28]

The price which had to be paid for this refusal to meet American fears became clear at the London Naval Conference. Britain had its light cruiser force reduced from 70 to 50, and the United States navy had to make do with fewer heavy cruisers than it wanted. Both measures decreased their ability to meet the growing threat from Japan, but the Japanese were nonetheless gravely disappointed. They were seriously estranged by the evident Anglo–American pre-conference collusion at Rapidan which precluded satisfying Japanese demands for 70 per cent of the Anglo–American standard for all classes of cruisers. The disgruntled Japanese held that the United States only wanted the heavy cruisers for prestige, and ultimately for aggressive war in the western Pacific. British naval representatives in

Japan tended to agree, but the price of Anglo–American harmony had to be paid.[29]

Hankey dissuaded Arthur Henderson, the Foreign Secretary, from bringing up the issue of belligerent rights at the 1930 Imperial Conference. In the planning for the 1932 General Disarmament Conference, he convinced MacDonald that it was bad policy to confuse a discussion of arms reduction by introducing the question of strategic use of arms.[30] The point was hardly logical, especially as the Admiralty was again asserting its need for 70 cruisers for trade defence. Mahan's assertion, however, that the need for a navy would disappear should it not be required for the defence of trade, is enough to alarm any naval professional.[31] No attempt was made to devise a politically acceptable defence rationale based on a need for defence against enemy attack on shipping, while denying Britain's own right to attack trade.

As international conditions came into sharper focus in the 1930s, the brighter lights in the American and British navies began to see that the two countries had more common ground than they had reason to fear each other. As early as 1929 Admiral Sir Herbert Richmond had prepared for Hankey a paper in which he catalogued Britain's 'private' wars since the beginning of the eighteenth century, and observed that Britain had, rightly, made virtually no attempt to protect its interests by the coercive effect of naval control of trade. Economic pressure, as opposed to contraband control, was not a strong instrument of policy. Richmond was not thanked for this paper, which did not blindly support Hankey's rigid position on belligerent rights, but he published his idea in 1932, in a monograph entitled *Imperial Defence and Capture at Sea in War*.[32] In the same year Admiral Pratt, Chief of US Naval Operations, sent Charles F. Adams, Secretary of the US Navy, a paper in which he presented a case for American acceptance of British ideas on belligerent rights.[33] Two years later Richmond published *Sea Power in the Modern World*, in which he developed the theme of the 'limitations of sea power'. He wrote:

> it is important to recognize that sea power possesses the strength which it demonstrated in the Napoleonic Wars and the recent war only when it is allied to land power. Single-handed sea power can do little against any great power. . . . When, on the other hand, the Maritime Power has been allied in a common cause with land powers, as Britain was in all but one of the great wars of the

> eighteenth century, and in the war of 1914, economic pressure becomes a far more powerful instrument. The financial needs and demands of the nations increase vastly.[34]

Richmond's idea was not new. Sir Julian Corbett had anticipated Richmond by many years, writing in 1907 that,

> Of late years the world has become so deeply impressed with the efficacy of sea power that we are inclined to forget how impotent it is of itself to decide a war against great Continental states, how tedious is the pressure of naval action unless it be nicely coordinated with military and diplomatic pressure.[35]

Richmond's intervention, however, was timely. Preliminary conversations between London and Washington, preparatory to the 1935 London Naval Conference, made it clear that both were determined 'at almost any cost', as Hankey noted, to avoid a naval arms race between themselves.[36] They were also agreed that Japan was a common danger. The Vinson Acts of 1934 and 1938 which enabled the US Navy to build up to treaty limits increased its self-confidence and reduced its need to perceive the British navy as a potential enemy.[37]

By 1939 the lesson had been learnt in London that first priority could not be given to the economic isolation of the enemy. In World War II, under the leadership of Winston Churchill, the balance of British economic warfare policy swung back towards something analogous to the mercantilist focus of the Napoleonic War. Even in the dark days of 1939–40 there was confidence in London that British war production would ultimately outpace that of Germany, provided there was no disruption of supply.[38] Armed force was not deliberately employed to channel trade into British hands; nevertheless, the official historian of Britain's economic war in World War II, Norman Medlicott, notes that one of the chief advantages of the blockade lay in the diversion of resources to Britain's own war production.

The diplomacy of this new mercantilism, if that is what it should be called, was necessarily complex, and it was distinguished by the overriding importance which Churchill gave to the maintenance of good relations with the United States. British blockade practice did not change in principle from that employed in World War I, during which avoidance of conflict with the United States was paramount. What had been a judicious restraint on blockade policy, however, was transformed into its central tenet. Nothing was allowed to injure the prospects of British forces receiving supplies from the United States. When in the summer of 1941 American interests complained that Britain was exploiting *Lend Lease* to compete with Americans in export markets, London announced an intention to reduce 'to the irreducible minimum' the pursuit of new markets.[39] It is clear that the lesson of the earlier centuries had been accepted as still valid. It was more productive to concentrate upon developing the belligerent's own wealth, even if the future had to be mortgaged to provide the needs of the present, rather than to attempt to maximise the enemy's poverty.

In effect, the 'new mercantilism' co-opted the United States as a partner. British factories, with American permission, were set up in the United States as well as in Canada. American shipyards were tuned up to the mass production of merchant hulls. Access to them for the repair of British warships was obtained.

In the first 15 months of war, 90.7 per cent of the munitions used by British Commonwealth forces were supplied by United Kingdom industry, but if the war is taken as a whole, 69.5 per cent was supplied by UK industry, 7.9 per cent came from Canada, and 21 per cent came from American industry.[40] Added to that must be the war supplies provided by the United States to the Soviet Union and China, and those used by United States forces themselves in the second half of the war. There is no way of knowing what would have been the consequences for Britain of an American refusal to contribute to the needs of war, but it is hard to imagine that Britain on its own could ever have defeated Germany. Britain's new mercantilist strategy, the foundations for which were the efforts at appeasement of the United States which extend back into the nineteenth century and drove British attitudes in the Washington and London naval conferences, was of fundamental importance.

An important aspect of the new mercantilism was the role of money. In October 1939 Maynard Keynes had written to the Director General of Economic Warfare, Sir Frederick Leith Ross, urging that the focus of British strategy be directed towards exploiting the expense of the German war effort.

> In the last war, both sides made the mistake of concentrating too much on specific goods and too little on money, . . . Our blockade was carried on to the grave impairment of our own financial resources and was apparently based on the assumption that the purchasing power of the enemy was inexhaustible. . . . It is almost

> as useful to force Germany to pay a high price for her imports as to prevent her from getting them. . . . corresponding to the policy of forcing her to buy her imports dear, there should be a policy of forcing her to sell her exports cheap by methods of cut-throat competition.[41]

The ministry did not believe that Keynes's ideas were operationally adequate. Purchasing power could not be used as an exclusive yardstick when dealing with a state capable of invading its neighbours. Keynes's insistence on the need to expand Britain's own purchasing power, however, even at the risk of permitting Germany some external economic activity, fell on more receptive ears. In February 1940 the Bank of England prepared a note on pre-emptive purchasing from Benelux countries which cautioned that 'the more we buy from them, the larger are the balances from which they can pay Germany in free exchange. So long as Germany is not seriously short of foodstuffs . . . free exchange may be more useful to her than extra food supplies.[42]

The expense of war was a major problem for Britain, not only because of the need for dollar payments to foreign suppliers, but also because of the need to prevent payment for goods and services leading to runaway inflation. Full employment, including the movement into employment of married women, was calculated in the Economic Section of the War Cabinet in March 1941 to be bringing an additional £100 million into the economy. Shipping shortages and production controls reduced the supply of goods and services by £400 million. To prevent disastrous social consequences from competition for scarce resources, income tax was raised to 10*s* in the pound. Purchase tax was introduced. Nevertheless, increased taxation could only raise £279 million against the £800 million increased war expenditure. Rationing had to be imposed, in part as a measure of control over inflation.[43]

British Treasury operations in financing the war effort were highly successful in the short term. British control of the money market ensured that interest paid on loans was not excessive. By 1944 taxation was paying 54 per cent of Britain's war expenditure, compared to 29 per cent in 1918. This was only possible, however, because of Canada's interest free loans under mutual aid from the end of 1941 of over $700 million per year, a further Canadian gift of $1 billion, and the American provision of supplies after the spring of 1941 under *Lend Lease*, the cost of which was eventually written off.

In late 1940, before those financial arrangements had been made by the Canadian and American governments, the British treasury war chest had been virtually exhausted. For five months, until President Roosevelt introduced the *Lend Lease* act to Congress, no new orders could be made to American suppliers to prepare for the 1941 campaign season.[44]

As will be shown later, the 'new mercantilist' policy pursued by Britain did not preclude the use of naval and administrative resources to restrict Germany's access to overseas sources of supply. Some importance has to be attached to the fact that Germany was not permitted to share with Britain access to American industry and raw materials. British expectations from their blockade of Germany in World War II, however, were never such as to challenge the priority given to the development of Britain's own war economy.

Britain's policy towards the United States was not entirely reciprocated. American fears of mercantilism backed by the British navy was not entirely submerged, and could be perceived throughout World War II, and perhaps as late as the Kennedy Administration. In the desperate days of 1940 Roosevelt's economic advisor Henry Morgenthau, although a Jew and sympathetic to the British cause, insisted that Britain must liquidate all the assets of the British Empire before the United States would offer any assistance.[45] Eventually he was obliged to see that American monetary regulations severely limited the proportion of British wealth which could be used to pay dollar debts, but he continued to demand that Britain should at any rate sell all its American assets. Inevitably, the suspicion was created that the United States was itself seeking to profit from the war, by selling munitions strictly on a cash and carry basis. Warren Kimball, the historian of the episode, discounts the idea.[46]

> It is misleading to state flatly that the American government used England's financial crisis as a means of substituting an American economic empire for the British one. Had this been a conscious policy of the Roosevelt Administration, far heavier pressures would have been applied. Although Morgenthau correctly accused the British of dragging their feet on the sale of British-owned investments in America, by the fall of 1940 the issue was largely forgotten since it would obviously be too late with too little.

On the other hand, the American public and their congressmen had fewer scruples about squeezing Britain, in order to end its economic dominance.

> Morgenthau's policy of forcing Great Britain to pay cash right to the end of their dollar resources found ample justification in the Congressional debate over Lend-Lease. The statistical evidence of Britain's dollar shortage overwhelmed opposition claims that the British could continue to fight against Hitler without aid from the United States.

The *Lend Lease* Act which empowered Roosevelt to furnish Britain with munitions free of charge was clearly not exploitive of Britain's predicament. However, it was not made law until two years of war had ensured that Britain was no longer an economic threat, and was repealed the moment war was over. It cannot compare with the generosity of Canada's mutual aid and billion-dollar gift to Britain, a sum five times the per-capita rate of American loans. The contrast can only be explained by the fact that Canadians hoped the end of the war would find Britain economically and militarily strong. Americans had mixed motives which, along with an awareness of a common purpose and need, included both greed and a distrust of British power. Later, when the United States became an ally of the British, the shadow of 1917–18 New Imperialism, and British navalism, can be seen in American resistance to British strategy in the Mediterranean, and to British plans to recapture Singapore prior to participation in the Pacific war.[47]

The mercantilism of neutrality has never gained the bad press attached to belligerent mercantilism, but post-war Britons have resented the long-term economic gains made by the United States as neutrals in the two world wars. The development of the New York money market from 1915 was matched by the erosion of London's *entrepôt* trade. The effect of war risk in the North Atlantic, and of the desperate shortage of tonnage which made it necessary to stop importing cargoes intended for re-export, encouraged the development of new trade routes direct to American markets, and dominated by American shipping.[48] In the second war, wartime British expenditure on armaments of up to 80 per cent of Gross National Product, compared with an American peak of 30 per cent, crippled British investment in peaceful commerce and ensured American economic supremacy following the war.[49] H. Duncan Hall, the official British historian of the arrangements made for obtaining supply from North America, blames British reticence to develop their case before the court of American public opinion, and Roosevelt's sudden death, for the failure of the American government to recognise an obligation to help British reconstruction.[50] The American historian Richard Gardner agrees.[51] The financial concordat concluded with the United States following the surrender of Japan was very generous, if the fact is kept in mind that the United States was a neutral for half the war, but it is also true that as a neutral the United States did very well out of the conflict, and that the savage wartime dislocations of its economy left Britain in 1945 in a difficult position for competing in the post-war world market.[52]

The Germans and Japanese were no less interested in maximising their wealth, again measured in goods and services. The Nazis had concentrated upon the development of economic autarchy. Hitler's obsession with the threat of blockade determined him to obtain direct control of the oil resources of Romania and the Soviet Union, and of the crop lands of the Ukraine. His strategic directives to the German Army in Russia were misguidedly influenced by the desire to obtain control of key mines with the least delay. The conquest of France proved to be profitable, because the German administration set bounds to its appetite, and was governed by economic considerations. In Norway the Germans even contemplated capital investment. In the east, on the other hand, Nazi ideology in general did not permit the organisation of the economy on a level above serf agriculture and slave labour. The Japanese occupation of China, and invasion of Indonesia, were also determined by the need to obtain control of supplies.[53] The only significant difference between the strategies of Germany and Japan, and that of Great Britain, was that the dictators attempted to obtain their wealth by force. The exception is of the greatest importance.

NOTES

1. See David F. Trask, *Captains and Cabinets*, pp. 309–58 *passim*; Seth P. Tillman, *Anglo–American Relations at the Paris Peace Conference of 1919*, pp. 44–52; and Charles Seymour (ed.), *The Intimate Papers of Colonel House*, vol. iv, pp. 159–60; and D. Lloyd George, *The Truth about the Peace Treaties*, vol. ii, p. 81.
2. S. W. Roskill, *Naval Policy Between the Wars*, p. 81.
3. See Marian Kent, *Oil & Empire*, pp. 136–57.
4. Quoted in S. W. Roskill, op. cit., p. 307.
5. Quoted in H. W. V. Temperley, op. cit., I, p. 133. See M. G. Fry, 'The

imperial war cabinet, the United States, and the freedom of the seas', *Journal of the Royal United Service Institute*, vol. 110 (1965), pp. 353–62.

6. Quoted in Harold and Margaret Sprout, *Toward a New Order of Sea Power*, p. 59.
7. Ibid.
8. See Gerald S. Graham, *The Politics of Naval Supremacy*, pp. 121–5.
9. Harold and Margaret Sprout, op. cit., pp. 59 to 117.
10. Ian MacGibbon, *Blue-Water Rationale, The Naval Defence of New Zealand, 1914–1942*, p. 90, Memo by Jellicoe, n.d. (forwarded by Parr to Coates on 18 Aug. 1927) NZ Archives, PM 111/17/1. 'Their incessant demands for parity had more behind them than prestige, he (Jellicoe) hinted darkly to Coates. The Americans were probably determined to ensure no interference by the Royal Navy with their trade in a future conflict in which the United States remained neutral', and see W. T. Mallison, op. cit., pp. 62–74.
11. Harold and Margaret Sprout, op. cit., pp. 186–212.
12. CAB 15/21 Committee of Imperial Defence; Standing Sub-Committee on the Co-ordination of Departmental Action on the Outbreak of War; Report of Sub-Committee on *Trading, Blockade and Enemy Shipping*, 30 May 1923; para. 11.
13. Ibid., para. 37.
14. Ibid. Appendix III, para. 13.
15. See CAB 21/319 Cecil E. Farrer, Department of Overseas Trade (Development and Intelligence) to Cmdr C. P. Hermon-Hodge, R.N., 20 May 1926.
16. Sir Edward Grey, *Twenty-Five Years, 1892–1916*, ii, p. 107.
17. S. W. Roskill, op. cit., p. 434.
18. Armin Rappaport, *The Navy League of the United States*, p. 113.
19. M. Vlahos, *The Blue Sword: The Naval War College and the American Mission 1919–1941*. Newport, 1980, pp. 107–8.
20. MacGibbon, op. cit., Chapter 8, note 90 (New Zealand Archives, PM 111/17/1, Memo by Jellicoe, n.d. forwarded by Parr to Coates on 18 Aug. 1927).
21. CAB 21/307 Belligerent Rights at Sea and the Relations Between the United States and Great Britain, 16 and 26 October 1927.
22. CAB 21/307 Sub-Committee Report, 14 January 1928.
23. CAB 21/310, Stamfordham to Hankey, 17 Dec. 1927; Salsbury to Hankey, 1 Jan. 1928; and S. W. Roskill, op. cit., p. 550.
24. Barry D. Hunt, 'British Policy on the Issue of Belligerent and Neutral Rights, 1919–1939', in *New Aspects of Naval History*, Craig L. Symonds (ed.), pp. 279–90; and *Sailor–Scholar*, pp. 175–88. See CAB 21/310, Hankey's draft dispatch to the US Government, 13 Feb. 1929, and CAB 21/328, Committee of Imperial Defence, Sub-Committee on Belligerent Rights at Sea, 'The Food Factor in Blockade', Dec. 1929.
25. H. C. Hoover, op. cit., Vol. II, p. 342. See also ADM 116/2686, Esme Howard to Austen Chamberlain, 9 May 1929; and *passim*.
26. See CAB 21/352, 'Memorandum respecting the Conversations Between the Prime Minister and President Hoover at Washington', 4 to 10 Oct. 1929.

27. S. W. Roskill, op. cit., vol. ii, p. 48.
28. John F. Naylor, *A Man and an Institution, Sir Maurice Hankey . . .*, pp. 173–7.
29. Malcolm D. Kennedy, *The Estrangement of Great Britain and Japan, 1917–35*, pp. 143–57.
30. S. W. Roskill, op. cit., Vol. 2, pp. 79 and 87. See CAB 21/352, Austin Chamberlain to Balfour, 10 May 1929, and CAB 21/328, Hankey to Sir Arthur Henderson, 21 Oct. 1930.
31. Admiral A. T. Mahan, *The Influence of Sea Power upon History*, p. 23. 'The necessity of a navy ... springs ... from the existence of a peaceful shipping, and disappears with it'.
32. CAB 21/310, Richmond to ? Hankey, undated, 10 pages. *Imperial Defence and Capture at Sea in War*, 1932, s.v. 'Employment of Maritime Force in War'.
33. S. W. Roskill, op. cit., ii, p. 84.
34. Pp. 71–2.
35. Sir Julian S. Corbett, *England in the Seven Years War: A Study in Combined Strategy*, pp. 5–6; noted by Barry D. Hunt in 'The Strategic Thought of Sir Julian S. Corbett', John B. Hattendorf and Robert S. Jordan (eds), *Maritime Strategy and the Balance of Power*, p. 120.
36. S. W. Roskill, op. cit., ii, p. 291.
37. Barry D. Hunt, 'Of Bits and Bridles: Sea Power and Arms Control Prior to World War II', paper given to the conference on Naval Arms Limitations and Maritime Security, Halifax, N.S., June 1990.
38. W. N. Medlicott, op. cit., ii, p. 631.
39. Robert Greenhalgh Albion, op. cit., p. 214.
40. H. Duncan Hall, *North American Supply*, p. 3.
41. F.O. 837/5, J. M. Keynes to Sir Frederick Leith Ross, 10 October 1939.
42. CAB 21/1244, Henry Clay (?), Bank of England, to Francis Hemming, 14 February 1940, covering draft of 'Pre-emptive Purchases and Exchange Resources'.
43. W. K. Hancock and M. M. Gowing, *British War Economy*, pp. 325–46. See also M. Kalecki, in *Studies in War Economics*, pp. 80–98; and J. R. T. Hughes, Review Article, 'Financing the British War Effort', of R. S. Sayers, *Financial Policy, 1939–45*, London, 1956; *Journal of Economic History*, XVIII, pp. 193–9, 1958.
44. H. Duncan Hall, *North American Supply*, pp. 239–42, 253ff.
45. Ibid., pp. 143ff.
46. W. F. Kimball, *The Most Unsordid Act, Lend-Lease 1939–41*, p. 237 *et seq.* See James W. Garner, 'The United States "Neutrality" Law of 1937', *British Yearbook of International Law*, 1938, p. 44; and Nils Orvik, op. cit., pp. 195–215.
47. See Mark A. Stoler, 'The American Perception of British Mediterranean Strategy, 1941–45', in Craig L. Symonds, *New Aspects of Naval History*, pp. 325–39; and Christopher Thorne, *Allies of a Kind*, pp. 408–18, and 450–5.
48. Robert Greenhalgh Albion, op. cit., pp. 280–96.
49. Philip Pugh, *The Cost of Seapower*, pp. 9–20.

50. H. Duncan Hall, *North American Supply*, pp. 489–92.
51. Richard N. Gardner, *Sterling–Dollar Diplomacy*, pp. 178–254.
52. W. K. Hancock and M. M. Gowing, op. cit., pp. 501ff and 546ff.
53. Alan S. Milward, op. cit., s.v., 'War and Policy', and 'The Economics of Occupation'; and W. N. Medlicott, op. cit., ii, pp. 641–6.

4 Trade Control and Blockade Between the Wars

Fear expressed by Americans at the end of World War I that British naval dominance would preclude the effective enforcement of the League of Nations Covenant was somewhat wide of the mark. Article 16 of the Covenant, paragraph 1, indicated that sanctions against an offending state were to follow the American wartime model. Commercial and financial transactions were to be severed at source. The effectiveness of the system would depend upon its universality. Paragraph 2 of Article 16 made provision for the possible need for military forces, but this was not conceived at the time of the Ethiopian crisis in 1935 as being intended to oblige members of the League to observe a sanctions rule. The extent to which naval blockade is a strategy which requires belligerent action against unoffending 'neutral' states made it inappropriate for League purposes. American hostility to naval blockade also ensured that it would be avoided.

In the first decade after the formation of the League, attention was focussed on the idea that trade embargo would serve as a demonstration of international opinion which would be capable of influencing world affairs. That concept was given prominence by pacifist feeling following World War I, although it is possible to trace the belief in the moral force of collective action back to the American non-importation agreements of the Revolutionary and Napoleonic wars. The League of Nations Union, formed in Britain in 1918, received enough support from pacifists that it came to promote the idea. Thus, it was hoped, the danger of war could be removed from collective security. The League of Nations International Blockade Committee which reported in August 1921 gave consideration to the idea.[1] The American government eventually rejected participation in collective security, but it nevertheless adopted the 'moral embargo' as an instrument of diplomatic suasion. Naval force was not required to carry out the demonstration, but it is probable that belief in the power of naval blockade lay behind the faith in demonstrative sanctions. In the instance of the League of Nations Union, conviction that the British blockade of Germany had won the war no doubt was the source of the belief that Britain had the decisive power needed to make collective security work.

The failure of the demonstrative method to put a stop to the Japanese invasion of Manchuria in 1931 discredited it. By the time of the 1935 Ethiopian crisis, the League of Nations Union leadership had decided that economic sanctions had to be something more.[2] The American government, however, continued to order 'moral embargoes' of trade with transgressors, and the demonstrative concept remains part of the vocabulary of suasive diplomacy. In the Rhodesian dispute of the 1960s and 1970s naval force was even used to impose the demonstrative sanctions.

In 1926–27 the British government had given serious attention to the potentiality of a pacific blockade against the Cantonese government, and also considered the advantage of belligerent blockade. However, the Committee of Imperial Defence's Advisory Committee on Trading and Blockade in Time of War had advised that 'a real difficulty would arise . . . if an attempt were made to interfere with the trade of states not participating in the blockade, such as Russia or the United States'. If war were declared, a blockade could be effectively enforced, but the committee warned that 'the opinion of the Chinese experts is that even such an effective external blockade would produce very little influence on the Cantonese, and that they could quite well get on without any foreign trade, as indeed they did during the 18th Century'. Furthermore, a blockade would severely hurt British financial interests because the bulk of Chinese customs receipts went to servicing foreign debts.[3] Because of these considerations, the first time that the coercive effect of trade control was tested in action following World War I was the Ethiopian crisis.

THE ETHIOPIAN CRISIS

The economic sanctions imposed on Italy in 1935 did not, strictly speaking, constitute an episode in the history of maritime strategy any more than had American non-importation legislation in the eighteenth and nineteenth centuries. Nevertheless, these events participate in its history. The intended function of trade boycott was comparable to that of Spanish trade war against the Dutch in the seventeenth century; the protracted pressure of economic constraint was intended to be incrementally instrumental in encouraging a positive response to the diplomacy of League members. Having changed its pacifist policy, the League of Nations Union was all for making Italy a test case, partly because Italy was weak enough that coercion was a realistic policy. The strategy of the British government, however, was to avoid blocking vital commodities such as oil, which would oblige Italy to make sudden decisions. By the end of May 1936 it was reported by Anthony Eden, British Minister of League Affairs, that sanctions had greatly increased Mussolini's domestic problems. By September economic deterioration would be serious, and by the end of the year, grave.[4]

Sanctions can be said to have been effective technically, but not politically. Eden had warned that one outcome of the pressure being placed on Italy could be an Italian resort to war. Already the British Mediterranean fleet had been moved from Malta to Alexandria to be safer from Italian attack. Coercion, in whatever form it was offered, had to expect a hostile response. The democracies, however, would not risk war. In 1936 Mussolini was seen as a necessary partner against Nazi Germany. Britain and France had to choose between sustaining the credibility of the League, and finding a formula by which Italy might be restored to partnership with the democracies. The latter was tried, and failure resulted. The League was mortally wounded, and Mussolini turned from the democracies towards alliance with Hitler.

The failure of sanctions against Italy can be attributed in part to the nature of fascist government. Absolutist states have considerable capacity to ignore the economic problems of businessmen. The Dutch had demonstrated that in the 1650s by their futile blockade of London. Mussolini, like Cromwell, had too strong a grip on the political process.

Naval force was not employed to enforce the sanctions against Italy. The Mediterranean Fleet at Alexandria had been well placed to prevent the Italian army passing through the Suez canal on its way to Ethiopia. Mussolini, however, decided correctly that he could count on Britain's avoiding war at all costs. American hostility to naval blockade also dissuaded the effective employment of the Mediterranean Fleet. It may well be argued, however, that the decision not to use naval force increased the danger implicit in economic sanctions. Probably a clear-cut *nolo proseque* delivered by naval forces would have been safer, because it would have been a more measurable force. All parties would have known their own limits. This conclusion becomes even more evident in the light of the attempt by the

American government at the end of the decade to use economic sanctions against Japan.

THE SPANISH CIVIL WAR

The humiliated British Mediterranean Fleet was on its way home from Alexandria when developments in the Spanish Civil War led to British nationals, and British shipping, coming into danger. Both the Republican government of Spain and the Nationalist mutineers led by General Franco attempted to use naval forces to deny to the other side access to foreign sources of supply. The Nationalists enjoyed the support of Mussolini and Hitler, and they also found sympathy in the British navy because the 'Red' Republican government had used junior officers to maintain its authority in the navy when the senior officers had mutinied. The British government attempted to maintain an impartial approach to the conflict, but impartiality implied acceptance of the legitimacy of the Nationalist mutineers. The Republican government was supported by many West European volunteers, and by the Soviet Union. The latter, however, was not in a position to provide organised military forces while Germany and Italy were, and did. The British and French governments attempted to enforce an international agreement that contraband should not be supplied to either side, and the Royal Navy was deployed on non-intervention patrols. They were inadequate, however, to prevent the arrival of Italian air force units, which significantly reinforced the Nationalist capacity to stop Soviet arms shipments. In late 1936 Nationalist aircraft sank a Soviet supply ship, and on 20 December Franco warned that the northern ports of Bilbao, Santander and Gijon were to be blockaded. It thus was critical to the outcome of the war what orders the British government would give to the Royal Navy.

The growing threat of war with Germany dominated British thinking. The First Lord of the Admiralty, Sir Samuel Hoare, continued despite the outcome of the Ethiopian crisis to set a high priority on detaching Italy from Germany, and persisted in this policy even when it became evident that Mussolini was employing Italian forces to support General Franco. So long as the Republican government possessed naval dominance the Admiralty preferred to deny Spain belligerent rights on the high seas, but when the Nationalists acquired significant naval assets of their own the Admiralty recommended to the cabinet that both sides be accorded the status of belligerents. This recommendation was not implemented, but in an attempt to make a policy of non-intervention compatible with a denial of belligerent rights British shipping was forbidden by act of parliament from carrying contraband to either side of the civil war.[5]

The Admiralty sought to undermine as little as possible the ability of Britain itself to employ a distant blockade of food supplies in future wars. It based its advice to the cabinet, that the blockade of Basque ports should be recognised, on the technical grounds that the Nationalists were able to mount an 'effective' blockade inside the three-mile limit. Dispatches from the admiral on station, however, indicated that in fact the Nationalists could not, because of the coastal guns of the Republican cities. The Nationalists had the power to enforce a distant blockade, but as they had not been recognised as a belligerent they could only be accorded the right of close blockade within territorial waters. The Royal Navy had the power, and eventually employed it, to escort ships up to the edge of Spanish territorial waters. In doing so, however, it came very close to violating the British policy dating back to the seventeenth century of not recognising the right of neutrals to escort their merchantmen through blockaded waters without submitting to search and arrest. The question of escorting food ships into Bilbao in April 1937 was especially provocative, given British resistance to President Hoover's efforts to obtain immunity for food ships in wartime. Public opinion in Britain forced the government's hand. The bombing of Guernica led to a further reversal of government policy, and orders to the navy to escort refugee ships leaving Basque towns.[6] The President of Rio Tinto Mining, Sir Auckland Geddes, had suggested in March 1937 that the navy also be used to prevent the transport out of Spain of iron ores seized from British-owned mines by the German trading contractor Hisma-Rowak in payment for German arms, and destined for German war production. The Admiralty, however, had rejected the idea as too likely to lead to war.[7]

Mussolini had earlier sold two submarines to the Nationalists and in August 1937 he provided four 'Legionary' submarines, and also ordered Italian navy submarines to make 'piratical' attacks on ships bound for Spanish ports. On 11 August Italian destroyers sank a Spanish tanker with a torpedo, and two days later sank another and shelled a Panamanian ship. In the last three weeks of August 1937 26 ships with British registry were attacked, and five sunk by submarine attack. Ships were also attacked by aircraft. The British government was obliged to take more forceful action. Following an attack by a submarine on a British destroyer, and the subsequent damage of the submarine, agreement was reached with other Mediterranean naval powers at a conference at Nyon on September 10 to 14 to set up anti-submarine patrols. Italy was invited to the Nyon conference, and the threat of collective action persuaded Mussolini's Foreign Minister, Count Ciano, to call off the attacks. The Nyon agreement was a rather feeble gesture of concerted action against the dictators, and it was the high-water mark in Anthony Eden's anti-appeasement policy. Ciano turned over two further Italian submarines to full Nationalist control, and attacks were resumed in January 1938. They were abandoned again in February when the Royal Navy adopted a policy of immediate attack on any submerged submarine. The naval patrols were technically effective because signal intelligence could identify submarine operational areas.[8]

After the collapse of the Basque Republic, the British government was all the more determined not to risk consequences by interfering with the Nationalist blockade of the remaining Republican cities. The Royal Navy reached a working agreement with the Nationalist navy that the latter would advise where their submarines were working, and the former would not attack them providing they behaved themselves. The French government was afraid to open the frontier to permit supply of the Republic overland, although for a while it was unofficially open during the night time. The smaller the territory left to the Spanish government the greater value to the Nationalists became their attacks on marine lines of supply. Finally the 'state besieged' was no more than the city of Barcelona in which the remnant of the Republic sheltered in dire distress. British food ships were not escorted into Barcelona as they had been into Bilbao. The British *chargé d'affaire* wrote:

> Humanitarian work in such circumstances comes perilously near intervention. It means, in fact, taking from Franco's hands the very weapon which we used against Germany with such grim effect twenty years ago.[9]

The economic privation of the Catalans during the last days of the Republic were extreme. In 1938 rations to Republican soldiers were reduced to less than a pound of bread, a third of a pound of meat, and a few vegetables. The civilian population were in a much worse condition; 600 000 children were refugees, but only 40 000 could be cared for by the Quaker International Commission. Unquestionably the blockade contributed significantly to the defeat, but it is difficult to assess its degree of importance. Blockade of contraband may have been less important than was the economic collapse which reduced the capacity of the Republic to purchase arms.[10]

SANCTIONS AGAINST JAPAN

The discovery which France and Britain had made during the Ethiopian crisis, that economic sanctions were a two-edged weapon which could only be employed if the risk was accepted that greater conflict could be provoked, was more than confirmed when the attempt was made to confront Japanese imperialism. These episodes, indeed, established the validity of the lessons of 300 years of experience with trade war. Japan is a country which is pre-eminently vulnerable to blockade because it is an island state which lacks a substantial domestic supply of iron or oil, and has a vast population which can only be fed by importation of food. In the early 1930s the Japanese Minister of War, General Sadao Araki, had been quoted in *Foreign Affairs* as making it clear that, since mankind had 'the right to live upon the earth', no country with abundant resources had the right to deny them to another country insufficiently endowed by nature. Japan's very vulnerability to economic blockade made that strategy, or the embargo of strategic commodities at source, a highly dangerous measure which could only be taken by a state prepared for war. Japan had long since recognised that only the growth of its military power could prevent other states turning off the tap. This had led to its takeover in northern China, and to the development of the military potential to seize the oil fields of the Netherlands East Indies. Ironically, the American embargo of iron ore in 1917 to compel Japan to provide shipping for the war effort had been one of the formative factors which determined the Japanese to acquire control of Chinese resources.[11]

Shortly after the Japanese attack on USS *Panay* in December 1937 President Roosevelt began serious consideration of the need to use naval force to restrain Japan. From 1911, the American navy had had a plan to conduct any war against Japan by the seizure of advanced bases from which an economic blockade could be mounted. Updated as War Plan *Orange* in 1922, it had then been superseded by more ambitious if less realistic plans.[12] In the *Panay* crisis, however, Captain R. E. Ingersoll, US Navy Chief of War Plans, was sent to London to discuss joint operations for a distant blockade of Japanese supply ships. A proposal was drawn up at the Admiralty by which Britain would send a battle fleet to operate in the South China Sea and east to the New Hebrides, while the US Navy blocked Japanese trade in the central Pacific. Roosevelt introduced the American public to the idea of 'quarantine' action against bandit states, and sought British agreement to a conference which would serve as a platform for developing American willingness to risk war in the defence of international ethics and American interests. British enthusiasm, however, soon waned. Neville Chamberlain did not believe that Roosevelt would deliver more than words, and he was intent on reducing the threat from European dictators. A heavy naval commitment in the Pacific might make a settlement with Mussolini unobtainable. Anthony Eden had been much more supportive, although he apparently preferred a naval demonstration to what would clearly be an act of war against Japan at the time when Italian and German warships were actively intervening in the Spanish Civil War. His inability to deflect Chamberlain's appeasement policy led to his resignation and put an end to the idea of blockading Japan.[13]

The US Atlantic fleet was deployed to the Pacific, and three American cruisers were sent to participate in the celebrations held to mark the completion of the Singapore defences, but the blockade plan was transformed into an embargo of American sources of supply of steel and oil. Roosevelt's advisors were divided in their opinions as to whether economic privation could ever drive Japan to war with the United States, with the result that American policy took shape gradually.[14] In December 1938 China was given a US $25 million loan, and in January 1939 a 'moral embargo' was instituted to discourage the sale of aircraft to Japan. In February there was a cessation of credits to Japan, and in July formal notice was given of the intention in six months to abrogate the 1911 commercial treaty. In July 1940 an export licensing system was established, but only some categories of petroleum distillates and of ferrous metals were placed under control. The limitations kept the embargoes from being a *causus bellum*, but in general they were counterproductive. Japan's southward drive for resources was accelerated, and on 27 September 1940 Japan signed the Tripartite Pact with Germany and Italy. On 26 July 1941 Roosevelt froze all Japanese assets in the United States, effectively cutting off Japan from American oil, which at the time was 59 per cent of the world supply. Possessing as it did an 18-month reserve stock of oil for naval war purposes, the Japanese government saw itself as presented with a deadline. Roosevelt expected capitulation, and his advisor on East Asian affairs, Stanten Hornbeck, retorted to a warning from an official of the US Embassy in Tokyo in November 1941 by asking to be told 'of one case in history where a nation went to war out of desperation'. As Prime Minister Tojo later phrased it, however, 'sometimes a man has to jump with his eyes closed, from the temple of Kiyomizo into the ravine below'. Rather than bow to the coercive effect of economic sanctions, the Japanese attacked the American fleet at Pearl Harbor, and invaded the Netherlands East Indies.[15]

The Ethiopian and Manchurian crises forcefully bring home the lesson that if sanctions are effective they are likely to lead to war, unless there are massive disincentives to restrain the victim. It may actually be more dangerous to impose economic sanctions by administrative means because it permits the victim an option of violent reaction, the consequences of which are unclear. Japan hopefully grasped the nettle at Pearl Harbor in 1941. Had the US and British navies been employed to effect economic sanctions by means of a sea blockade, proper military precautions would certainly have been taken to guard against counterattack. As a result all states would most likely have been acutely aware of the limits to their capacity, and have governed their behaviour accordingly.[16]

NOTES

1. Philip C. Jessup, op. cit., vol. iv, p. 93.
2. Donald S. Birn, *The League of Nations Union*, s.v., 'The Manchurian Crisis' and 'The Ethiopian Crisis'.
3. CAB 21/299, CID Advisory Committee on Trading and Blockade in Time of War, *Possibilities of Exerting Economic Pressure on the Nationalist Government of South China*, Feb. 1927.
4. George W. Baer, *Test Case Italy, Ethiopia, and the League of Nations*, pp. 7–9, 245, 287 and 302–3. See also George Martelli, *Italy Against the World*.
5. Jill Edwards, *The British Government and the Spanish Civil War, 1936–1939*, Ch. 4, s.v., 'Naval Attitudes to the Spanish Civil War'.
6. James Cable, *The Royal Navy & the Siege of Bilbao*, pp. 8–14, 55–76, 87 and 91–8.
7. C. E. Harvey, 'Politics and Pyrites during the Spanish Civil War', *Economic History Review*, s2, vol. 31, pp. 89–104, 1978.
8. Jill Edwards, loc. cit.; S. W. Roskill, op. cit., ii, ch. 12; Peter Gretton,

'The Nyon Conference – the naval aspects', *English Historical Review*, no. 354 (1975), p. 103; and (unattributed) 'The Nyon Arrangements – Piracy by Treaty?', *British Yearbook of International Law*, 1938, p. 198.

9. Quoted in Jill Edwards, op. cit., p. 129.
10. Hugh Thomas, *The Spanish Civil War*, pp. 859–65.
11. Jeffrey J. Safford, *Wilsonian Maritime Diplomacy 1913–1921*, pp. 127–40.
12. Malcolm H. Murfett, 'Are We Ready? The Development of American and British Naval Strategy, 1922–39', in John B. Hattendorf and Robert S. Jordan, *Maritime Strategy and the Balance of Power*, pp. 220–1.
13. J. M. Haight, 'Franklin D. Roosevelt and a naval quaranteen of Japan', *Pacific Historical Review*, vol. 40, pp. 203–56, May 1971.
14. J. H. Herzog, 'Influence of the United States Navy in the Embargo of Oil to Japan 1940–1941', *Pacific Historical Review*, vol. 35, pp. 317–28, Aug. 1966.
15. Norman A. Graeber, 'Japan, Unanswered Challenge, 1931–41', in M. F. Morris and S. L. Myres (eds), *Essays on American Foreign Policy*.
16. See Walter R. Thomas, 'Pacific Blockade: A Lost Opportunity of the 1930's?', *United States Naval War College International Law Studies*, p. 197.

5 World War II

THE BRITISH BLOCKADE OF GERMANY

The British government had secretly collected economic intelligence during the 1920s and 1930s. In 1929 a Ministry of Blockade had been formed at the Foreign Office, and in 1931 an Industrial Intelligence Centre had been established under the direction of Major Desmond Morton, which became the Intelligence Division of the Ministry of Economic Warfare when it was officially established on 3 September 1939.[1] A 'Handbook of Economic Warfare', prepared by the Advisory Committee on Trade Questions in Time of War, had been printed the previous July.[2] The Intelligence Division was subdivided into a Blockade Branch responsible for the minutiae of contraband control and an Enemy Branch which was tasked with appraising the expected performance of the German economy.[3] Concern about the American attitude to restraints on trade, however, and also the feeling that coercion of small neutral states was inappropriate in a war which was being fought to defend the freedoms of small states, led to the blockade Britain ordered against Germany on the outbreak of war in 1939 being restricted to contraband control as it had been in 1914. No attempt was made to recreate the apparatus for rationing the imports of neutral states bordering Germany, nor was pre-emptive purchasing of war supplies pursued. German trade agreements with Russia, signed in August 1939, February 1940 and January 1941, gave Germany access, not only to Russian sources of supply, but also to those of China and elsewhere in the Far East. After the fall of France, the Vichy regime provided another channel of supply to Germany, one the British were afraid to block entirely for 'fear of an incident which would precipitate French hostility and the active use of their fleet and ports against us'.[4] Aerial attack on industry was the new dimension of economic warfare, but it too was restricted. The strict rules of conduct for operations against trade had been renewed by the London Protocol of 1936. Britain applied them rigorously on ships and aircraft, which latter were at first forbidden to attack any enemy ships other than warships, troopships, and 'auxiliaries in direct attendance on the enemy fleet'.

Prize courts functioned in virtually the same manner as they had in World War I, but the destructive nature of the conflict meant that relatively few cases were brought before them. The precedents established in World War I were in general applicable to World War II.[5] The reprisal orders of World War I having lapsed, the Declaration of Paris was recognised as protecting enemy goods in neutral ships. The distinction between contraband and conditional contraband was recognised as part of the course of Admiralty, but the Declaration of London was not recognised following its denunciation in 1916.[6]

Even the 1914 level of blockade could not be sustained in the new conditions. The American government was not willing to provide passive support for British economic warfare, although it did amend its own neutrality legislation to permit British ships to load munitions in American ports. It imposed restrictions on American ships, and American nationals, to reduce the risk of being drawn into war as it had been in 1917, but it defended the rights of American shipping to conduct its trade unrestricted by the demands of the belligerents. Americans, and American ships, were ordered to stay outside a war-zone which was drawn around most of Europe and included Halifax and ports in Canada east of it. An exception was made of Bergen and the North Norwegian coast, and strong protests were made when British cruisers brought American traders to Bergen into Kerkwall for inspection. In agreement with the Latin American states, Washington declared an American neutrality zone which included southern Nova Scotia. Canadian consent was not considered necessary. Efforts to allow American shipping to be examined in a safe Canadian port were thereby frustrated. The United States Treasury forbade shippers to make agreements with the British government to restrict their cargoes to those covered by a British Navicert. Eventually in January 1940, as a necessary concession to Anglo–American relations, Winston Churchill was constrained to order the Admiralty to stop bringing in American ships. The less powerful neutrals could complain with good reason that Britain showed special deference to American might.

When in April 1940 the American government banned sailings to Bergen, that particular problem was shelved. The *blitzkrieg* of the next few months ended the freedom of most border neutrals, and reduced American resistance to the British blockade. The fall of France enabled Britain to obtain American consent to compulsory navicerting of cargoes, and the establishment of bunker control. Nonetheless, the proviso in the Lend-Lease Act, that it would only come into effect when Britain had exhausted all its dollar credits, reflected the continued American suspicion of preferential British trading. American hostility to naval control remained unchanged, but the fall of France left Britain with little other means of blocking imports to Germany.[7] Throughout the winter of 1940–41 British efforts at blocking leaks were again and again frustrated by the Americans who objected to Britain basing trade control ships in its own West Indian colonies. Only the German attack on Russia put an end to the leak of cargoes into Germany through Siberia. And only when the United States began to impose embargoes on commodities at source, and to encourage the Latin American states to do so as well, was it possible to attack with any effect the economic base of the German war machine. Until late in 1942, however, the United States government had no agency to provide it with intelligence for economic warfare purposes. Although Washington had secretly advised Latin American states in February 1941 that it wished to further British war efforts by pre-emptive purchasing of strategic commodities, US policy tended to be swayed by domestic political considerations.

The Japanese attack at Pearl Harbor which brought the United States into the war put an end to the need for London to be cautious of neutral reaction. Traditional American dislike of economic blockade was preserved only in the preference of Washington for political intervention in the neutral capitals, and for black-listing of neutral businesses, rather than interception of merchant ships at sea.[8] The United States Board of Economic Warfare became an advocate of extreme measures. The British Ministry of Economic Warfare, however, did not entirely abandon its restraint. Apparently more aware of the permanent damage which could be done to post-war trade, London was more solicitous for the trading rights of Europe's remaining neutrals. The British War Cabinet also found itself under considerable moral pressure to relax the blockade when Germany seized the food supplies in occupied countries, notably in Greece.[9]

Measurement of the utility of the British blockade in World War II is as difficult as it is for World War I. In May 1940 the Defence Committee had ordered the Ministry of Economic Warfare to prepare a study of Germany's economic situation in the event that France collapsed and the French fleet fell into enemy hands. It somewhat optimistically calculated that with full American co-operation external trade control, at source, would produce a shortfall of food in the *reich*, and a decline in German war potential because of shortages of oil, non-ferrous metals, alloys, rubber and fibres. F. H.

Hinsley writes that 'at the time the paper was drafted British economic intelligence assessments exaggerated the results that might be expected from economic warfare'.[10] Soon, more sober analysis began to suggest that German war losses were not affecting its military capacity, and by the end of 1940 the Joint Intelligence Committee held out little hope of Germany's being forced by economic factors to seek peace. Oil was increasingly seen to be the weakest link in the German economy, and that could only be attacked by bombing the synthetic oil plants and by interfering with the supply from Romania and Russia.

The selection of iron ore as a target turned out to be a mistake. In 1938 Germany imported 5.4 million metric tons of iron ore from Sweden, over half of its entire imports. Sweden was inaccessible to British power, however, and could not be compelled to stop exports. German stockpiles were adequate to fill any shortfall until after the capture of French iron mines.[11] Attempts to incapacitate German war industry by blockading rare metals was no more successful because of German stockpiles, and because of resources in the defeated states occupied by German forces.

By the time the Americans became active in economic warfare against Germany, Berlin controlled far too extensive a coastline for the blockade to be effective, and far too vast economic resources to be incapacitated by external constraint. The prestige of the German Army by then was such that the few remaining border neutrals could not be brought to embargo strategic materials. It was not until the balance was decidedly tilted in favour of the Allies that Turkey could be persuaded to stop its supply of chrome, Sweden to cut off ball-bearings, and Spain and Portugal to embargo wolfram.

Alan S. Milward has concluded that an important cause of the relative failure of allied economic warfare 'was the lack of consistency with which . . . it was carried on'. 'Although weak links in the German and Japanese economies were in fact discovered, they were never attacked for long enough, or frequently enough . . .'

> Both individual national economies and the international economy proved to be systems more complex than was allowed for in most plans of economic warfare. In retrospect these plans can be seen as drastically inaccurate simplifications of economic existence.[12]

In any case, the German war economy did not present a good target. Gerd Hardach's findings about the impact of the British blockade of Germany in World War I are equally applicable to World War II, and are supported by those of Mancur Olson, who concluded that the decisive factor in a state's economic survival in wartime is the degree of administrative virtuosity of which it is capable. Albert Speer's control of German production and distribution in the last years of the Third Reich greatly surpassed anything achieved in Wilhelminian Germany.[13]

The historian of the Economic Blockade, W. N. Medlicott, concludes that

> The broad record of Allied economic-warfare policy shows therefore that while the pre-war plans were formidable on paper they could be fully carried out only when the Allies possessed a qualitative and quantitative superiority in armaments which would ensure victory by more direct methods in the field. Even without victory in the field an air superiority so overwhelming as to put German transport and industry out of action would have either ended the war abruptly or at least deprived the blockade of most of its purpose.

However, the blockade was not without some value. As Medlicott wrote,

> the various modes of direct attack on [the] German economy did not become overwhelming until the second half of 1944, and the importance and proportions of the blockade were directly due to the relative failure of these other means of sapping the enemy's economic power in the middle years of the war. It was an improved Maginot line which encircled the economy of the Axis powers, and by placing permanent limits on their resources and expansion achieved the primary aim of containment, the essential purpose of any good defensive strategy.[14]

Had Germany had access to American sources of supply in the first years of the war, its outcome might have been very different. In comparison to the strategic bomber campaign, the blockade was relatively cost-effective, and it proved to be a major strategic catalyst. The passionate, extravagant, German reaction to it was their undoing when they invaded Russia.

In World War II economic warfare was not confined to action outside the enemy frontier. Direct attack on enemy industry from the air had been experimented with in World War I, and was the most visible aspect of economic warfare in World War II. Milward's observations on the inadequacy of allied target selection are applicable to the bomber operations as they are to naval blockade. Air power failed to meet the expectations of pre-war strategists. Technical developments in air defence undermined the premise that the bomber would carry out its raids with ease. Effective selection of targets was frustrated by the limited understanding there was of the German war economy. Only at the end of 1944, when German retreat in the East had increased the importance of German synthetic oil production, did the bombers find in the oil industry a target which disabled the enemy.

THE ALLIED BLOCKADE OF JAPAN

The economic campaign against Japan was much more effective than was that against Germany, because Japan could not hope for autarchy, because it was a relatively easy task to isolate it from outside sources of trade, and because, in Mancur Olson's view, the Japanese economy had not developed an innovative virtuosity which could have contended with the problem of blockade. Immediately after receiving news of Pearl Harbor, Churchill wrote a strategy paper in which he noted that 'The resources of Japan are a wasting factor'.[15] The resources of Anglo–American sea power could be built up, especially with submarines and naval aircraft. Although Japan's neighbour, the Soviet Union, was neutral until the last days of the war, it was a hostile neutral which was desperately short of supplies to sustain its own war effort. Soviet dependence upon Britain and the United States for its imports ensured that Japan would get little from that source.

The blockade of Japan was conducted by the American and British navies without any attempt to conform with the Declarations of Paris and London, or even with the restraints embodied with so much trouble in the 1936 London Protocol on the use of submarines. On receipt of word of the Japanese attack on Pearl Harbor, Admiral Stark, US Chief of Naval Operations, signalled 'Execute Unrestricted Air and Submarine Warfare against Japan'.[16] Japanese militarist barbarism, and no doubt racism, eradicated any sense of a humanitarian morality behind international law. This violation of the Hague convention ultimately served at the Nuremburg War Crimes trials to justify the earlier German resort to unrestricted U-boat operations. American resort to unrestricted war on trade freed the British from their restraint in the European theatre. Whole areas of ocean were declared to be 'dangerous to shipping', within some of which enemy vessels were liable to be sunk on sight. This departure from international law was justified as reprisal for German excesses.[17]

The Japanese Navy had not developed either the weapons or the doctrine for attacking merchant shipping. Japanese submarines were designed for operations against very high value naval targets, and the Japanese Navy never abandoned its aversion to attacking civilian shipping. Crediting its potential enemies with a similar attitude, it had failed before the war to make preparations to defend Japanese shipping. By the end of 1942 Japan was obliged to begin in a half-hearted way to devise means of protecting merchant shipping, but these were never very effective, in part because Japanese naval officers hated the inglorious task.[18] In February 1944 Admiral Takagi concluded that the Allied campaign against merchant tonnage was going to lose the war for Japan. He contemplated assassinating Prime Minister Tojo in protest.[19] By the time the American and British fleets were closing for the invasion of the Japanese home islands, the Japanese Navy was nearly immobilised for lack of fuel oil.

American submarines sunk over five million tons of shipping during the war, and by the end were in control of the Sea of Japan. The battle fleet raided the Pacific coastline. Bombers sewed fields of naval mines off the Japanese coast, sinking 609 000 tons. Army and navy aircraft sank another million tons by direct attack.[20] In the view of the officers who compiled the United States Strategic Bombing Survey of the War against Japanese Transportation, American strategy had not fully grasped the importance of merchant ship targets. Only 1.5 per cent of air strikes by land-based aircraft were directed at merchant shipping, and American naval forces concentrated their efforts unduly against enemy warships. The B-29 mine-laying operations off Japanese harbours did not begin until March 1945. In the end, however, these efforts had a devastating effect on the Japanese economy. Iron ore imports, which had totalled 6 073 000 metric tons in 1940, was reduced to 341 000 tons in 1945. Rice was reduced from 1 694 000 to 151 200 tons. Total imports fell from 22 million metric tons to 2.7 million. In April 1945 the Japanese had to restrict imports almost exclusively to food.[21] By July 1945 sailings from Kobe and Osaka had fallen to 44 000 tons from the March figure of 320 000 tons. The Shimonoseki Strait was closed entirely for 16 days during the period 1 July to 14 August, and Japan was unable to continue traffic to mainland Asia.[22]

Perhaps greater concentration on economic warfare at an earlier date could have obviated much of the hard fighting ashore during the Pacific war. It is possible that surrender could have been exacted by close blockade alone. By the summer of 1945, however, there was little patience in Washington to await the slow workings of blockade to bring Japan's surrender. Considering the scale of effort which had already been expended, that attitude has some justification. Callous disregard for the suffering of Japanese people by their own military could have protracted the campaign for many months. The American public might not continue to support a war effort which was not yielding spectacular results. Experience with the Versailles treaty, extorted by blockade of an enemy which could claim it had not been defeated in the field, was a strong disincentive to accept anything but virtually unconditional surrender. To achieve that, resort was made to the atomic bomb, and the Russians invaded Manchuria.

THE GERMAN U-BOAT *GUERRE DE COURSE*

Winston Churchill, writing of the U-boat war on shipping in World War I, called it 'among the most heart-shaking episodes of history', and a 'turning point in the destiny of nations', but he also disputed that it had 'nearly succeeded' in defeating the *Entente*.

> Where as any one of a score of alternative accidents would have given the German Army Paris in 1914, the seafaring resources of Great Britain were in fact and in the circumstances always superior to the U-boat attack. Moreover that attack was inherently of a character so gradual that these superior resources could certainly obtain their full development.[23]

As British prime minister for most of World War II, he had to contend with the full weight of a much better directed U-boat campaign, and in his memoirs he wrote that 'the only thing that ever really frightened me . . . was the U-boat peril'. However, his judgment of World War I is equally applicable to World War II.[24] Admiral Carl Dönitz, the commander of German U-boats in 1939 and later Commander-in-Chief of the German Navy, was convinced that attack on trade was the only means by which Germany could defeat Britain.[25] This belief had been supported by articles on the 'new conception of naval war as economic warfare' published by the German navy's historian, Vice-Admiral Kurt Assmann, shortly before the outbreak of war.[26] In the end, however, Dönitz proved to be wrong. Allied naval resources were put under tremendous strain by the U-boat operations, but they were adequate to contain the problem, while simultaneously conducting offensive operations. These latter were indeed affected by shipping shortages, but not so much as to prevent altogether the mobilisation of British Empire and American resources to participate with the Soviet Red Army in the defeat of Germany and Japan.

When hostilities resumed in 1939 between Britain and Germany, the most effective defence against U-boats, the convoy, was at once put into operation. The German U-boat campaign in World War II, however, was conducted with much greater sophistication and concentration. The techniques and technologies of trade defence worked out in World War I, and in the inter-war years, were discounted by the tactical use of U-boats in night group attacks on the surface.[27]

The Germans no longer pinned their strategy upon the idea that ship-owners could be panicked into keeping their ships in port. The measures taken by the British government in World War I, to keep British and neutral shipping operating on services necessary to the British war effort, indicated that strategic planning could not expect to exploit the capacity of ship owners to make the voluntary decisions based on considerations of risk and profit. In 1938 the British government belatedly concluded an agreement with the War Risk insurance clubs which provided shippers in World War II with a minimum of protection for dangerous wartime trades.[28] German strategy, accordingly, was based upon the effect of the loss to Britain of the tonnage which could actually be sunk by German U-boats, and by other forces. Shipping was to be attacked wherever it was least well defended, in the expectation that greater losses could be inflicted than could be made good by new construction in British and American yards. Dönitz wrote in his diary at the end of 1942: 'The tonnage war is the main task of the U-boats . . . It must be carried on where the greatest successes can be achieved with the smallest losses'.[29]

Loss of shipping to U-boat attack was only part of the wartime pressure put on shipping. Surface attack, mines, and aerial bombing all played parts. Bombing of east coast British harbours forced the diversion of shipping to western ports. Inadequate provision in those ports for handling the wartime cargoes, and especially the inability of the railways to handle the diverted traffic under wartime conditions of blackout, led to a loss of 2.3 to 3 million tons of cargo a year in

1940–41.[30] Despite desultory efforts during the 1920s and 1930s to profit by the administrative lessons of World War I, in 1939 Britain did not have a central economic planning system adequate to the needs of war. Ports, ships and railways were separately administered and, as Martin Doughty has shown, the inter-departmental committee system could not overcome the limitations of that arrangement. It was only in 1941 that the Ministry of War Transport was established to co-ordinate the work of other departments.[31] The need to hold ships in harbour while convoys were made up, to sail convoys at the speed of the slowest ship, and to give circuitous routing to convoys and to the ships sailing independently all reduced the amount of cargo which could be delivered, by up to 30 per cent.[32]

In the four months up to June 1941 the U-boats sank 282 000 tons per month, against which Commonwealth shipbuilding could only supply one million tons per year. Although Britain had the world's largest merchant marine, Britain's ship-building yards were incapable on their own of compensating for ships sunk by the Germans. The first British orders to American yards were made in late 1940.[33] Lend-lease orders for shipping from rapidly expanded American yards exceeded 1200 hulls in 1941. These ships could not be ready for service, however, until 1943.[34] In the first years of the war losses could only be offset by purchase from neutrals, by seizure of Axis ships in American harbours, and by increased efficiency of operation. After the German invasion of Russia in July 1941 the need to carry military stores to Russia added to the demand for shipping. Between June 1941 and September 1945, 17 million tons of supplies were shipped to Russia, primarily via Murmansk, Archangel, and the Persian Gulf, and by American ships under Russian colours through Vladivostok.[35]

The 1941 shipping crisis was dramatically ended by the success of British cryptography at Bletchley Park in breaking the 'Home Waters' setting of the German Navy's *Enigma* cypher machine. The British Submarine Control Room was able to maintain a plot of all U-boat positions, and route merchant shipping to avoid contact. In the second half of 1941 loss to U-boats dropped to 120 000 tons a month. Nevertheless, a total of four and a half million tons of shipping were destroyed in 1941, and in February 1942 Sir Arthur Salter, Head of British Merchant Shipping Mission to Washington, drew up an alarming memorandum in which the strategic implications were spelt out.[36]

The US and British building programmes amount to about 7 million gross tons. But the new ships only become gradually available, and a large proportion will only make one completed voyage in the year. Allowing for this, and the fact that we start the year with 2 million tons less than 1941, it is clear that, even if losses do not exceed 4½ million tons, the *USA and Great Britain cannot carry more in 1942 than in 1941*.

The *extra* demands for 1942 can therefore only be met by corresponding reduction of the services carried out in 1941.

Those *extra* demands are:

(a) The Russian programme, requiring for its full execution at least 1 million tons of shipping.

(b) The needs of the Pacific War.

(c) The transport and maintenance of additional US forces.

(d) Naval demands for additional Merchant ships (as air carriers, etc.) . . .

The volume of UK imports affords a good measure of the stringency of shipping. The UK imported (excluding oil) 52 million tons in 1938. . . . 44 million tons in the first year of the war. . . . [but] only 30½ in 1941. . . .

The prospects for 1942 are much worse. In the first quarter of the year the Ministry of War Transport estimate that, with the shipping now at their disposal, they can only load for the UK from all sources 5¼ million tons. This is equivalent to an annual rate of only 21 million tons – and a still lower rate of *imports* since some cargoes will be lost enroute. . . . If losses continue at this rate it is evident from the figures given above that we shall be no better able in 1943 than we are in 1942 to undertake substantial overseas operations; and indeed that the danger of starvation or of shutting down munitions factories in the UK will be a very great. [sic]

In February 1942 German U-boat command fundamentally changed its cryptographic machine and Bletchley Park was not able to break the code again until December. At the same time the German Navy succeeded in breaking the British Naval Cypher #3 which controlled North Atlantic operations.[37] The significance of this intelligence success, however, was obscured by the opportunity presented U-boat command following the American entry into the war to concentrate upon ships sailing unconvoyed along the American east coast. In the first six months of 1942 504 unconvoyed ships were lost to the U-boats.[38]

The scene was set for a maximum effort on the part of the German U-boat fleet when in January 1943 Admiral Dönitz was appointed Commander-in-Chief of the German navy. Re-establishment in December 1942 of Bletchley Park's ability to read the *Enigma* code enabled the British to avoid the first onslaught of the new U-boat attack, but the growing numbers of U-boats, increasing German cryptographic prowess which provided operationally valuable intelligence of convoy operations, and a short-term failure of British cryptography in March, dramatically increased sinkings in the North Atlantic at the end of the winter.[39] In January only 15 ships were sunk in convoy, but in March the number rose to 72, totalling 477 000 tons. By February 1943 British food stocks, which had risen slowly from 4.3 million tons in March and April 1941 to 6.3 million tons in May and June 1942, were down again to 5.4 million tons. Commercial bunker fuel was down to a critical level, and on 1 March Lord Leathers, the Minister of War Transport, wrote to the Chiefs of Staff that

> The shipping shortage is not only inhibiting the deployment of our forces, but if we cannot very substantially increase our imports above the level achieved in the last three months, we shall be unable to maintain our war production on anything like the present scale . . . The situation which now faces us is entirely different; the volume of shipping engaged on military operations has increased and is increasing, and we are now more seriously short of shipping than at any previous stage of the war.[40]

On 10 March the Lord President of the Council, Sir John Anderson, warned the War Cabinet that:

> in order to achieve the target set by the Shipping Committee it would be necessary during May and June for our food imports to be at a monthly rate nearly twice as great as, and for our material imports to be at monthly rate more than twice as great as, the average monthly rate likely to be achieved for the first four months. It is improbable that so great an improvement will occur.[41]

Alarming as it was at the time, however, the U-boat campaign did not in fact come within reach of destroying Britain's defensive capacity. Assessment of the impact of the tonnage war upon British food supplies and industrial raw materials can only be done intelligently if the deliberate sacrifices made by the British government in order to make a military offensive possible are taken into account.

Ministry of Food imports dropped from 20 689 000 tons in 1939–40 to less than half that figure in 1942–43. To a very considerable extent that must be viewed as a measure of the successful domestic agricultural production policy.

In February 1940 the Lord Privy Seal, Sir Kingsley Wood, had reported to the War Cabinet that the expected deficit in imports should be met by immediate economies.

> Any attempt to deal with this problem in a piecemeal fashion would not only be foredoomed to failure but would also aggravate the difficulties in which we find ourselves. . . . with the passage of every week the likelihood grows that some of the imports which are arriving are imports which in the last resort we could do without, with the result that at the end of the first year of the war we may find that we have failed to obtain imports which are absolutely vital to our war effort. . . .[42]

In June the Ministry of Shipping was optimistic that they were in a position to employ shipping control as a means of economic warfare, but that optimism did not long survive the fall of France.[43] The First Report of the Shipping Committee on 22 June 1942 estimated that non-tanker imports for the year would be 25½ million tons, 35 million until mid-1943. This was 8.4 million tons less than planned consumption for the period. Again a 'very early decision to enforce economies' was required.[44] Churchill was not prepared to take the gamble of running down stocks. He set out to persuade the Americans that United Kingdom imports were a first charge on allied shipping, but at the same time rigorous economies were put into effect.[45]

Ultimately, the tonnage saved on food imports reduced the total tonnage requirement for British imports by 32 per cent.[46] At the worst, during the January to March 1943 period, only 9.1 per cent of this can be accounted as the result of loss at sea. There was indeed a restriction on comforts in Britain, but wartime food control actually increased the nutritional quality of food available to the average family. Tactical success in the U-boat operations, economies in military use of shipping, and greater allied co-operation, eventually eased the shipping situation. In the second quarter of 1943 loss of food at sea was reduced to 3.4 per cent of imports, and to 0.8 per cent in the third quarter.[47]

The convoy battles of April and May 1943 decisively improved the allied position. Losses were reduced to 245 000 and 165 000 tons respectively. The defeat of the U-boats was the outcome of tactical and technical developments which began effectively to exploit the weaknesses of the U-boats – their slow speed and limited ability to acquire tactical information when submerged. Cryptoanalysis contributed ever more effectively to the capacity of Western Approaches command to evade U-boat attack. The belated redeployment of aircraft from 'offensive' patrols to the direct defence of convoys had an even more dramatic effect than had the introduction of convoy in 1917.[48] The futile use of escort vessels in 'offensive' sweeps was also reduced so that support groups could be formed to reinforce the close escort of convoys under attack. Improvements in radar contributed to the triumph of the escorts. In March only 15 U-boats had been sunk, and an equal number in April. In May, however, 41 U-boats were sunk, a number which amounted to about 30 per cent of all U-boats at sea. Dönitz withdrew the survivors to the area west of the Azores where they could avoid air reconnaissance, but also where they could have little effect. In June new additions to the British merchant fleet exceeded losses to all causes, including the U-boats. New construction in American yards was already outpacing total allied losses by more than 4 to 1.[49] In July the Admiralty introduced a new code for operational control which remained secure for the rest of the war. Although there were later times of anxiety caused by new U-boat technologies and tactics, by the summer of 1943 it was clear that the U-boat *guerre de course* had been contained.[50]

Unfortunately, improvement in the shipping situation came too late to avert tragedy in Bengal. During the winter months of 1942–43 there were repeated alarms that there might be famine in the Indian Ocean area. It turned out that there really was little or no shortfall of agricultural production throughout the wider area, but there was crop failure in Bengal. The lack of shipping in the cross-trades, the inefficiency of the British civil government of India, and panic-induced hoarding, made this local problem a disaster; 1.5 million people in Bengal died from starvation and related diseases. The U-boats, however, were at most but a contributing factor in this tragedy. In any case, the brutal truth is that the localised famine did not delay the allied victory.[51]

Only overwhelming losses at sea could have denied Britain the shipping tonnage needed to supply the food, fuel and munitions needed for home defence. Given the determination of the British Empire to defend itself against attack on its sea routes, and the support provided by the United States, the Germans never had much chance of destroying Britain's defence by that means.[52] The outcome of the U-boat campaign discredits the *Jeune Ecole*, and supports the Mahanian conviction that a minor naval power can never defeat a greater by sporadic raids on shipping.

Inadequate as it proved to be to defeat the British Commonwealth by siege, the U-boat war was a powerful instrument as an auxiliary to the direct military defence of the Reich. The wastage of merchant ship assets exacerbated the strategic problems of an alliance which had to conduct its campaigns on the far side of oceans. In World War I only the Eastern Mediterranean theatres had had to be sustained entirely by sea. In World War II, after the fall of France in June 1940, any offensive conducted by British forces, and later by American forces, had to be delivered and sustained that way. The most easily attained strategic objective which the German government could pursue by means of naval attack on merchant shipping was the reduction of the allies' capacity to deploy forces to distant theatres, and to sustain them there. In this they had some considerable measure of success. The Joint Planning staff had to advise in 1941 that 'no new large-scale military commitments involving an ocean passage can be justified'.[53]

At the beginning of 1942 it appeared that the greatest problem for the Allies was shortage of troop transports. It was decided in London that Churchill should make an appeal to President Roosevelt.

> You know we are moving very large numbers, including an Australian corps of three Divisions and the 70th British Division, from the Middle East across the Indian Ocean. To make good the depletion of the Middle East and to send large reinforcements both land and air to India and Ceylon, we would like to ship from the United Kingdom 295,000 men in the months February, March, April and May. A convoy of 45,000 men sailed in February. Another convoy of 50,000, including the 5th division and seven squadrons of aircraft, will sail in March. Two further convoys totaling 85,000 men will sail in April and May. To achieve this we are scraping together every ton of personnel shipping we can lay our hands on and adopting every expedient to hasten the turn-round and increase the carrying capacity of the shipping. Even so, we shall fall short of our aim by 115,000 men.
>
> This is the situation in which I turn to you for help.[54]

However, with some diversion of American transport capacity from the Pacific, the 'W.S.' troop convoys supplying British theatres in the Middle East and Far East transported in 1942 half a million men, and at the same time a quarter of a million US troops were brought over to Britain to prepare for the invasion of France.[55] More than half of the American troops were then re-embarked to participate in the Allied invasion of North Africa. Improvements in management of resources ensured that there were adequate troopships for the purpose, and relatively few were lost to enemy action because of the very strong escorts provided and because of their higher speeds.

In 1942–43 it became evident that the weak link in strategic mobility was the requirement for dry cargo ships to carry the supplies needed by the troops. In the winter of 1942–43 the Germans came close to achieving the limited objective of preventing Allied use of the sea for offensive purposes. A War Cabinet Paper concluded in March 1942 that

> Geography, the enemy submarines and, to some extent, enemy air power have created a naval and mercantile tonnage shortage which, for the whole of 1942 as a minimum, must severely condition allied strategy and limit to a grave degree the deployment overseas of our war strength. . . . Geography (11,000 miles) has beaten us and will continue to beat us in 1942. The dangers of a German success in the next six months in Russia means that time is not with us but with the enemy.[56]

Enough tonnage was assembled to enable the Allies to land forces in Morocco and Algeria in November 1942, but the operation proved to be even more expensive in terms of shipping than had been expected. Churchill was obliged, as a result, to order the cancellation of all sailings on the long ocean run to India around the Cape of Good Hope so that the tonnage could be used to sustain imports to Britain. That meant that the 8th Army in Egypt had to live on its reserves, which it proved to be more than able to do. The civil authorities in India proved to be less capable of handling the shortage. At the Casablanca conference in January 1943 plans were made for the invasion of Italy and the reconquest of Burma, as well as the continued build-up of American troops in Britain. It was soon found, however, that there was inadequate dry-cargo tonnage for the Burma campaign, and the flow of US troops to Britain had to be reduced to a trickle because there was no point in transporting troops if it were impossible to bring in supplies for them. By the end of 1942 there were only 96 537 American troops in the UK instead of the 539 000 which were to have been deployed the previous July.[57]

Churchill tried to explain to Stalin that the Western allies were doing all they could. On 26 June 1943 he wrote

> although all shipping has been fully occupied it has not been possible to transport the American Army to Britain according to the programme proposed in June 1941. Whereas it was then hoped that 27 American Divisions would be in Great Britain by April 1943, in fact there is now, in June 1943, only one, and there will be by August only five. This is owing to the decision to go to North Africa and other causes. Moreover, the landing craft which in January of this year we proposed to make available for a cross Channel enterprise have either not materialised up to date or have all been drawn into the great operation now impending in the Mediterranean.[58]

On 20 November 1943 he confessed to the Foreign Secretary, Anthony Eden, who was in Moscow, that

> The disposition of our forces between the Italian and the Channel theatre has not been settled by strategic needs but by the march of events, by shipping possibilities, and by arbitrary compromises between the British and Americans. Neither the forces built up in Italy nor that which will be ready in May to cross the Channel is adequate for what is required, and only transferences of the order of 7 or 8 divisions can physically be made between them.[59]

A contributing factor to the supply management problems experienced by the Anglo–American allies was the inadequacy of British and inter-Allied machinery for the distribution of shipping between British and American, and between civilian and military uses. The armed forces of Britain and the United States were nowhere near as efficient in their employment of shipping as the British civilian services had become. The 8th Army, for instance, was found to have a four-year reserve of ground transport, and a 14-year reserve of rifles. In March 1943 Churchill tartly advised the Chiefs of Staff:

> Everywhere the British and Americans are overloading their operational plans with so many factors of safety that they are ceasing to be capable of making any form of aggressive war. For six or eight months to come Great Britain and the United States will be playing about with half a dozen German divisions. That is the position to which we are reduced, and which you should labour sedulously to correct.[60]

American military hoarding of shipping for the Pacific theatre increased British difficulties.[61] Field Marshall Dill wrote from Washington to the Chiefs of Staff on 18 March 1943,

> We *think* that the Americans mis-use ships in the Pacific, but we do not *know*. They *think* that we may be using too many ships for British imports, but they do not *know*. In fact neither side feels that the other is being quite open, and there is distrust. I feel sure that we shall both have to put *all* our shipping cards on the table very soon.[62]

Eventually all British-controlled shipping was placed in a common pool, but American ship management continued to frustrate London. American theatre commanders had independent control of 'their' shipping, which was wastefully used as floating warehouses, and left in long queues awaiting loading. C. B. Behrens, the British official historian of merchant shipping in the war, estimates that American mismanagement of shipping cost the Allies about 9 million tons annually, about three times the total American tonnage lost during the entire war.[63]

> The Americans could have saved far more by good management than ever they lost from enemy action. . . . If at the end of 1944 the kinds of waste described . . . had been put a stop to, enough American ships must have been released to make good a very large part and quite possibly the whole of the *net* losses sustained up to date by the fleets of Great Britain and of the European nations who put their ships at her disposal.

At the Argonaut conference in January 1945, the American Chiefs of Staff successfully retained independent control of shipping despite a concerted British effort. The impending crisis failed to materialise, however, because US commanders responded to an appeal from Roosevelt that shipping economies be effected. These rather typical frictions of war were made highly significant by the pressure of U-boat operations.

Careful management of resources on the part of the British ensured that shipping shortages served more to determine the theatre of operations chosen for the Allied offensive, than to delay victory. The invasion of northwest Europe was delayed for a year, although the U-boat attacks were only a contributory reason for the decision to do so, but during that year the war was carried to the enemy in the Mediterranean. The number of German divisions which could be engaged in the Mediterranean theatre was limited, and that could have been disastrous if the German army had been able to defeat the Soviet Union in 1943. It was not, however, and the British and American armies learnt much in that year which was to serve them well in 1944. Constraints imposed by shipping limitations also contributed to the decision that the British counterattack against Japan should be predominantly a land operation in Burma.[64] In the light of the shipping resources unnecessarily held by American commanders for their use in the Pacific, however, there is a suspicion that lack of sympathy for British hopes to reconstruct the empire in South East Asia may have been a factor in preventing the release of the necessary tonnage. The success of the Mediterranean operations in 1943 permitted the use of shorter routes to the Middle and Far East, and greatly eased the shipping crisis.[65]

The U-boat operations against merchant shipping did not have a more decisive effect on military strategic movement because the concept of the 'tonnage war' was too ambitious. With the benefit of hindsight it can be seen that the German U-boat campaign was too widely focussed. In effect, general cargo was permitted to provide cover for military logistics, and British planners were given the option of sacrificing the needs of the general public to those of the military. In the course of World War I the distinction between contraband and general economic activity had been obscured. Industrialisation, and modern chemistry which allowed for the substitution of raw materials in manufacturing, meant there could be no logical distinction. Functionally, however, it is evident that the inability to observe a distinction reduced the utility of action against logistics. As early as September 1942 Dönitz's Naval Staff had suggested that it might be impossible to sink the entire output of Allied ship-building yards, and that the U-boats should change their strategy to a 'supply war' against particular high-value cargoes. Probably the most valuable strategy would have been the classic one of attack on troop convoys. The German navy, however, was ill-equipped for that purpose and Dönitz never abandoned his faith in the 'tonnage war'.[66]

The conduct of Britain's strategic bombing campaign against Germany produced a similar lesson. The arguments of the pre-war advocates of air power, Guilio Douhet and his followers, that general economic dislocation of the enemy through air attack could disable his war machine, only became an operational reality with the invention of the thermonuclear bomb. During the war it was belatedly discovered that bombing was more effective when it was directed specifically at the logistic needs of the enemy armed forces.

Besides the important, but limited, value to Germany of the U-boat campaign in constraining Allied strategic mobility, the war in the trade routes was also seen as a means of containing Allied resources which might otherwise have been employed for offensive purposes. The strategic idea of the post-Crimean War Imperial Russian Navy, that trade warfare could contain enemy resources, was demonstrated by the U-boat war. An impression can be gained of the strategic value to Germany of the war at sea by looking at the statistics of British warship construction. In 1940 Britain completed construction of 75 889 tons of escort ships and only 9929 tons of landing craft, shortage of which was to have a profound effect on strategy in 1943 and 1944.[67] In 1941 were built 158 150 tons of escorts and 34 899 tons of landing craft. In 1942 the balance began to change. Only 93 887 tons of escorts were built compared to 108 279 tons of landing craft, although late in 1942 the Admiralty recognised an urgent need for an ocean escort force of 1050 vessels, of which they already had only 445. The War Cabinet agreed to divert labour into ship-building to the maximum which the shipyards could effectively employ.[68] In 1943 the tide of war turned strongly; 134 275 tons of escorts were completed, but so were 250 771 tons of landing craft. In the first six months of 1944 the discrepancy became even greater, with 76 108 tons of escorts and 168 216 tons of landing craft.[69]

The material and man-hours expended on construction of mercantile hulls to replace those sunk also reduced the resources available for offensive purposes. One of the major contributions made by the United States to the Allied war effort was the construction of merchant tonnage, of which 22 218 000 displacement tons were built between 1939 and 1945; 9 412 000 tons of this were series-built Liberty ships, designed for inexpensive construction, and for service on the North Atlantic. Twenty per cent of all the steel produced in the United States was employed in ship-building, of which 70 per cent was used by the Maritime Commission for construction of merchant tonnage. The needs of the US Navy and Army were in direct competition, and in 1942 Admiral Land, Chairman of the Maritime Commission, had to appeal to President Roosevelt. Early in 1943 the US Joint Chiefs of Staff were able to reconcile the needs of the civilian and service establishments, but only the immense capacity of American steel production ensured that the American war effort was not more significantly affected by the containment of resources occasioned by the U-boat tonnage war.[70]

In 1942 1 302 000 gross tons of merchant shipping were constructed in Britain. Repair of damaged ships took half the total dockyard energies. Ship-building is an assembly industry. Much of the materials and labour put into outfitting the ships with weapons and sensors could have been used for other purposes. Containment of Allied human resources was no less significant.[71] When the investment which Britain had to make in capital ships to guard against German surface raiders is taken into account, it can be seen that a very high proportion of British and allied naval effort served defensive functions.

Pursuit of more precise statistics might not contribute much to wisdom because of other less quantifiable considerations which might be obscured. The naval defensive effort was entirely necessary and useful. It was the *sine qua non* of offensive action. In contrast, the offensive effort of bomber forces operating against Germany was dreadfully wasteful, and in several important respects counterproductive.

In the last two years of the war, the Germans continued the U-boat campaign at a reduced level. Although it could no longer be thought of as decisive to the outcome of the war, it was still thought to have significant effects on the economics of war, and it could continue to reduce Allied strategic mobility. It could still reduce the rate of tonnage growth, and hence effected tonnage limitations upon Anglo–American operations. The threat of attack required the Allies to continue to use convoy which, in all respects except those of defence, is inefficient of tonnage. Defence of convoy continued to tie up Allied warships and aircraft which might otherwise have been a greater threat to German interests, and required the continued construction of defensive types of warships using materials which might otherwise have been available for offensive purposes. Hitler made clear his policy of containment when he said to Dönitz on 31 May 1943

> There can be no talk of a let-up in submarine warfare. The Atlantic is my first line of defence in the West, and even if I have to fight a defensive battle, that is preferable to waiting to defend myself on the coasts of Europe. The enemy forces tied up by our submarine warfare are tremendous, even though the actual losses inflicted by us are no longer great. I cannot afford to release these forces by discontinuing submarine warfare.[72]

The containment of Allied resources by the U-boat war was real enough, but Philip Pugh suggests that it might be mistaken to believe that German investment in naval attack on trade was a cost-effective strategy. It cost Germany a very great deal to mount the U-boat operations. An exhaustive measurement of the total consumption of resources on defence of trade, and that consumed in attacking it, poses insuperable problems. It would also fail as a test of the relative efficiency of attack and defence because there is no way of determining whether the effort devoted to the defence was in excess of the minimum needed to defeat the attack. Instead, Pugh has preferred to account the monetary cost of ships and aircraft employed by attack and defence during a period of apparent equilibrium, October 1942 to June 1943.[73] Pugh concludes that the total German monthly expenditure on the U-boat war was in the order of 10.72 million pounds, against 9.99 million for the total monthly cost of Allied surface and air action against them, and the cost of the merchant ships. Although the nature of the statistical evidence makes it necessary to allow a margin of error in the area of 20 to 30 per cent it is apparent that these figures

> show that nowhere were the Allies suffering economic defeat in the sense of putting forth substantially greater efforts than Germany. In interdiction efforts they were winning a battle of attrition while elsewhere the economic efforts of enemies were in rough balance. Even RAF Bomber Command's attacks on naval targets were causing economic loss to Germany commensurate with their cost to Britain – which cannot be said of its much larger effort in area bombing of cities.

It must be remembered that the scale of German investment was based on the false expectation of ultimately destroying Britain's war economy and defensive capacity. Had the limited strategy of containment been adopted at the outset, and adhered to, the balance of expenditure might have been more evidently in Germany's favour. Pugh calculates that the point at which the overhead costs of running convoys would come to exceed the cost of attack would have been at a level of effort 1/12th of that actually expended by Germany. At that point the German attack would have been a cost-effective use of resources, measured in monetary terms.

Against these figures must be set the consideration that strategy, as an art of the possible, must be as concerned with opportunity costs as with monetary costs. To what extent could the Germans in fact have diverted resources from the U-boat war to other aspects of defence? At what percentage should be accounted the loss of efficiency consequential upon diverting the resources of the U-boat war to other purposes? Skilled shipwrights might be more productive working on U-boat hulls than if given the job of building tanks, and certainly would be wasted as cannon fodder in Russia. If the shipyard itself was not constructing U-boats, what other tasks could it carry out? Another aspect of opportunity costs lies in the more strictly military field. The brake the U-boat war put on Allied strategic mobility may well have been worth the cost. It almost certainly would have been had Germany been able to defeat the Soviet Union in 1943. Pugh's figures are sufficient, however, to suggest that Clausewitz's observation, that the defensive is the stronger form of warfare, is supported by the economics of, as well as by the outcome of, the German war against British trade.

The cost in diplomatic terms to Germany of conducting an unrestricted war on shipping is less easily perceived than it was in World War I. American neutrality laws were in part conceived with the specific objective of ensuring that the United States would not be dragged into war by attacks on American ships. The brutality of the *blitzkrieg* and the bombing raids on cities, and the horrors of the Nazi regime, set the sufferings of seamen in perspective. When eventually the United States did intervene in the war, it was as a result of the general consideration that American security depended upon the survival of Britain. It is significant, however, that American forces first became directly, if unofficially, engaged in the war in 1941 when the 'Neutrality' patrols began to be employed to support the Anglo–Canadian defence of merchant shipping.[74]

The conduct of trade warfare in World War II profoundly affected conceptions of acceptable naval practice. The violence perpetrated by British military action in World War II against merchant shipping had been justified by the right of making reprisals for German violation of the 1936 London Protocol. The German unrestricted U-boat warfare against maritime trade, however, was itself justified by the claim that the British convoy system virtually converted all merchantmen into auxiliary warships. The order was not given to sink shipping without warning until 17 October 1939, after the German U-boats had experienced the defensive measures used by the British, although it appears that from the beginning of the war the Germans intended to abandon the Hague Convention as soon as an excuse could be found.[75] Admiral Dönitz was able to defend himself at the Nuremberg War Crimes trial with the argument that merchant shipping had abandoned its non-belligerent status. The Tribunal ruled that merchant ships did not lose their mercantile status by carrying defensive arms, but if they act like warships by manoeuvring in company, and by sending sighting and radio intercept reports, then they might be attacked as though they were warships. Dönitz's more important defence, however, was the fact that the United States ordered unrestricted submarine operations against Japan on the first day of the war. Submarines and aircraft are still not legally exempt from the general requirement to place the crews of merchant ships in a position of safety, but, in practice, attack on merchant ships without warning is accepted in the late twentieth century as a fact of war. More attention is now given in 'just war' analysis to defining the right to employ force, *jus ad bello*, than to restraining the conduct of states once at war, *jus in bello*.

NOTES

1. Minister of Economic Warfare Order, 1939 (SR & O 1939 no. 1188) under the Ministers of the Crown (Emergency Appointments) Act 1939 (2 & 3 George VI Chap. 77). The Ministry was dissolved 28 May 1945. See Martin Doughty, *Merchant Shipping and War*, p. 82, and Barry D. Hunt, 'British Policy on the Issue of Belligerent and Neutral Rights, 1919–1939', in *New Aspects of Naval History*, Craig L. Symonds (ed.), pp. 279–90.
2. F.O. 837/3 and 4.
3. F. T. Hinsley, *British Intelligence in the Second World War*, vol. 1, pp. 223–48.
4. Uncited official contemporary paper quoted in J. M. Gwyer, *Grand Strategy*, vol. iii, pt. 1, p. 23.
5. G. G. Fitzmaurice, 'Some Aspects of Modern Contraband Control and the Law of Prize', *British Yearbook of International Law*, 1945, p. 75; S. W. D. Rowson, 'Italian Prize Law, 1940–1943', and 'Prize Law During the Second World War', *British Yearbook of International Law*, 1946, p. 282 and 1947, p. 160.
6. Joseph L. Kunz, 'British Prize Cases, 1939–41', *The American Journal of International Law*, 36 (1942), pp. 204–28. Judge Admiral Dr. Curt Eckhardt asserts that Britain did not recognise the protection extended by the Declaration of Paris to German exports; see 'International Law and Germany's Economic Warfare at Sea' by Judge Admiral Dr. Curt Eckhardt, in *World War II German Military Studies*, Donald S. Detwiler (ed.), vol. 20, part 4, 'MS D–177'.
7. MT 59/285, 'Memorandum on Economic Pressure Through Control of Shipping', 11 July 1940; and War Cabinet, 'Economic Warfare', First Monthly Report.
8. Alan S. Milward, *War, Economy and Society*, s.v., 'Economic Warfare', pp. 305–8.
9. See CAB 66/17 ff 233, 235, /20 f. 191, and /22 f. 45.

10. F. H. Hinsley, op. cit., p. 235.
11. See Patrick Salmon, 'Churchill, the Admiralty and the Narvik Traffic, September–November 1939', *Scandinavian Journal of History*, vol. 4, pp. 305–26 (1979).
12. Alan S. Milward, op. cit., p. 299. See also Patrick Salmon, 'British Plans for Economic Warfare against Germany 1937–1939: The Problem of Swedish Iron Ore', *Journal of Contemporary History*, vol. 16, pp. 53–71, 1981.
13. Mancur Olson, op. cit., pp. 144–5.
14. W. N. Medlicott, *The Economic Blockade*, ii, p. 641.
15. J. M. A. Gwyer, op. cit., vol. III, p. 330.
16. W. T. Mallison, op. cit., pp. 87–91.
17. See William O. Miller, 'Belligerency and Limited War', United States Naval War College International Law Studies, Vol. 62, *The Use of Force, Human Rights and General International Legal Issues*, p. 164.
18. See Clay Blair, *Silent Victory*, pp. 359–64, 551–6, and *passim*.
19. John Toland, op. cit., p. 475.
20. Table II, The Joint Army–Navy Assessment Committee, *Japanese Naval and Merchant Shipping Losses During World War II by all Causes*, p. vii.
21. United States, *Strategic Bombing Survey*, vol. IX, 'The War Against Japanese Transportation, 1941–1945 (Pacific Report 55)'.
22. Alan S. Milward, op. cit., pp. 317–21; S. Woodburn Kirby, *The War Against Japan*, vol. v, pp. 161–9, s.v., 'The Bombing and Blockade of Japan', pp. 465–81, s.v., 'The Japanese Economy 1937–1945'; and Ellis A. Johnson and David A. Katcher, *Mines against Japan*, *passim*.
23. Winston S. Churchill, *The World Crisis*, vol. iv, pp. 63–4.
24. Winston S. Churchill, *Their Finest Hour* (*The Second World War*, vol. II), p. 598.
25. See Peter Padfield, *Dönitz, The Last Fuhrer*, p. 266.
26. Holger H. Herwig, 'The Failure of German Sea Power, 1914–1945: Mahan, Tirpitz, and Raeder Reconsidered', *The International History Review*, Vol. 10 (February 1988), No. 1, p. 95.
27. Carl Dönitz [R. H. Stevens, translator], *Memoirs, Ten Years and Twenty Days*, pp. 18–24.
28. Martin Doughty, op. cit., pp. 115–31.
29. Carl Dönitz, op. cit., p. 264.
30. C. B. A. Behrens, *Merchant Shipping and the Demands of War*, pp. 146–7.
31. Martin Doughty, op. cit., pp. 177–97 *et passim*.
32. See CAB 21/1237, Report by the Lord Privy Seal, *Loss of Importing Capacity Inseparable from the Convoy System*, 23 Feb. 1940; and CAB 66/5 f. 231, 'The Extent to Which Shipping Considerations Call for a Review of Our Import Programme'.
33. See CAB 66/11 f. 219, 'Merchant Shipbuilding', 9 September 1940.
34. See CAB 66/25 f. 198, 'The Shipping Situation', Joint Memorandum by the First Lord of the Admiralty and the Minister of War Transport, 22 June 1942.
35. C. B. A. Behrens, op. cit., pp. 245–6, 265 and 275; T. H. Vail Motter, *The Persian Corridor and Aid to Russia*, Appendix A, pp. 481–5; and

Richard M. Leighton and Robert W. Coakley, *Global Logistics and Strategy 1940–1943*, pp. 58–9 and Appendix D, p. 731.
36. CAB 120/398, *Relation of Merchant Shipping Losses to the Prosecution of the War*, Memorandum by Sir Arthur Salter forwarded by the British Chiefs of Staff to the Combined Chiefs of Staff, 14 February 1942.
37. Ibid., p. 178.
38. S. W. Roskill, *The War at Sea*, vol. 2, p. 378.
39. F. H. Hinsley, op. cit., vol. 2, pp. 547–72.
40. C. B. A. Behrens, op. cit., pp. 336–8, and see pp. 312–56.
41. CAB 66/35 f. 24, 'The United Kingdom Import Programme, Memorandum by the Lord President of the Council', 10 March 1943.
42. CAB 66/5 f. 231 – 'Report by Lord Privy Seal on the extent to which shipping restriction calls for a review of import programmes', signed S.H., 23 February 1940. See MT 59/285, 'Draft Statement for the Advisory Council', 4 July 1940.
43. MT 59/285, 'Control of World Shipping', 27 June 1940.
44. CAB 66/26 f. 117, 'Shipping Committee, First Report', 22 June 1943.
45. CAB 66/26 f. 194, 'A Review of the War Position, Memorandum by the Prime Minister', 21 July 1942; CAB 66/33 f. 193, 'Memorandum by the Lord President of the Council', 29 January 1943; CAB 66/35 f. 24, 'The United Kingdom Import Programme, Memorandum by the Lord President of the Council', 10 March 1943; CAB 66/36 f. 10, 'Fifth Report by the Shipping Committee', 14 April 1943.
46. Mancur Olson, op. cit., p. 129. See CAB 66/26 f. 124, 'The Shipping Situation, Memorandum by the Lord President of the Council', 14 July 1942.
47. R. J. Hammond, *Food*, vol. 1, table 8, p. 396. See also CAB 66/49 and /51, 8th, 9th and 10th Reports of the Shipping Committee, 25 April, 23 June and 7 November 1944.
48. Peter Gretton, 'The U-boat Campaign in Two World Wars', in *Naval Warfare in the Twentieth Century 1900–1945*.
49. See Richard M. Leighton and Robert W. Coakley, op. cit., Appendix H, p. 741.
50. S. W. Roskill, op. cit., vol. 2, pp. 351–82 and Appendix J, pp. 469–71; and C B. A. Behrens, op. cit., p. 293.
51. Ibid., pp. 345–53; and see CAB 21/1240, Shipping Committee, General Correspondence (Amery, Anderson, Woolton correspondence 15–17 December 1943); CAB 66/39 f. 191, /43 f. 17, /49 f. 65 War Cabinet papers on India's need for imported grain; and CAB 120/398, Prime Minister to Ismay and to Minister of War Transport, 16 February 1943.
52. This assessment is supported by the recent analytic work of Peter Padfield, op. cit., pp. 250, 264, 278, 306, 484.
53. F. H. Hinsley, op. cit., vol. 2, p. 168.
54. CAB 120/398, Draft Telegram from Prime Minister to President, n.d., forwarded by Keenlyside to G. N. Flemming, Offices of the War Cabinet, 2 March 1942 – the draft had been seen by Harriman, and amended. See also CAB 120/400, 'Estimates of Practicable Personnel Movement Overseas During 1942', 3 February 1942; and CAB 120/398, 'The Shipping Situation', Memorandum by the Chiefs of Staff,

Dudley Pound, C. Portal, and A. F. Brooke, 13 February 1942, and 'Draft Telegram to President Roosevelt', 26 February 1942.

55. See CAB 120/398, President to Prime Minister, 8 March 1942; CAB 120/405, Foreign Office to Washington, 23 March 1943; CAB 120/410, Most Secret and Personal From Prime Minister to Generals Wavell and Auchinlech, 22 March 1942.
56. CAB 120/410, 'An Outlook Justifying a New Short Term War Policy', 14 March 1942.
57. See Michael Howard, *Grand Strategy, August 1942–September 1943*, pp. 271–2, 291–7, 397–8, and 632–6, s.v., Appendix IV, 'The Shipping Position [COS(W)511 of 7th March 1943] Note by Prime Minister and Lord Cherwell'.
58. CAB 120/412, Churchill to Stalin, 26 June 1943. See also CAB 120/411, Prime Minister's Personal Telegram to Premier Stalin, February 1943; 'Memorandum by the Foreign Secretary', 17 February; Prime Minister's Personal Telegram to Stalin, 11 March 1943; CAB 120/412, Prime Minister to Field Marshal Dill, 25 April 1943; and Stalin to Churchill, 24 June 1943.
59. CAB 120/412, Prime Minister to Mr Eden, 20 November 1943.
60. CAB 120/398, Prime Minister to General Ismay for COS Committee, 3 March 1943; and see CAB 66/26 f. 190, 'Shipping Committee, Second Report', 21 July 1942.
61. See CAB 66/30 f. 234, 'Shipping Assistance from USA, Present Position in Washington', Note by Minister of War Transport, 7 November 1942.
62. CAB 120/398, Field Marshal Dill to Chiefs of Staff, 18 March 1943.
63. C. B. A. Behrens, op. cit., pp. 415–18, 424–6. See CAB 120/398, Prime Minister's Personal Minute to Minister of Production, 'Military Overseas Supply Requirements', 21 November 1944; and S. W. Roskill, *The Strategy of Seapower*, p. 150.
64. See CAB 120/398, Prime Minister to General Ismay for COS Committee, 3 March 1943; 'Shipping', Draft Telegram to Joint Staff Mission, 7 March 1943; Ismay to Prime Minister, 9 March and 1 April 1943; Draft, Former Naval Person to President, 12 March 1943; Churchill to Ismay, 18 March; Lord Leathers, Minister of War Transport, to Ismay, 19 March; President Roosevelt to Prime Minister, 30 March and 2 April; Secretary of State to Prime Minister, 29 and 30 March 1943; CAB 120/410, Personal from Prime Minister to Field Marshal Dill, 14 March 1942.
65. CAB 120/398, 'Opening of the Mediterranean', Minister of War Transport, 7 April 1943.
66. Peter Padfield, op. cit., p. 250. See also Keith W. Bird, *German Naval History, A Guide to the Literature*, pp. 678–80.
67. See CAB 120/398, Ismay to Prime Minister, 3 April and 8 September 1943.
68. CAB 66/30 f. 69, 'Increase in Corvette Construction, Memorandum by the First Lord of the Admiralty', 26 October 1942; CAB 66/31 ff 200 and 259, 'Man-Power, Note by Prime Minister and Minister of Defence', 28 November 1942, and 'Man-Power, Memorandum by First Lord of the Admiralty', 9 December 1942.

69. CAB 66/56 f. 109, *Statistics Relating to the War Effort of the United Kingdom*, HMSO 1944, *DRAFT*.
70. Frederic C. Lane, *Ships for Victory*, pp. 5, 311–12, 335, 347–8 and 352.
71. See Great Britain, House of Commons, Nov. 1944 CMD 6564, *Statistics Relating to the War Effort of the United Kingdom*.
72. *Fuehrer Conferences on Naval Affairs*, Vol. 2, p. 46. See Carl Dönitz, op. cit., pp. 406–8.
73. Philip Pugh, 'The Battle of the Atlantic: an analysis of its economics', August 1988 [read in ms]:

Monthly costs in £M at 1938 price levels

Activity	Strategic warfare	Inter-diction	Direct defence	Total cost
Allied Air forces				
RAF Coastal Command				
: A/S Aircraft		1.43	1.21	2.64
: A/A patrol		0.05		0.05
RAF Bomber Command	0.82			0.82
Other A/S aircraft			0.19	0.19
Total	0.82	1.48	1.40	3.70
Allied Navies				
Escort vessels			0.73	0.73
Allied Merchantmen				
All merchantmen			5.56	5.56
Allied Total	0.82	1.48	7.69	9.99
German Air force				
A/ship strike & U-boat co-op.			0.48	0.48
A/A patrol		0.07		0.07
vs. RAF Bomber Co	0.21			0.21
Total	0.21	0.07	0.48	0.76
German Navy				
U-boats lost to RAF bombing	0.52			0.52
U-boats at sea		2.36	7.08	9.44
Total	0.52	2.36	7.08	9.96
German Total	0.73	2.43	7.56	10.72
German/Allied				
: all costs	0.89	1.64	0.98	1.07
: excluding merchantmen	0.89	1.64	3.55	2.42

See Pugh, *The Cost of Seapower*, p. 243, fig. 8/15.

74. See Patrick Abbazia, *Mr. Roosevelt's Navy*, *passim*; and Holger H. Herwig, 'Prelude to *Weltblitzkrieg*: Germany's Naval Policy Towards the United States of America, 1939–41', *The Journal of Modern History*, vol. 43, pp. 649–68 (1971).
75. See W. T. Mallison, op. cit., pp. 113–22; and Padfield, op. cit., pp. 190–206.

6 Naval Blockade and Trade War Since 1945

W. N. Medlicott concluded his official history of the economic war with the observation that

> the great interest in blockade during the last forty or more years has been due to the peculiar combination of opportunities and challenge [which] might never, perhaps, recur.[1]

The exaggerated expectations which had led the British in the years following World War I to prize blockade as their great instrument of policy, and had no less propelled the American determination to have a navy 'second to none', evaporated in the blazing heat of total war against fully mobilised war economies. Faith in the effectiveness of besieging enemy states to starve them into submission had been shaken. The Charter of the United Nations, Article 2(4), put an end to the right of states to carry out acts of reprisal. Pacific blockade remains a sanction available to the Security Council of the United Nations, but by 1945 experience of economic sanctions as an instrument of collective security had revealed how limited a one it could be.[2] As D. P. O'Connell might have said, however, attack on maritime trade has remained a phenomenon notwithstanding.

KOREA

In the Korean War, United Nations forces mounted a coastal blockade of both North Korean coasts, that on the east being the first blockade operation mounted under US Navy command since the Civil War. The focus of United Nations action was upon battlefield logistics, but the only limitations placed on the blockade were geographical. There was no general economic campaign mounted on the high seas. Because of North Korea's long border with China, and because of the economic support provided by the Soviet Union and China, the naval blockade could be of strategic value only to the extent it obliged the North Korean government to devote more inland transport to military and civilian food supplies. Its only utility was as a multiplier of the simultaneous efforts which were made with aircraft and gunfire to isolate the Korean battlefield.

As with the British blockade of Germany after the 1918 armistice, naval action was directed against fishing vessels. By the decision of the United States Supreme Court in 1898 based on the 'comity of nations', and by the provision of the 11th Hague convention of 1907, these should have been exempt from attack. In World War I, a British prize court had disallowed this protection for ocean-going trawlers, but it clearly applied to the small coastal craft of Korea.[3] Apparently the blockade brought extreme privation to the already hard lot of the coastal fishermen who made desperate attempts at escape. The line which can be drawn between economic warfare and military interdiction is never clear. In the Korean War, however, the latter was unquestionably the principal objective. When it was found that the North Korean capacity to repair transport systems surpassed that of the United Nations to put them out of action, by a margin which was adequate for the very limited supply needs of the Asian armies, the economic privation produced by the blockade became significant only as a barbarity of war. The fishermen could have been left at peace for all the good their sufferings did the United Nations.[4]

North Korea and its allies also gave geographic restrictions to their military operations. Evidently both sides recognised that military operations on the high seas against trade had too great a potential for escalation. In the context of the Korean War there were no great neutral states which might be transformed by attack on shipping into an enemy. A new factor was at work, however, to create a similar danger. The states of the United Nations did not attempt full mobilisation for war, in part because of public disinclination. Military action with a high public profile, such as attack on shipping, might be calculated to transform a hitherto 'neutral' public into a bellicose democracy demanding total war and total victory. As it was President Truman was vilified for his decision not to use the atomic bomb.

CUBA

On 22 October 1962 the United States ordered a formal naval blockade of Cuba. This was not an extension of the American attempt to coerce Fidel Castro through economic restraint. Euphemistically referred to as a 'quarantine', President Kennedy's blockade was intended as a minimum display of a resolve to see that the Soviet Union withdrew the strategic missiles for which emplacements were being built on Cuban soil.[5] The blockade was confined to 'offensive equipment under shipment in Cuba'. This is certainly the most dramatic occasion in recent history, at least until the 1990 Kuwait crisis, when blockade has been used as an instrument of international dispute, but in practice it may be a less instructive episode than is the earlier economic sanctions against Cuba which led to the initial transformation of Cuba into a Soviet base. Kennedy's 'quarantine' was primarily demonstrative, although the diversion of Soviet merchant ships *en route* to Cuba suggests that not all the equipment needed to complete the missile sites had been landed before the imposition of control. Cuban civilian imports were not blocked, but insurance for voyages to Cuba became hard to get. That the quarantine constituted a demonstration of resolve, whatever other direct purpose it may have served, is not open to question. The measure of its success was that the Soviets eventually agreed to withdraw the weapons.

One of the honorary editors of *The American Journal of International Law*, Quincy Wright, demolished the special pleading which was used in Washington to justify the quarantine. In particular, he dismissed the claim that it was an instance of Pacific Blockade. It was applied to the ships of all states and was employed before recourse had been made to all diplomatic means of resolving the conflict. 'The episode', he concluded, 'has not improved the reputation of the United States as a champion of international law'.[6] Neutrals were not inclined to support the legality of the quarantine. The Canadian government withheld assent to the blockade but saw that its objective was met by inspecting ships and aircraft in Canadian ports before granting clearances for Cuba. Sweden refused to acknowledge the justice or the fact of blockade, but Poland said it would comply although it could not agree to the quarantine's legality.

It would be a mistake to suggest that international protest was based on any principle of neutral rights. In the circumstances of the nearest approach to nuclear war to which the world has been brought attention was concentrated upon the simple fact that the United States was conducting an exercise of naked force. The British press was especially hostile to Kennedy's action, which stood in such stark contrast to American denunciation of the Anglo–French operation at Suez, and to Kennedy's denunciation of India's take-over of Portuguese Goa. The Canadian Prime Minister, John Diefenbaker, reacted to the American assumption of authority by ignoring it, leaving it to his Minister of National Defence to alert Canadian forces on his own responsibility. Most of the US Air Force requests for permission to overfly Canadian airspace were rejected. However, not all opinion was condemnatory. Mexico was exceptionally helpful to the United States. Even President de Gaulle, no great friend of the United States, pledged the 'understanding and support of the French Government'. Prime Minister Macmillan of Britain expressed the predominant view when he told the House of Commons that the American action was 'designed to meet a situation which is without precedent' by means which were 'studiously moderate'.[7] The quarantine was an illegal resort to force, but it was generally recognised to be a soft option compared to the alternatives available to President Kennedy. Because of the special circumstances, the Cuban quarantine contributes little to understanding of the value of blockade but it played a part in establishing it as acceptable behaviour.

VIETNAM

The American undeclared war against North Vietnam provides an important example in recent history of the employment of a sea denial strategy, and emphasises once again the problem of making such a strategy compatible with continued peaceful relations with neutrals. The problem was at least in theory vastly increased by the fact that the war had never been officially declared, which meant that the established legal right of a belligerent to blockade an enemy port could not be exploited.[8] Presumably that reason, and fear of hostile neutral reaction to interception of merchant shipping, compounded by the 200-year history of American protest at interference with maritime trade, contributed to the initial decision of the United States not to attempt naval control of the seaward approaches to the North Vietnamese port of Haiphong through which came the supplies of munitions from the Soviet Union and East Europe. Naval forces were used to enforce municipal law within territorial sea of South Vietnam in an attempt to control the import of contraband into enemy-controlled harbours, but in the north the United States attempted to realise the strategic objective by conducting air strikes against the roads from North Vietnam which supplied the communist armies in the south. The bombing raids were extended to the perimeter of the port of Haiphong.

The restraint on the use of naval means to arrest the flow of contraband continued until 8 May 1972, when President Nixon announced that the US Navy would close the entrances to Haiphong and other North Vietnam ports by laying mine fields. A renewed, and intensified, series of air operations against the landward communications of the North Vietnam ports was also ordered.[9] A secondary motive for the blockade was the hope that it would coerce the North Vietnamese government into making serious efforts at negotiating peace. As such it was a reaction to the failure of Dr Kissinger's talks on 2 May in Paris. Six months had been spent in preparatory work but Le Duc Tho nonetheless had confined himself to bombast. Talks in Moscow had been no more fruitful. This coercive purpose gives the episode a place in a study of economic warfare, but in any case the diplomatic history of the event is of considerable importance.

Nixon appealed to the Soviet Union to respect the American determination to protect their soldiers fighting in South Vietnam by arresting the flow of arms, but both Moscow and Peking criticised the 'blockade'. TASS, on 11 May, described the mining and bombing as 'fraught with serious consequences for international peace and security'. The Chinese Foreign Ministry declared that the mining 'grossly violates the freedom of international navigation and trade and wantonly tramples upon the charter of the United Nations and international public law'. The British supported the Americans, but the French were more critical. The French Foreign Minister, Maurice Schumann, warned of the 'risk of confrontation between the great powers'.[10]

The use of mines to effect the 'blockade' helped to ensure that there would be no confrontation with the great allies of North Vietnam. On 9 May Kissinger said that 'the instructions are to warn all foreign ships of the existence of these minefields, but not to interfere with them if they decide to proceed into the minefields at their own risk'. This tactic and technology virtually put it out of the power of a neutral to create a crisis by sending ships to challenge the blockade. Modern influence mines are so difficult to sweep that the possibility of a neutral escorting his merchant ships with minesweepers could be discounted. After the three days warning which the US supplied, the mines were activated, and no ships attempted to enter or leave the harbour. Some Soviet ships were damaged by the American air attacks, but even that did not create serious difficulties.

The effectiveness of the blockade in serving its two objectives is difficult to assess. Reportedly, traffic on the Chinese railway system was stepped up, but that could hardly compensate for the loss of seaborne supplies which accounted for 80 per cent of North Vietnam's imports. George Kahin, who was present in Hanoi at the time as an observer, has stated his opinion that the Vietnamese road system to China had been developed to such an extent that it was able to replace marine transport.[11] The bottom line is that a ceasefire was negotiated, US troops were withdrawn, and the mines were cleared by the US Navy, beginning on 6 February 1973. The operation was protracted, deliberately, as a means of applying continuous pressure to the Hanoi government.[12] Ultimately, however, South Vietnam fell to the armies of the north. The minefields may have helped to persuade Hanoi to negotiate, just as the mounting anti-war demonstrations forced Washington's hand. If Hanoi's final victory is borne in mind, however, the function of the mining operation becomes less clear. To what extent was it intended to serve a domestic political function in the United States? In assessing the value of the mining operation as part of a campaign to interdict supplies to the North Vietnamese Army, it should be borne in mind that the timing was ill-chosen. The mines were laid at the beginning of the wet season. The campaigning season was over, and the Vietnamese armies would have become inactive in any case. The rain was a more effective means of isolating the battlefield than were bombs or mines. Probably the most important result of the mining of North Vietnam ports was the establishment of the precedent that mining, and blockade, was a legitimate aspect of limited war in the nuclear age.

RHODESIA

Economic boycotts, such as that imposed by the United States on Cuba in 1960, and the United Nations sanctions against Rhodesia, like the 1935 League of Nations action against Italy, participate indirectly in the history of naval action against trade. The American Ambassador to Cuba in 1960, Philip Bonsal, believes that the effect of the American boycott of Cuban sugar exports was largely counterproductive because it obliged the Cubans to depend on the Soviet Union.[13] Moscow's prompt intervention ensured that the results of this exercise of 'economic warfare' was unusually quick acting. In the Rhodesian episode, on the other hand, it took the better part of 14 years for coercion to produce useful results.

This study must interest itself primarily with the use which has been made of warships for trade control, and leave aside the larger question of the utility of economic constraint in conditions of relative peace. It is relevant, however, and in keeping with the general experience of economic warfare, to note that the sanctions against Rhodesia were easily violated by business interests. There is good evidence that the Prime Minister of Rhodesia, Ian Smith, was assured by a *Shell Oil* executive prior to the unilateral declaration of independence that means would be found of getting around any oil embargo.[14] The Portuguese Foreign Minister advised London in 1966 that half the oil being shipped into Rhodesia was being shipped by British companies, *Shell UK* and *BP*, and on 15 February 1968 President Kaunda of Zambia reiterated the information.[15] On 21 February 1968 *Shell* and *BP* finally admitted something like the truth to the Commonwealth Secretary George Thomson, but the latter made it clear that he was not interested in trying to make the sanctions effective. He only wanted to be able to say that the oil was not being delivered by a British firm, and he lent at least tacit approval to an arrangement by which *Shell* and *BP* disguised the oil under the French *Total* marque. This evidence of mixed British motives, that London was primarily concerned to protect British interests in the multi-racial Commonwealth rather than to compel Rhodesian submission, and that the economic requirements of the British state conflicted with its political purposes, is consistent with the general history of trade war that positive motives of gain generally outweigh the negative ones of inflicting deprivation on the enemy.[16]

Eventually, a combination of political and economic events increased the effectiveness of the sanctions. On 3 March 1976 the newly independent government of Mozambique closed its frontier with Rhodesia. After that, all supplies of oil had to be routed through South Africa. An arrangement was concluded by which the South African state oil company *Sasol* provided Rhodesian needs, and the international oil companies increased their sales to the South African market. The increasing revelations in the press about how oil was reaching Rhodesia, however, put pressure on the South African government. In June 1976 there was 'congestion' in the South African railway system which led to Rhodesia's oil stockpile falling to about 20 days' supply. South African pressure, and the increasing success of the black guerrillas operating from the northern borders, led the Salisbury government to waver in its resolve. The expense of the military equipment which had to be purchased, the loss of skilled manpower as a result of conscription, and the economic recession in the Western world which reduced markets for Rhodesian exports, exacerbated the situation.[17] In September 1976 the United States Secretary of State, Henry Kissinger, finally brought Ian Smith to agree to the establishment of a majority government within two years. South Africa's own difficulties in obtaining oil were intensified by the revolution in Iran in 1978. The implications for Rhodesia were self-evident. After several conferences in London, a British governor flew to Salisbury to administer the transfer of power at the end of 1979.

Although the Rhodesian sanctions had been imposed largely by political action at source, there was a naval component to the campaign. The British Royal Navy was deployed between December 1965 and June 1975 to the Mozambique Channel to ensure that Rhodesia was unable to receive oil through the pipeline from the port of Beira. Between March 1966 and June 1971 a British air reconnaissance squadron was based at Majunga in the Malagasy Republic. Once the United Nations had made it clear that the British navy was entitled to use force, the patrol did close the port, but because of the mixed motives of the British and other governments Rhodesia was able to import oil via the South African railway system. The naval blockade of Beira was intended largely for demonstrative purposes and for other purposes unconnected with Rhodesia. The participation of the British government in the campaign against Rhodesia's racial policies provided political cover for the deployment of British warships into the Indian Ocean where they could be used to monitor the activities of the Soviet Navy.[18]

ARAB–ISRAELI INCIDENTS

Economic warfare has formed part of the general Arab strategy against the state of Israel. Israeli commodities have not been accepted across Arab borders. Commercial concerns in neutral states which dealt with Israel have been placed on a black list. Passage through the Suez canal has been denied to ships which touched at Israeli ports. An interesting technicality is that Egypt claimed belligerent rights despite the armistice with Israel.[19] On several occasions Egypt also declared a blockade of the Red Sea and Gulf of Aqaba, access routes to the Israeli port of Eilat. The most important instance of the last occurred in 1967, on 22 May, and triggered the outbreak of the Six-Day war. More than economic motives, however, lay behind the declaration of the Israeli government that blockade would be considered a *causus belli*. By 25 May, in the view of Jonathan Trumbull Howe, Israel had decided that a pretext for war was necessary.

The British and American governments attempted to form an international naval force to keep open the Straits of Tiran. Interference in a belligerent's rights has rarely been part of British foreign policy, but Prime Minister Harold Wilson explained that the Cabinet were moved by a belief that they might be able to avert war. The diplomatic moves to create the force were matched by naval preparations. The Americans were also primarily motivated by the hope of averting war, although they were to become the principal champions of the free use of international straits in the next decade. Israel, however, did not want this intervention on its behalf, and moved quickly to forestall it. Once it became evident that the resolution of the blockade issue would do little to affect events in the Middle East, the naval and diplomatic preparations were discontinued.[20] British economic vulnerability to Arab action, and American commitments in Vietnam, discouraged the vigorous prosecution of an aggressive policy.

INDO–PAKISTAN WAR

In the 1971 Indo–Pakistan war the Indian navy closely blockaded the coast of East Pakistan (Bangladesh), although no blockade order was gazetted, and in naval operations against Karachi the Indian navy accidentally sank with all hands a Liberian freighter 26 miles off shore. Because the war lasted only a few days there was no time for concerted neutral reaction, and there was no protest following the event. D. P. O'Connell attributes that tolerance to the effectiveness of the marine insurance system which spreads the losses.[21]

OCTOBER WAR

In the 1973 'October War' there occurred two episodes which contribute to the recent history of belligerent action against shipping. Both are ill-defined incidents. Egypt used naval forces to close the straits of Bab-el-Mandeb, intercepting an American ship to do so. The legal basis of the action is unclear because the strait is within the territorial waters of the Republic of South Yemen, an ally of Egypt.

Egypt, true to the traditions of belligerents, avoided legal squabbles by not stating whether it was conducting a blockade of Israel.[22]

The second episode may have greater importance to this study, or none. When Israeli ground forces successfully outflanked the Egyptian army the Soviet Union despatched reinforcements through the Dardanelles. The United States Sixth Fleet interposed itself between Egyptian ports and the Soviet military convoy, which eventually turned back. At the height of the crisis, however, the Soviet Northern Fleet deployed a large submarine force into the Atlantic. These may have been moving to war stations to act against units of the North Atlantic Treaty Organization, NATO's, navies, but it is possible that their potential targets were merchant ships. If the latter, the objective could have been economic blockade, blockade of logistics, or distraction of NATO strategy by sporadic attacks on shipping. Sporadic attacks might also have been viewed as a demonstration of Soviet determination, but if so, it would not have been consistent with the apparent Soviet policy of avoiding conflict at sea.

THE FALKLAND ISLANDS WAR 'TOTAL EXCLUSION ZONE'

In the 1982 operations of British forces to expel the Argentine invaders of the Falkland Islands, the British government declared a two hundred mile exclusion zone around the archipelago, and actually sunk an Argentine cruiser, the *General Belgrano*, which was manoeuvring apparently to conduct operations within the zone. Later the zone was redefined as a 'Total Exclusion Zone' within which an Argentine trawler carrying military supplies was sunk without warning. The international community made no objection to the declaration of the exclusion zone, and only four states objected to the more comprehensive total exclusion zone. While these precedents are not directly related to questions of economic warfare, especially because the Falklands are British territory, nevertheless they are a sequel to the Haiphong closure by the United States and are not without significance.

THE GULF WAR

The Iran/Iraq war which broke out in 1980 has produced a final example of *guerre de course*, motivated by the objectives of contraband control, and of general economic warfare, but also by a fundamentally new motive of exploiting the potential for lateral escalation. In a most bloody and protracted war the operations against shipping constituted a relatively small part of belligerent activity. They were nonetheless on a formidable scale. In 1984 alone Iraqi forces carried out 53 attacks on shipping. Iran responded with 18, and intercepted cargo vessels entering the Arabian Gulf to inspect them for contraband bound for Iraq.[23] By the end of 1987 the total number of attacks on shipping reached 451, and the navies of six powers were involved in the defence of neutral trade.[24] The tanker war in the Arabian Gulf area became a major international problem.

The declared Iraqi motive for attack was to deny Iran the revenue from crude oil sales that was needed to pay for the war effort. Ships approaching the Iranian oil terminal at Kharg Island were attacked by aircraft firing *Exocet* missiles. The weapon homed on the most prominent part of the ship's superstructure, and tended to strike in the engine room of tankers two metres above the water-line. Crude oil does not burn easily. Accordingly it was generally possible to tow damaged ships into port. Clearly the Iraqi *modus operandi* was intended to panic world shipping, and so to multiply the effects of sporadic raids.

Iran could use its location at the entrance to the Gulf to carry out an economic war strategy which conformed to the traditional laws of war. Because the Iranian fleet base at Bandar Abbas is near the Straits of Hormuz it was possible for the Iranian Navy to intercept shipping at sea, carry out inspection, and if necessary bring in ships for further examination. In April 1987 the commander of the Iranian Navy, Commodore Mohammed Hoseyn Malekzadeyan, said that since the beginning of the war Iran had boarded 1200 ships, and seized 30 cargoes.[25] Iran, however, did not possess the necessary naval power to enforce a formal blockade in defiance of neutral attitudes. It was not able to establish a navicert system to minimise confrontation at sea, although there is some indication that it attempted to do so, and the United States did not recognise as legitimate Iranian efforts to examine ships under US Navy escort. Had the political climate been more supportive of Iranian exercise of belligerent rights, the utility of the strategy would nonetheless have been limited because Iraq was able to export oil via pipelines through Jordan and Turkey.

Economic warfare considerations were not the principal motive for

Iranian resort to more violent methods against trade ships. The General Council of British Shipping *Guidance Notes for Owners with Vessels in the Arabian Gulf* observed that the pattern of war up to the end of 1984 indicated that Iran's motive for violent attacks on shipping appeared to have been that of retaliation, perhaps with the objective of deterring further Iraqi attacks.[26] When in May, July and September 1987 Iraq briefly suspended its attacks on shipping Iran did so as well.[27] Iran warned shipping to keep south of a line drawn through points in the middle of the Gulf, although shipping was attacked by Iranian aircraft well outside the closed area. Iranian attacks were extended to shipping trading to Kuwait and Saudi Arabia, which were *de facto* allies of Iraq. Because those countries were not able to make use of pipelines for exporting their oil, Iran could hope to generate an indirect economic pressure on Iraq.[28] The *Maverick* missile employed by Iran up to mid-1985 is less effective than the *Exocet* against shipping.

In 1986 a new motive for Iranian attacks on trade became evident, that of intercepting munitions thought to be reaching Iraq via Kuwait. Ships were rarely brought into port for inspection, perhaps because of the difficulty of inspecting containerised freight, or simply because the area of operations had been extended to the coast of the United Arab Emirates. On several occasions positive identification of ships trading to Kuwait was followed two or three hours later by attack without warning using *Sea Killer* missiles with a night-firing capability. Before 16 January 1987 the Iranian navy made nine night attacks on shipping. The ability of Iranian intelligence to identify ships carrying contraband is not clear. The Iranian assertion that Kuwait acted as an *entrepôt* for arms shipment to Iraq, however, appears to have been correct.[29]

It appears possible that Iranian objectives may have included a hope to bring about great-power intervention, or at least to pose that possibility. The Iranian Ambassador to the United Nations asserted

> that since the initiation of Iraqi attacks on ships in the Persian Gulf, we have repeatedly announced in international fora the readiness of the Islamic Republic of Iran to co-operate in every possible way with the Secretary-General of the United Nations and/or other relevant international organisations in securing the freedom of navigation in and the security of the Persian Gulf.[30]

Inconsistencies in Iraqi operations suggest that their motives for attacking shipping may also have included a hope of drawing neutral governments into the war.[31]

The threat of neutral intervention has always been the greatest fear of belligerents conducting economic warfare, not least because it can greatly reduce the effectiveness of the economic strategy. The period of superpower thermonuclear confrontation which developed after World War II, however, effected changes which could make it expedient for a belligerent deliberately to exploit the long history of attacks on neutral commerce leading to a widening of the field of war in order to draw in the active participation of one or more superpowers into a regional conflict. In some circumstances the value to the belligerent of intervention by great powers may be very great, perhaps because it provides an excuse for radical changes of policy. Only the paralysing effect of the nuclear stalemate which existed whilst American and Soviet policies were locked in the 'Cold War' made this use of attack on shipping a possible strategy for a small power.

No doubt a principal consideration in determining the course of events before 1987 was the limited economic consequences to the outside world of the Gulf War. Because of the very large numbers of ships operating into Gulf ports, the 451 ships attacked by the end of 1987 represented only 1 to 2 per cent of the whole. Glut in the world market for oil prevented the reduction in Iranian exports creating shortages to consumers. The shipping industry was able to compensate to some extent for the costs of war. The British National Maritime Board declared that any ship passing west of 55°E in the Gulf entered an area of 'Warlike Operations' in which crews of British ships were entitled to an additional allowance equivalent to 100 per cent of their rate of pay, for a minimum of five days. Crew members who wished to leave the ship before entering the zone might do so without breaking contract. The terms were acceptable to crews, who continue to man British ships in the area. On 4 January 1985 the British War Risks Association announced premiums of .25 per cent on seven-day cover for all Gulf ports, .5 per cent for Sirri and Lavan Islands, and 10 per cent for Kharg Island. The Kharg rate was too high for British registered shipping, but ships of other registration operated a shuttle service between Kharg and Sirri. Iran reduced the price of its crude oil to compensate for the cost of insurance, or as an inducement to those prepared to take the risk without insurance. The current glut in the shipping market increased the incentive to take such risks. The change in international attitudes to the Gulf War in 1987 was a product of American domestic politics, and of the new Iranian tactics, rather than a result of any increase in the economic significance of the constraint on trade.

In the first five years of the war there occurred no major neutral intervention in defence of shipping, although the regional potential which was built up by the armed forces of the United States, the Soviet Union, Britain and France no doubt was influential. France and the United States provided escort on occasion for their merchant ships within the war zone.[32] The United States did not permit Iran to bring in for inspection ships under US Navy convoy. Great Britain, on the other hand, was careful not to undermine its doctrine that convoy does not impede the belligerent's right to inspect ships for contraband. In effect, Britain was less interested in this war than in a possible future one in which it as a belligerent might wish to employ traditional belligerent rights. British warships co-ordinated their passages through the war zone with those of British merchant ships to provide some defence and deterrence against violent attack. Given the difference in American and British rules of engagement, and their different political policies, it is not surprising that American demands for NATO co-operation in the defence of Arabian Gulf merchant shipping were ineffectual. France flatly rejected a Kuwaiti request in June 1987 that it join the United States in convoying tankers.[33]

In 1987 the scale of Iranian attack on shipping increased, and new forms of attack were carried out, some of them by the Islamic Revolutionary Guards. In February 1987 Iranian warships were reported to be firing *Sea Killer* missiles at tankers bound for Kuwait even after Iranian officers had visited the ships and given clearance. The victims included a British registry liquid petroleum gas carrier which had not communicated its arrival in the war zone to the British frigate on station.[34] The Iranian government threatened to close the Gulf to shipping, and did locate Chinese *Silkworm* surface to surface missiles in the Gulf of Hormuz area and the Faw peninsula where Kuwait could be threatened directly.[35] Raids were carried out by Islamic Revolutionary Guards using small craft firing light anti-tank missiles, and naval mines were laid.

In mid-1987 the United States began to abandon its policy of neutrality. Paradoxically, it was an accidental Iraqi attack on the USS *Stark* in May 1987 which catalysed the hardening of American policy against Iran.[36] American relations with Iran were under very severe strain as a result of the disclosure of an American deal to ransom hostages in the Lebanon by supplying Iran with arms. Instinctive American hostility to the Soviet Union played an important part because Kuwait had asked the Soviet government to charter merchant ships protected by Soviet warships. In response, the United

States government undertook to transfer Kuwaiti ships to the American flag, and the United States Navy provided escort for a ship reportedly loaded with tanks to Kuwait.[37] In so impeding Iranian enforcement of the doctrine of continuous voyage, the American government was departing from a policy of neutrality in a manner reminiscent of American support for Britain in 1940. In May 1987 the American government threatened to attack the *Silkworm* missile sites.[38]

Iran succeeded in laying a field of naval mines before the arrival of the first convoy of reflagged Kuwaiti tankers under US Navy escort, and the tanker *Bridgeton* was damaged.[39] As a result of the mining of the tanker routes, and in particular the discovery of mines in the holding area outside the Gulf, British, French, Netherlands, Italian and Belgian minesweepers were dispatched to the Gulf to support the minesweeping operations conducted by American helicopters. On 21 September American forces identified an Iranian landing craft laying mines. Army helicopters operating off naval frigates opened fire on it; the ship was captured and subsequently scuttled.[40] In October Iran used its *Silkworm* missiles against shipping targets and the Kuwait sea island oil terminal. When eventually a reflagged tanker was hit, the US Navy responded by retaliatory action against an Iranian offshore oil installation being used as a base by the Islamic Revolutionary Guards. The violence between American and Iranian forces began to escalate. In April 1987 the US frigate *Samuel B. Roberts* was seriously damaged by an Iranian mine while escorting a convoy. In response, the US Navy attacked another Iranian offshore oil platform. During the operation, an Iranian warship *Joshan*, which fired on the USS *Wainwright*, was sunk. Later, Iranian gunboats were attacked from the air. When two Iranian frigates counterattacked, one, the *Shahand*, was sunk and the *Sabalan* was seriously damaged.[41] In July 1988, while the US Navy and the Iranian Navy were engaged in direct combat in which the Iranian's were decidely outgunned, an Iranian civilian airliner was accidentally shot down by the USS *Vincennes*.[42]

Iran alone sustained significant economic loss from the tanker war. Unlike Iraq, Iran was not able to purchase expensive Western munitions such as the *Exocet*. The shuttle service did not sustain Kharg at full export capacity. In consequence the Iranian government declared its intention to construct a pipeline diverting oil exports to southern Iran. A barter arrangement with the North Korean government, in which oil was exchanged for arms, collapsed when in the 19

September 1985 raid on Kharg Island North Korea's only supertanker was sunk.[43] However, the economic cost to Iran did not produce critical political effects. Iran was able to continue to export oil at discounted prices despite the Iraqi attacks, and despite embargoes eventually imposed by France and the United States. The Iranian government's credit was still good when it was obliged for other reasons to agree to a truce.

There is some reason to think that the increased scale of Iranian attacks on shipping in 1987 was intended to produce the results it did, the increased intervention by the United States in the area and limited co-operation between the United States and the Soviet Union in the United Nations with the purpose of imposing a ceasefire.[44] The Iranian government cited the tragic loss of the airliner, which threatened to engulf innocent civilians in the war, as a reason for accepting a ceasefire with Iraq. Any regime which has been demanding sacrifice from its people needs a credible excuse for seeking peace. The US involvement in the war, which was catalysed by the attacks on shipping, served that purpose.

SOVIET ATTITUDES

John G. Hibbits has observed that Admiral Sergi Gorshkov, until 1985 the Commander-in-Chief of the Soviet Navy, has given scant attention in his polemical writing to interdiction of maritime trade. He makes only one reference to it as a contemporary mission of the Soviet Navy, and he tempers any enthusiasm for the role with the observation that no interdiction campaign has had a decisive impact on the course of war in the twentieth century.[45] Soviet theorists did not share the belief of Britons and Americans that blockade had been decisive in World War I. Peter Vigor points out that the 'Mahanist' concept of naval dominance, based on a capacity to win a decisive battle, and leading to political supremacy, finds no favour in a Soviet Union, which at the time lacked an effective fleet. World War II reinforced the Soviet policy of belittling 'Command of the Sea'.[46] It would be foolish to view this policy as no more than propaganda without a basis in fact. World War II did little to enhance the reputation of sea power for its offensive capacity against a great continental state. Admiral Richmond's observation in 1934 that 'Single-handed sea power can do little against any great power' (*vide supra*) was amply borne out. The space Gorshkov devotes in *The Sea*

Power of the State to detailing the economic resources of the sea, and its value as a medium of transport, is implicit recognition of the potential of sea control in grand strategy.[47] No doubt bureaucratic commitment to the rhetoric abusing sea power added to Gorshkov's difficulties in devising an acceptable rationale for naval expansion. However, his failure to reverse the official opinion on the offensive capacity of sea-based economic warfare 'is not accidental'.

As a practical strategist, Gorshkov is evidently more interested in the capacity of navies to attack military logistics. Nevertheless, the ability of great powers to ensure they receive the necessary military supplies despite the efforts of their enemies has generally been evident in the last resort. Gorshkov relegates attack on logistics to a low order of priority in military planning. He attributes Germany's failure in World War II not to the ultimate inadequacy of the U-boat campaign, which was bound to fail, but to Germany's inability to achieve decisive results quickly, before the Atlantic powers were able to muster the logistic support of the world. By implication, he suggests the need for the Soviet Union to plan for a quick war of conquest which would make unnecessary naval attack on shipping. The torpedo-armed submarine force of the Soviet navy, the ships which would undoubtedly have the greatest role to play in an interdiction campaign, are being steadily reduced in number.

Not all naval analysts are content to accept on face value the evidence of Soviet strategic attitudes. The German Navy went to war in 1914 and 1939 with scant preparation for attacking maritime trade but they quickly obtained the necessary equipment and devised the tactics, although they lost in the end. Military doctrine calls for preparation to contend with an enemy's capabilities, rather than being content to assess his intentions. In a total-war scenario, however, an obsession with defence of supply lines may be counter-productive.

It is probable that tacit acceptance of the relatively limited role of naval attack on trade in a nuclear war scenario lies behind a change of emphasis by Western naval professionals. The emphasis now is upon circumstances short of total war. Fears are expressed about the political implications of Soviet capacity to attack maritime logistics whether or not that potentiality is ever put to the test. Admiral Zumwalt wrote in 1971

> The mere sufficient evidence in peacetime of Soviet capability to do this would be enough to start the erosion of our alliances and lay the basis for accommodations by our allies with the USSR.[48]

To borrow the definitions of James Cable, blockade and *guerre de course* can be used for 'purposeful' and for 'expressive' purposes.[49] In Edward Luttwak's usage, the 'purposeful' act would be one of 'active coercive suasion'. 'Expressive' action may be 'latent coercive suasion', or it could relate entirely to domestic political manoeuvre.[50]

Zumwalt's hypothesis is too unmethodical to be very convincing. If the usual arguments are stood on their head, however, the idea that economic war at sea has a continuing potentiality may be taken seriously. Gorshkov's assertion is unquestionably correct, that attack on logistics, let alone economic blockade, has not had a decisive effect on any twentieth-century war. What effect economic blockade has had has been too slow-acting to yield political results distinct from those produced by other forces. Assumptions generally made about the potential course of nuclear war suggest that even less is to be expected from economic war operations under such severe conditions. However, strategic analysis in the nuclear age must not become obsessed with the idea of general nuclear war. Strategy is primarily interested in less apocalyptic events. Nuclear powers inevitably must seek to protect their interests by means which do not threaten other nuclear powers with the prospect of destruction. Economic war operations, because they are so slow-working, have a history of leading to negotiated settlements. In effect, the very limitations which the twentieth century has shown to exist in the strategy of naval action against shipping has contributed to its attractiveness as a mode of coercive diplomacy, but it remains a relatively high profile *modus operandum*.

It certainly appears that naval attack on trade ships is a growth area in the strategic application of force. As the limitations of economic warfare become more evident, and the alternatives more devastating, the legal and political restraints on its use are being modified. The most notable exception to this trend, however, is the foreign policy of the Soviet Union which continues to avoid this use of sea power.

NOTES

1. W. N. Medlicott, *Naval Blockade and Attack on Shipping Since 1945*, vol. ii, p. 661.
2. Max Sorensen (ed.), *Manual of Public International Law*, p. 754. See

Philip C. Jessup, op. cit., vol. iv, p. 112; brief by M. Giraud, League of Nations Secretariat.

3. D. P. O'Connell, *International Law*, vol. 1, p. 21; and James Wilford Garner, op. cit., p. 240.
4. Malcolm W. Cagle and Frank A. Manson, *The Sea War in Korea*, pp. 222–373.
5. See H. M. Pachter, *Collision Course*. See also Neil H. Alford, op. cit., s.v., 'Analysis of the Quarantine', pp. 269–83.
6. Quincy Wright, 'The Cuban Quarantine', *The American Journal of International Law*, 57 (1963), p. 547.
7. Carlo Q. Christol and Charles R. Davis, 'Maritime Quarantine: The Naval Interdiction of Offensive Weapons and Associated Materiel to Cuba, 1962', *The American Yearbook of International Law*, 57 (1963), p. 528.
8. William O. Miller, loc. cit.
9. W. Knappman (ed.), *South Vietnam, U.S.–Communist Confrontation in Southeast Asia 1972–1973*, vol. 7, pp. 80–1.
10. Ibid., pp. 82–3.
11. Seminar at the Institute of Southeast Asian Studies, Singapore, 10 July 1985.
12. Gareth Porter, *A Peace Denied*, pp. 234–6.
13. P. Bonsal, *Cuba, Castro, and the United States*, p. 165.
14. M. Bailey, *Oilgate, the Sanctions Scandal*, p. 110 *et seq.*
15. Ibid., pp. 174 and 190.
16. Harry R. Strack, *Sanctions, The Case of Rhodesia*, pp. 24–33.
17. Ibid., p. 89.
18. Ibid., p. 19; and conversation with Admiral Sir Edward Ashmore, First Sea Lord, 12 Nov. 1975.
19. See William O. Miller, loc. cit. See also Howard S. Levie, 'The Nature and Scope of the Armistice Agreement', *American Journal of International Law*, 50 (1956), pp. 885–6.
20. Jonathan Trumbull Howe, *Multicrisis*, part II.
21. D. P. O'Connell, *The Influence of Law upon Seapower*, p. 160.
22. Ibid., p. 101.
23. General Council of British Shipping, *Guidance Notes for Owners and Masters with vessels in the Arabian Gulf*, 1 October 1985. *The Times*, 6 February 1987 reported that a total of 98 ships were attacked in 1986.
24. Detailed statistics are printed by Ronald O'Rourke in 'The Tanker War', USNI *Proceedings*, May 1988 (114/5/1033), pp. 30–4.
25. Anthony H. Cordesman, *The Gulf and the West, Strategic Relations and Military Realities*, p. 334.
26. General Council of British Shipping, *Guidance Notes for Owners and Masters with vessels in the Arabian Gulf*, February 1987 edn, p. 14.
27. Ronald O'Rourke, loc. cit.
28. Wesley L. McDonald, 'The Convoy Mission', USNI *Proceedings*, May 1988 (114/5/1033), pp.36–44.
29. *The Independent*, 28 May 1987, p. 8.
30. Ibid., p. 16.

31. See Efraim Karsh, *The Iran–Iraq War: A Military Analysis*, Adelphi Papers #220, London, 1987; pp. 28–30.
32. *Straits Times*, 14 January 1986.
33. Anthony H. Cordesman, op. cit., pp. 349–50.
34. *The Times*, from Robert Fisk, Dubai, 6 February 1987.
35. Anthony H. Cordesman, op. cit., pp. 332–3.
36. Michael Vlahos, 'The Stark Report', USNI *Proceedings*, May 1988 (114/5/1033), pp. 64–7.
37. *The Independent*, 28 May 1987, p. 8; *The Times*, 30 May, p. 5, 3 June pp. 1 and 5; *The Guardian Weekly*, 7 June 1987, vol. 136, no. 23; and Anthony H. Cordesman, op. cit., pp. 325–31.
38. *The Times*, 30 May 1987, p. 5; and Anthony H. Cordesman, op. cit., p. 346.
39. Frank C. Seitz, 'SS Bridgeton: the First Convoy', USNI *Proceedings*, May 1988 (114/5/1033), pp. 52–7; and Anthony H. Cordesman, op. cit., pp. 365–6.
40. *The Globe and Mail*, 26 September 1987, p. A4; and Ronald O'Rourke, loc. cit.
41. Anthony H. Cordesman, op. cit., pp. 434–8.
42. Norman Friedman, 'World Naval Developments', *Proceedings*, August 1988, p. 123.
43. *Straits Times*, 28 January 1986.
44. Ibid., 26 March 1987, p. 24, 'King Faid in talks on the Gulf War'.
45. John G. Hibbits, 'Admiral Gorshkov's Writings: Twenty Years of Naval Thought', in Paul J. Murphy (ed.), *Naval Power in Soviet Policy*, Studies in Communist Affairs, Volume 2, The United States Air Force, 1978.
46. Peter H. Vigor, 'Soviet Understanding of "Command of the Sea"', and Michael MccGwire, 'Command of the Sea in Soviet Naval Strategy', in Michael MccGwire, Ken Booth and John McDonnell (eds), *Soviet Naval Policy*.
47. S. G. Gorshkov, *The Sea Power of the State*.
48. *Military Posture and H.R. 3818 and H.R. 8687*, Hearings before the House Committee on Armed Services, 92 Cong. 1 sess. (1971), Pt. 1, p. 2762. Quoted in Barry M. Blechman, *The Changing Soviet Navy*.
49. James Cable, op. cit.
50. Edward N. Luttwak, op. cit.

7 General Conclusions

The economics of warfare is concerned with the resources and requirements of opposing belligerents, measured in fiscal terms and also in terms of *matériel* and manpower. The conduct of economic warfare, accordingly, not only involves devising means of impoverishing the enemy, but also calls for the maximisation of resources, and their most economic expenditure. Decisions have to be made whether the emphasis of effort will be on the negative objective, or on the positive one. Each involves peculiar difficulties. The decision will be influenced by the nature of the available forces. The historical record does not present consistent answers to these questions, because of environmental changes. It is possible, however, to identify at least some of the factors which produced a strategic pattern, and which led to its modification over time. In this conclusion the more consistent observations which may be made about employment of naval forces of economic warfare will be noted, and also some of the less constant ones, the disappearance of which affect the utility of the strategy.

The principal theme running through this study is that naval action to deny an enemy the use of the sea for his trade is a strategy which only has decisive military and political significance when it is undertaken by the strong against states which are at once weak and economically vulnerable, and which cannot count on the support of powerful neighbours. Admiral Mahan's thesis, that the capacity of navies to have decisive impact on international relations is dependent upon their capacity to sustain operations in the trade routes regardless of the sorties of the enemy, has been supported by the evidence of the two world wars.[1] At the same time, however, it is evident that the determinant of success is less the strength of the attacking force than it is the vulnerability of the victim. Admiral Richmond correctly observed in 1934 that, 'Single-handed sea power can do little against any great power'. The sporadic raiding of the trade routes by submarine was not decisive in either world war, but neither was the methodical if distant blockade mounted by Britain. The extent of territory controlled by Germany in World War II reduced the significance of the British blockade, but even in World War I external economic constraint did not have a decisive effect because the capitalist system could adjust to operation within a smaller economy.

Studies of the economic impact of Britain's blockade of Germany in World War I, and of the economic campaigns against Britain in the wars of the nineteenth and twentieth centuries, have suggested that the degree of administrative efficiency a state has reached is a principal factor in determining its vulnerability to blockade. Gerd Hardach described the vital quality as the 'liberal-capitalist' framework, and Mancur Olson uses the term economic 'virtuosity' which enables a state to be innovative under pressure. Japan suffered from American action against its trade more because of a lack of that virtuosity in the period 1941–45 than from the fact of its dependence upon imported raw materials. Olson's conclusions have particular relevance to the problem of food supply, which has rarely been a weak link in national defences because of the capacity of states to make direct or indirect substitutions for the products in short supply.

One of the factors which determines the degree of vulnerability of the victim is its ability to defend its shipping with skill and activity. It is a paradox, but nonetheless true, that great states need navies more to defend their own trade than they do to influence world events by controlling the trade of others.

Inevitably, this paradox can be exploited by navies pursuing other strategies. Defence of trade is a demanding commitment, and it is to the advantage of a state at war to compel its opponent to undertake it. Before the Declaration of Paris, navies could devote relatively little effort to trade defence because part of the function of privateers was defence against those of the enemy. The development of high performance naval *matériel* in the nineteenth century made it more difficult for navies to maintain the resources needed both for trade protection and for offensive purposes. The twentieth century development of the submarine greatly increased the potential of the strategy of containment by trade attack because anti-submarine operations require the construction of specialist vessels, using scarce material resources, which thus become permanently unavailable for most other naval or military purposes.

In World War I very large numbers of British naval trawlers were deployed in trade defence. When in 1917 the Admiralty came under pressure to introduce convoy, it objected that it could not do so without immobilising the Grand Fleet by depriving it of escort destroyers. It was later found that a convoy system could be organised, but at a cost in warships which the British and American navies both hoped could be obviated by the new anti-submarine technologies developed in the inter-war years. In World War II great efforts were made to confine the use of convoys to slow traffic on dangerous routes. These restrictions were not always well advised. The Americans tried to avoid the use of convoy on their east coast in early 1942 and the losses were prodigious. After the German defeats of 1943, it could no longer be hoped that the U-boats could prevent Allied preparations for a military offensive, but the U-boat operations contained a large part of Britain's naval and air effort on trade defence, and were continued to the end of the war.

An important aspect of this strategy is the restraint imposed by attack on trade upon the availability and economics of mercantile shipping. Although the waste of resources which occurred when it was attempted in the two world wars to sail shipping without convoy was even greater than was that occasioned by the operation of a system of convoy, convoy is anything but an optimum means of operating shipping services. An enemy seeking to reduce either the cost-effectiveness of trade, or the strategic mobility of forces, can achieve disproportionate results by a limited investment in the means of attack.

The containment of resources in trade warfare, however, is not restricted only to one belligerent. The attacker also has to commit resources which might have been used in other ways. Only at a very low level of naval attack, when the costs of naval forces employed in attack and defence are outweighed by the overhead cost of convoy, is the mathematics clearly in favour of the attack. The German commitment of resources to the U-boat campaign in World War II may actually have exceeded those of the Allies in their defensive effort, measured by monetary cost. It appears that Clausewitz's observation, that the defensive form of warfare is intrinsically stronger than the offensive, may be applicable to naval trade warfare.[2]

Dislike of trade defence persists because it absorbs resources that might be devoted to attacking the enemy. Nevertheless, the task has been unavoidable, and constitutes a major rationale for the maintenance of the navy. In the context of potential nuclear war in Europe it is by no means clear that defence of trade is relevant, especially as destruction of port areas is all too probable. As a means of distracting and containing the naval forces of NATO, however, it is not at all improbable that the Soviet Navy has a plan to implement the same strategy of commerce raiding which their Imperial forebearers developed.

A second, and related, theme is that interdiction of trade is a strategy which, at least in its most comprehensive forms, and when conducted in accordance with British interpretation of belligerent rights, must be conducted against neutrals for the ultimate discomfiture of the enemy. Inevitably, it has had the tendency to transform neutrals into enemies. Different motives for conducting the attacks on trade, and different circumstances, affect the extent of the escalatory problem for the belligerent. The doctrine favoured by lesser naval powers that belligerents should not interfere with neutral shipping, except when closely blockading an enemy port, certainly reduces the probability of widening the conflict. The 'free ships make free goods' doctrine, however, means that the strategic value of interdiction of trade can be accounted only in the commercial value of the enemy ships and cargoes, and in the political effects of their seizure. General economic blockade to deny the enemy access to resources must confront the problem of neutral reaction head on. Only a combination of great military power and judicious concessions to the needs of neutrals will permit the belligerent to pursue his strategy. A mercantilist strategy which aims at maximising the wealth of the belligerent, and only incidentally at the impoverishment of the enemy, requires a less complete interference with trade. However, mercantilism will always be regarded as injurious to neutrals because of the economic power which it ultimately puts in the hands of the victor.

The positive objective of economic warfare, the mercantilist one of enriching the belligerent, harnesses the natural forces of commerce. A third theme in the history of war on trade may be characterised by a borrowed, and transformed, aphorism to the effect that 'The businessman will always get through'. Over the history of naval and administrative blockade there has been a steady improvement in the technology of enforcement, but there has never been a blockade of a major state which was impermeable. The motivation of those who wish to continue trading is greater than is that of those who wish to block it. Governments connive at wartime trade with the enemy, either because it is recognised that the belligerent itself must trade to live, or because business interests suborn government. International business has little interest in respecting a blockade, preferring to profit from high wartime prices, and providing itself with insurance against war loss. Because the armed forces of the victim state will generally ensure that they receive whatever supplies are available in preference to civilian needs, even small deficiencies in a blockade intended to impoverish the enemy may well negate its usefulness. For mercantilist trade war to be a profitable endeavour, on the other hand, it may only be necessary to effect a limited change in the efficiency of the economic system of the enemy.

Mercantilist and related concepts dominated naval strategy from the sixteenth century. Adam Smith showed that Britain's overseas trade paid for victory in the Seven Years' War. In the Napoleonic War a mercantilist strategy served to finance the defeat of the French Empire. Napoleon was less successful in his own mercantilist 'Continental System'.

Mercantilism is a discredited system of economics because it obstructs the growth of the total world economy. However, for the purposes of military strategy the decisive consideration is the relative wealth of states to each other rather than the aggregate wealth of all. For a brief period in the mid-nineteenth century Britain was able to pursue the ends of mercantilism by means of Free Trade, because the British economy was so successfully competitive. The Ango–French policy of free trade in wartime during the Crimean War, to minimise the impact of war upon the trade which was paying for their war effort, amounted to a mercantilist strategy conducted by free-enterprise means. This experiment was not repeated by the belligerents of the American Civil War, or by those of the two World Wars, but following World War I the dichotomy between 'mercantilism' and 'free trade' become increasingly unclear. In World War II Germany, Japan, and Britain all focussed on the need to maximise the wealth of the belligerent. Britain did so most effectively because the means employed were diplomatic and persuasive. In the circumstances London was obliged to restrict Britain's own long-term economic development in order to sustain in the shorter term the political forces in the United States which supported *Lend-Lease.* American profits from the two World Wars, first as neutral and then as belligerent, resemble the success of eighteenth-century mercantilism. Neither British nor American policy was mercantilist trade war in the traditional form, but it was analogous to it.

Mahan described the action of naval operations on a state's war economy as 'noiseless, steady, exhausting pressure'. The capacity of such action to precipitate decisive political results is evidently much more restricted than Mahan understood to be the case, but there is no disputing that such effect as is produced tends to be the result of protracted periods of trade war. Blockade and mercantilist trade war can only produce rapid results if the deprivation is not absorbed by the enemy community at large, and if the direct victims have significant political power. As that has rarely been the case, it has almost always taken years for results to be significant. In the instance of Britain's great mercantilist trade war, it took a century and a half between the Navigation Act of 1651 and the final defeat of Napoleon by European armies financed by British subsidies. The economic effects of the American blockade of Japan between 1942 and 1945 were more quickly felt. Nevertheless, it had not produced decisive political results by the time the Americans were faced with a choice between invasion of Japan and the use of atomic bombs. Because economic deprivation will rarely produce a time-urgent crisis such as that implicit in invasion or threatened bombardment it is to be expected that the political product eventually reached will be in the nature of a negotiated settlement. For that very reason economic warfare may continue to have appeal in the nuclear age.

The manipulation of international law has been an important aspect of the belligerent's propaganda campaign to reconcile its needs with those of neutrals. War against trade has been difficult to reconcile with the established concept of the 'just war' which stipulates that methods must be discriminating and proportional. Attempts to define by treaty the rights of belligerents has been an important means of limiting the injury suffered by neutrals. The most nagging question has been whether neutral shipping may legally be stopped, searched, and possibly condemned as a prize. The concept of continuous voyage, conceived in the eighteenth century and still accepted as a justification for the arrest of shipping, is under pressure from the development of containerised freight services. Britain and the United States continue to disagree over the right of neutral warships to extend protection over merchantmen which may be carrying contraband.

Underlying the disputes over the laws of war has been the shifting sand of the concept of law itself. Until the Declaration of Paris in 1856, the principal basis of law was the Roman code, which was at once pervasive and unalterable. Treaties between states had, from the Middle Ages, modified the application of belligerent law. The nearly universal agreement of states to the Declaration of Paris, however, introduced a period when treaties came to exceed in importance the pervasive influence of Roman law. The paradoxical result was that law lost its foundation of respect and became a matter of convenience. World War I presented a spectacle of states seeking excuses for altering the laws of war to suit their immediate needs. Following that war, international society began to struggle towards a new pervasive concept of law, based on the common humanity of man. Nevertheless, World War II reduced the extent to which legal forms affect the conduct of operations against trade. More attention is now given in 'just war' analysis to defining the right to employ force, *jus ad bello*, than to restraining the conduct of states once at war, *jus in bello*. The means employed by states in conducting their wars continue to have importance in determining international political reactions, but the air war and the extermination camp have put the horrors of attack on shipping in a new context.

The ultimate consideration has always been the danger of escalation. The desire for legitimacy is to be seen as an aspect of the need to reconcile the needs of neutrals and belligerents. Recently the danger of vertical, or qualitative, escalation has had more of a restraining influence, but the underlying problem remains that of lateral escalation by the alienation of neutrals. The protracted time which is generally required before results can be obtained from economic warfare exacerbates the problem of retaining political acceptance of the legitimacy of the belligerent act.

Because interference with trade has long been recognised as being escalatory, there is a long history of self-imposed restraint on the part of belligerents. Only those with exceptional military strength have been able to ignore neutral feelings. The proxy wars the Soviet Union has fought against the United States since 1945 have shown a consistent pattern of restraint at sea. The only difference between this restraint and the earlier instances, is that Soviet concern is with the danger of qualitative, rather than quantitative, escalation. The danger lay in the prospect of an American political 'spasm reaction' which might escalate the level of violence above that which was useful to Soviet objectives. The Americans risked escalation in the Cuban Missile crisis and the Haiphong blockade, but in both instances the disruption of trade was generally recognised to be a 'soft' reaction compared to the recommendations of American military leaders. The employment of naval action against shipping by Iran and Iraq during the Gulf war may have been motivated, in part, by the hope of involving neutrals in the war. That tactic is a product of the nuclear age, but depends for its effectiveness upon the long history of such action indeed precipitating neutral intervention.

One of the observations the historian can make about the effects of the strategy of attack on maritime trade is that the political linkage, from the belligerent act of power through the investors in maritime trade to the victim's government, is a weak one. Shipowners have been shown to have little power to bring changes in the war policies of states, neither as a lobby group, nor as independent agents. As agents within a state, shipowners have been more notable for their ability to devise means of compensating for attacks on trade than for the capacity to withdraw services. If they attempt the latter, government can be expected to devise its own controls forcing the ships back to sea. The most that can be said in the shipowner's favour is that powerful, democratic states with a strong trading lobby tend to provide themselves with strong navies.

Changes in geopolitical circumstances and domestic tax structure have affected the motivation of states. No longer is attack on trade valuable to governments as an instrument of foreign policy because it is cost-free to the exchequer. The long history of naval attack on trade up to the Declaration of Paris, which outlawed the use of privateers in 1856, can be most misleading. No doubt the most outdated motive for directing the naval forces of a state to attack seaborne trade is the need to stimulate private investment in warships, and the enlistment of seamen and officers. In the twentieth century the apparatus of the totalitarian, and quasi-totalitarian, state not only is able to pay for naval forces out of tax revenue, but can also employ coercion to conscript personnel. No state at present relies upon prizes for those purposes. It is true that torpedo-firing submarines, and other naval weapons, took the place of privateers in trade warfare. The fact remains that there is no longer a fiscal reason why states should prefer to conduct a naval strategy against trade rather than invest in some other strategic system. It should be noted in passing that there does remain a fiscal reason for employing administrative measures of economic warfare. The indirect cost of the economic and political dislocation created thereby, however, may be a greater consideration than is the fiscal saving.

Changes in the inland transportation systems of continental states have had a profound impact on the utility of 'Mahanist' maritime strategy. Mercantilist trade manipulation, efforts to deny an enemy access to trade, and interdiction of logistics are all affected. Soviet analysts have never been convinced by the potential of 'Command of the Sea' for economic warfare, and Admiral Gorshkov did not employ that conception as a rationale for naval expansion. Nor was Gorshkov impressed by the strategic utility of operations against military logistics, that is, contraband. The value of naval forces in providing oceanic logistic links for land forces, and in their denial to an enemy, is increasingly restricted to specific circumstances. In the eighteenth century armies became unusually dependent upon maritime transport because of the development of a supply system to replace foraging, and because of the poverty of inland transport systems. The development of canals and railways changed the strategic requirements of armies, and in many circumstances reduced their dependence on navies. The great mechanical armies of the twentieth century continue to depend upon sea transport, but only if they are being deployed overseas. Limitations imposed by shipping shortages, exacerbated by the U-boat war and by the overhead costs of convoy, had powerful effects upon the strategic mobility of the Western allies. On the other hand, Asian armies have demonstrated in Korea and Vietnam that they can continue to function with very limited sea transport and with their logistic supplies under continuous air attack.

The idea current in the 1920s, that economic sanctions could constitute a demonstration of protest by the international community, was discredited by the Ethiopian and Manchurian crises. Embargoes placed on exports from time to time following World War II have been intended primarily to produce economic effects, or to deny access to technology, rather than to express disapproval. That embargo also has a demonstrative effect, however, can hardly be denied. What is true for embargo at source is even more true of naval blockade. The Beira patrol is an example of a naval blockade mounted for demonstrative purposes, although it had other purposes besides the nominal one of bringing Rhodesia to renounce its rebellion.

Used as 'expressive' coercive diplomacy, naval attack on shipping would always be a major demonstration. If conducted with vigour by a major navy it would be a demonstration with very great political significance. Such a demonstration would hardly constitute an act of economic warfare, but it would acquire its political significance at least in part from the long history of belligerent action at sea against trade, and of escalatory neutral reaction to it. The Soviet deployment of submarines into the Atlantic in 1973 during the confrontation with the United States over military support for Egypt has been interpreted as the first moves in such a demonstration, although a more convincing explanation is that it was a preparatory deployment made in case war should be the outcome of the manoeuvres in the Mediterranean. Measures of economic warfare have, notably in 1775 and 1941, and also in 1990–91, constituted a transitional stage between peace and war.

The Ethiopian and Manchurian crises forcefully bring home the lesson that if sanctions are effective they are likely to lead to war, unless there are massive disincentives to restrain the victim. It may actually be more dangerous to impose economic sanctions by administrative means because it permits the victim an option of violent reaction, the consequences of which are unclear.

There is no reason to depart from W. N. Medlicott's conclusion in 1952 that the interest felt in the strategy of blockade during the interwar years was a product of an unusual combination of opportunities and challenges, which may recur only at rare intervals. Nevertheless, it is apparent that naval action against trade remains part of the vocabulary of war. It may be a valuable means of containing enemy forces. Action against trade vessels inevitably constrains logistic movement by sea. Attack on shipping may be used as a demonstration. The involvement of neutrals is an inevitable and possibly a welcome consequence of its use. The positive, mercantilist, form of trade war has serious long-term significance. The negative form, economic blockade, may yet be effective against some especially vulnerable victims. As though to highlight this point, the Iraqi invasion of Kuwait in August 1990, and the rapid organisation of naval squadrons and battle-groups to enforce a blockade of Iraq, occurred just as this book was being sent to press.

THE 1990–91 KUWAIT CRISIS

In this instance, several factors contribute to the potential of blockade as a form of coercion. The underlying reason for the Iraqi invasion of Kuwait, and threatened invasion of Saudi Arabia, was the cost of the recent war with Iran. Having been unable to persuade Kuwait and Saudi Arabia to force up the price of crude oil, Iraq sought to acquire Kuwait's share of the market, and its liquid assets at one blow. A blockade of Iraq's oil exports hits directly at its greatest problem. It can be argued, as Maynard Keynes did in 1939, that the blockade will be most effective if Iraq is permitted to purchase all the imports required for its civilian economy, because its fiscal problems would be exacerbated, and the Iraqi government would not be able to make political capital out of food shortages.

The most important factor in determining the effectiveness of the blockade must be the virtual unanimity of the world community in its determination to resist the Iraqi threat. The United Nations Security Council agreed on 7 August to impose a total ban on trade with Iraq, without any vote against, and the Soviet Union and United States acting in agreement. There was some doubt about whether this resolution permitted the use of force by warships to impose the ban, but Britain declared that the request of the Emir of Kuwait for assistance justified Britain taking military action under the United Nations Charter, Article 51, which permits collective self-defence 'until the Security Council has taken measures necessary to maintain international peace and security'. The United States, which avoided the word 'blockade' because it is only a legitimate action for a state at war, declared its intention to use the 'minimum amount of force necessary' to enforce the 'interdiction of trade', but also obtained the agreement of the Security Council for doing so, co-operating with other nations through the mechanism of the UN Military Staff Committee. By mid-September seven other nations had sent warships to the area to co-operate with the Anglo–American blockade, or at least to demonstrate opposition to Iraqi aggression.

Iraq can only export its oil by pipeline, because its Gulf terminal was destroyed in the Iran War, and these pipelines cross Saudi Arabia and Turkey, which have closed them down. The military potential assembling in the region is primarily required to ensure that those countries can continue to do so despite the menace of Iraqi arms, and to enforce the ban on the imports of military equipment into Iraq which might otherwise pass through bordering neutral states such as Jordan which has divided political reactions to the crisis. Naval forces are also necessary, however, to prevent Iraq shipping oil out of the port of Kuwait, possibly to Iran, for transhipment to the world market. Traditionally the United States respects the right of neutral warships to escort convoys through a war zone, but whether Iran will be permitted to do so is problematic. There is no question of the technical ability of the blockading forces, and the Iraq government ordered its tankers to obey their instructions.

On past record it is fairly safe to predict that the effectiveness of the blockade of Iraq will depend upon the extent to which the blockading nations are united and committed to what amounts to an act of war, and upon the extent to which Iraq demonstrates entrepreneurial virtuosity in countering its impact. It is also safe to predict that blockade alone will generate only enough political pressure to bring about a negotiated settlement in which Iraq will retain enough of the fruits of its aggression to save face at home.[3]

NOTES

1. See Sir Herbert Richmond, *Economy and Naval Security*, pp. 61–72.
2. Carl von Clausewitz, *On War*, pp. 357–9.
3. *The Times*, August 7, 14, 18 and 23, 1990.

Bibliography

UNPUBLISHED DOCUMENTS

Public Record Office, London

Admiralty Papers:
ADM 116/1079, 1087, 1233, 1236, 1319, 1320B, 1715, 2466, 2686, 3159, 3303
Cabinet Office Papers:
CAB 15/21
CAB 21/299; 307; 310; 319; 320; 352; 1237; 1240; 1244
CAB 66/5; 11; 25; 26; 30; 31; 33; 35; 36; 39; 43; 49; 51; 56
CAB 120/398; 400; 405; 410; 411; 412
Foreign Office Papers:
F.O. 837/5
Ministry of War Transport Papers:
MT 59/285
State Papers:
SP 94/175 no. 26
SP 84/561 no. 6

PUBLISHED DOCUMENTS

Admiralty, [from Captured Tambach archives], *Fuehrer Conferences on Naval Affairs*. 2 vols., London, August 1947

Supplement to the American Journal of International Law, Diplomatic Correspondence between the United States and Belligerent Governments Relating to Neutral Rights and Commerce. Vols. 9–11, New York, July 1915 to October 1917

S. L. Bane and R. H. Lutz (eds), *The Blockade of Germany after the Armistice, 1918–1919, Selected Documents*. Stanford, California, 1942

James Scott Brown (ed.), *The Controversy Over Neutral Rights Between the United States and France, 1797–1800, A Collection of American State Papers and Judicial Decisions*. New York, 1917

The Declaration of London, February 26, 1909, A Collection of Official Papers . . . . New York, 1919

Calendar of State Papers, Foreign. Vols XV–XXIII, London, 1907–50

James Frederick Chance (ed.), *British Diplomatic Instructions, 1689–1789*. (Camden 3rd Series, Vol. 32 and 33); Vol. 1 (Sweden), London, 1922

Donald S. Detwiler (ed.), *World War II German Military Studies*. 24 vols., New York, 1979

Carl Doenitz [R. H. Stevens, translator], *Memoirs, Ten Years and Twenty Days*. Westport, Connecticut, 1976
England, *Queens Regulations for the Royal Navy*. Revised, 1967; London, 1967
C. H. Firth and R. S. Rait (eds), *Acts and Ordinances of the Interregnum 1642–1660*, vol. II, London, 1911
G. P. Gooch and H. Temperley (eds), *British Documents on the Origins of the War*, vols III and VIII. London, 1932
Great Britain, House of Commons, Nov. 1944 CMD 6564, *Statistics Relating to the War Effort of the United Kingdom*
Mrs E. Green (*née* Mary Anne Wood) (ed.), *State Papers Domestic, Elizabeth*, CCLIX no. 12, and CCLXIII no. 102. London, 1856–71
Allen B. Hinds (ed.), *Calendar of State Papers, Venice*, vols 8 and 34 nos. 379 and 398. London, 1864
H. C. Hoover, *The Memoirs of Herbert Hoover*, vols I and II. New York, 1951–52
The Joint Army–Navy Assessment Committee, *Japanese Naval and Merchant Shipping Losses During World War II by all Causes*. February 1947
Peter K. Kemp (ed.), *The Papers of Admiral Sir John Fisher*. 2 vols, London, 1964
Edward Fairfax Taylor and Felix James Henry Skene (eds), *Manuscripts of the House of Lords*. London, 1900–
A. Temple Patterson (ed.), *The Jellicoe Papers*. 2 Vols, London, 1966–68
Charles Seymour (ed.), *The Intimate Papers of Colonel House*. 4 vols, Boston, 1926–28
J. R. Tanner (ed.), *Samuel Pepys Naval Minutes*. London, 1926
United States Naval War College International Law Topics; *The Declaration of London of February 26, 1909*. Washington, 1910

NEWSPAPERS

The Guardian Weekly, Manchester periodical, 7 June 1987, vol. 136, no. 23.
The Globe and Mail, Toronto periodical, 26, 30 September 1987
The Independent, London periodical, 28 May 1987
Straits Times, Singapore periodical, 14, 28 January 1986
The Times, London periodical, 6 February, 30 May and 3 June 1987

THESES

Richard D. Bourland Jr., 'Maurepas and his Administration of the French Navy on the Eve of the War of the Austrian Succession (1737–1742)', PhD Dissertation, Notre Dame, Indiana, 1978
Ralph A. Leitner Jr., 'International Considerations in the French Blockade of Formosa (1884–1885)', PhD Dissertation, St John's University, New York, 1979

M. R. Pitt, 'Great Britain and Belligerent Maritime Rights from the Declaration of Paris, 1856, to the Declaration of London, 1909', University of London PhD, 1964
David J. Starkey, 'British Privateering, 1702–1783, with particular reference to London', University of Exeter PhD, 1985
Carl E. Swanson, 'Preditors and Prizes: Privateering in the British Colonies During the War of 1739–1748', PhD University of Western Ontario, 1979

MONOGRAPHS

Patrick Abbazia, *Mr. Roosevelt's Navy: the Private War of the U.S. Atlantic Fleet*. Annapolis, Maryland, 1975
Ephraim Douglass Adams, *Great Britain and the American Civil War*. Gloucester, Mass., 1957
Robert Greenhalgh Albion, *The Timber Problem in the Royal Navy, 1652–1862*. Cambridge, Mass., 1926
with Jennie Barnes Pope, *Sea Lanes in Wartime*. U.S.A., 1968
Neil H. Alford, Naval War College International Law Studies, 1963, *Modern Economic Warfare (Law and the Naval Participant)*. Washington, 1967
Olive Anderson, *A Liberal State at War*. London, 1967
Kenneth Raymond Andrews, *Elizabethan Privateering*. Cambridge, 1964
George W. Baer, *Test Case Italy, Ethiopia, and the League of Nations*. Stanford University, California, 1976
M. Bailey, *Oilgate, the Sanctions Scandal*. London, 1979
Thomas A. Bailey, *The Policy of the United States Towards the Neutrals, 1917–1918*. Gloucester, Mass., 1966
Paul W. Bamford, *Forests and French Sea Power 1660–1789*. Toronto, 1956
C. J. Bartlett, *Great Britain and Sea Power*. Oxford, 1963
Daniel Baugh, *British Naval Administration in the Age of Walpole*. Princeton, 1965
George Louis Beer, *British Colonial Policy, 1754–1765*. New York, 1907
C. B. A. Behrens, *Merchant Shipping and the Demands of War*. London, 1955
A. C. Bell, *A History of the Blockade of Germany, 1914–1918*. London, 1937 (Confidential to 1961)
Elbert J. Benton, *International Law and the Diplomacy of the Spanish-American War*. Baltimore, 1908
Stuart L. Bernath, *Squall Across the Atlantic*. Berkeley, 1970
T. S. Bindoff, *The Schelt Question*. London, 1945
Hans Binnendijk, *et al.*, *War in the Gulf*, A Staff Report to the Committee on Foreign Relations, August 20, 1984
Keith W. Bird, *German Naval History, A Guide to the Literature*. New York, 1985
Donald S. Birn, *The League of Nations Union*. Oxford, 1981
Karl E. Birnbaum, *Peace Moves and U-boat Warfare*. USA, 1970
Jeremy Black and Philip Woodfine (eds), *The British Navy and the Use of Naval Power in the Eighteenth Century*. Atlantic Highlands, N.J., 1989

Clay Blair, *Silent Victory, The US Submarine War Against Japan*. Philadelphia, 1975
Barry M. Blechman, *The Changing Soviet Navy*. The Brookings Institution, Washington DC, 1973
Ernest L. Bogart, *Direct and Indirect Costs of the Great World War*. New York, 1919
Philip Bonsal, *Cuba, Castro, and the United States*. Pittsburgh, 1971
R. Arthur Bowler, *Logistics and the Failure of the British Army in America, 1775–1783*. Princeton, 1975
Charles R. Boxer, *The Dutch Seaborne Empire 1600–1800*. London, 1977
Francis B. C. Bradlee, *Blockade Running During the Civil War, And the Effect of Land and Water Transportation on the Confederacy*. Salem, Mass., 1925
Fernand Braudel, *The Mediterranean and the Mediterranean World in the Age of Philip II*. New York, 1966
John S. Bromley, *Corsairs and Navies, 1660–1760*. London, 1987
E. H. Buehrig, *Woodrow Wilson and the Balance of Power*. Gloucester, Mass., 1968
Kathleen Burk, *Britain, America and the Sinews of War, 1914–1918*. London, 1985
J. R. M. Butler, *Grand Strategy*, vol. II, September 1939–June 1941. London, 1957
James Cable, *Gunboat Diplomacy, Political Applications of Limited Naval Force*. London, 1971
The Royal Navy & the Seige of Bilbao. Cambridge, 1979
Malcolm W. Cagle and Frank A. Manson, *The Sea War in Korea*. Annapolis, Maryland, 1957
Alice Clare Carter, *Neutrality or Commitment: The Evaluation of Dutch Foreign Policy, 1667–1795*. London, 1975
The Dutch Republic in Europe in the Seven Years War. London, 1971
David G. Chandler, *The Art of War in the Age of Marlborough*. London, 1976
E. Keble Chatterton, *The Big Blockade*. London, 1932
Winston S. Churchill, *The World Crisis*. 6 vols, New York, 1927
Their Finest Hour (vol. II of *The Second World War*). Boston, 1947
G. N. Clark, *The Dutch Alliance and the War Against French Trade*. Manchester, 1923, and New York, 1971
Anna Cornelia Clauder, *American Commerce as Affected by the Wars of the French Revolution and Napoleon, 1793–1812*. Philadelphia, 1932
Carl Marie von Clausewitz, *On War*. Peter Paret and Michael Howard (eds). Princeton, 1976
Hamilton Cochrane, *Blockade Runners of the Confederacy*. Indianapolis, 1958
Sir Julian S. Corbett, *England in the Seven Years War: A Study in Combined Strategy*. London, 2 vols, 1907
Some Principles of Maritime Strategy. Old Woking, England (reprint), 1972
Anthony H. Cordesman, *The Gulf and the West, Strategic Relations and Military Realities*. Boulder, 1988

Richard H. Cox, *Locke on War and Peace*. Oxford, 1960
Patrick Crowhurst, *The Defence of British Trade 1689–1815*. Folkstone, England, 1977
George Dalzell, *The Flight From the Flag*. Chapel Hill, N. Carolina, 1940
H. W. Carless Davis, *History of the Blockade. Emergency Departments*. London, 1920
Ralph Davis, *The Rise of the English Shipping Industry*. London, 1962
David Donald, with Richard N. Current, T. Harry Williams, Norman A. Graebner and David M. Potter, *Why the North Won the Civil War*. Louisiana, 1973
Martin Doughty, *Merchant Shipping and War*. London, 1982
M. P. Doxey, *International Sanctions and International Enforcement*. London, 1971
H. Duncan Hall, *North American Supply*. London, 1955
W. J. Ecles, *Canada under Louis XIV, 1663–1701*. London, 1964
Jill Edwards, *The British Government and the Spanish Civil War, 1936–1939*. London, 1979
John Ehrman, *The Navy in the War of William III 1689–1697*. Cambridge, 1953
Goffrey Ellis, *Napoleon's Continental Blockade*. Oxford, 1981
Marjorie Milbank Farrar, *Conflict and Compromise, The Strategy, Politics and Diplomacy of the French Blockade, 1914–1918*. The Hague, 1974
C. Ernest Fayle, *The War and the Shipping Industry*. London, 1927
Seaborne Trade. 3 vols, London, 1920–24
Philip S. Foner, *British Labour and The American Civil War*. New York, 1981
W. Freeman Gilpin, *The Grain Supply of England During the Napoleonic Period*. New York, 1925
David French, *British Economic and Strategic Planning 1905–1915*. London, 1982
Richard N. Gardner, *Sterling–Dollar Diplomacy, Anglo–American Collaboration in the Reconstruction of Multilateral Trade*. Oxford, 1956
J. W. Garner, *Prize Law During the World War*. New York, 1927
General Council of British Shipping, *Guidance Notes for Owners and Masters with vessels in the Arabian Gulf, Confidential*. London, 1 October 1985; and February 1987
Guidance Notes on the Protection of Shipping against Terrorism and Sabotage, In Confidence. London, August 1986
R. H. Gibson and Maurice Prendergast, *The German Submarine War*. London, 1931
S. G. Gorshkov, *The Sea Power of the State*. Oxford, 1979
Dominic Graham and Shelford Bidwell, *Firepower*. London, 1982
Gerald S. Graham, *The Politics of Naval Supremacy*. London, 1965
William D. Grampp, *The Manchester School of Economics*. Stanford, 1960
Robert M. Grant, *U-boat Intelligence*. London, 1969
Leo Grebler and Wilhelm Winkler, *The Cost of the World War to Germany and to Austria Hungary*. New Haven, USA, 1940
Sir Edward Grey, *Twenty-Five Years, 1892–1916*. 2 vols, New York, 1925
Sir Peter Gretton, *Former Naval Person*. London, 1968

Hugo Grotius, *The Rights of War and Peace*. A. C. Campbell (ed.), New York, 1901
De Jure Belli Ac Pacis. [Francis W. Kelsey Translation, Introduction by James Brown Scott], New York and London, 1964
Louis Guichard, *The Naval Blockade 1914–1918*. London, 1930
John Francis Guilmartin, *Gunpowder and Galleys*. Cambridge, 1974
J. M. A. Gwyer, *Grand Strategy*, vol. III. London, 1964
R. J. Hammond, *Food*, vol. 1. London, 1951
W. K. Hancock and M. M. Gowing, *British War Economy*. London, 1949
Lord Hankey, *The Supreme Command*. 2 vols, London, 1961
Gerd Hardach, *The First World War*. London, 1977
D. Hargraves and S. Fromson, *World Index of Strategic Minerals*. Aldershot, UK, 1983
Lawrence A. Harper, *The English Navigation Laws*. New York, 1964
John B. Hattendorf, *England in the War of the Spanish Succession, A Study in the English View and Conduct of Grand Strategy, 1701–1713*. 1987
and Robert S. Jordan (eds), *Maritime Strategy and the Balance of Power, Britain and America in the Twentieth Century*. London, 1989
E. F. Hecksher, *The Continental System*. Oxford, 1923
Mercantilism. [Translator, M. Shapiro], 2 vols, London, 1931
Holger H. Herwig, *Germany's Vision of Empire in Venezuela, 1871–1914*. Princeton, 1986
L. M. Hill, *Bench and Bureaucracy*. Stanford, 1988
F. T. Hinsley, *British Intelligence in the Second World War*. 3 vols, Cambridge, 1979
Albert E. Hogan, *Pacific Blockade*. London, 1908
Daniel Horn, *The German Naval Mutinies of World War I*. New Brunswick, USA, 1969
Michael Howard, *The Continental Commitment*. London, 1972
Grand Strategy, August 1942–Sept. 1943, vol. V. London, 1972
War and the Liberal Conscience. Oxford, 1981
Jonathan Trumbull Howe, *Multicrisis*. Cambridge, Mass., 1971
Barry D. Hunt, *Sailor-Scholar, Admiral Sir Herbert Richmond 1871–1946*. Waterloo, Canada, 1982
Archibald Hurd, *The Merchant Navy*. 3 vols. London, 1921
Samuel J. Hurwitz, *State Intervention in Great Britain, A Study of Economic Control and Social Response, 1914–1919*. New York, 1949 and 1968
Jonathan I. Israel, *The Dutch Republic and the Hispanic World, 1606–1661*. Oxford, 1982
Walter Wilson Jennings, *The American Embargo, 1807–1809*. University of Iowa Studies in Social Science, Vol. 8, No. 1, Iowa City, 1921
Philip C. Jessup and Francis Deak, *Neutrality, its History, Economics and Law*. 4 vols, New York, 1935
Ellis A. Johnson and David A. Katcher, *Mines against Japan*. US Gov. Printing Office, 1973
Efraim Karsh, *The Iran–Iraq War: A Military Analysis*. Adelphi Papers #220, London, 1987
Robert W. Kenney, *Elizabeth's Admiral*. Baltimore, 1970

Peter Kemp, *Prize Money*. Aldershot, 1946
Malcolm D. Kennedy, *The Estrangement of Great Britain and Japan, 1917–35*. Manchester, 1969
Paul Kennedy, *The Rise and Fall of British Naval Mastery*. London, 1976
H. S. K. Kent, *War and Trade in Northern Seas*. Cambridge, 1973
Marian Kent, *Oil & Empire*. London, 1976
W. F. Kimball, *The Most Unsordid Act, Lend-Lease 1939–41*. Baltimore, 1969
David Kinley, *Influence of the Great War upon Shipping*. New York, 1919
Bernard Knollenberg, *Growth of the American Revolution 1766–1775*. New York, 1975
W. Knappman (ed.), *South Vietnam, U.S.–Communist Confrontation in Southeast Asia 1972–1973*, Vol. 7. New York, 1973
Dudley W. Knox, *A History of the United States Navy*. New York, 1936
Charles W. Koburger, Jr., *Sea Power in the Falklands*. New York, 1983
Carl J. Kulsrud, *Maritime Neutrality to 1780*. Boston, 1936
Frederic C. Lane, *Ships for Victory, A History of Shipbuilding Under the U.S. Maritime Commission in World War II*. Baltimore, 1951
Agnes M. C. Latham, *Sir Walter Raleigh*. London, 1964
Norbert Laude, *La Compagnie d'Ostende et son activité coloniale au Bengale 1725–30*. Bruxelles, 1944
Richard M. Leighton and Robert W. Coakley, *Global Logistics and Strategy 1940–1943*. Washington, 1955
James R. Leutze, *Bargaining for Supremacy, Anglo–American Naval Collaboration 1937–41*. Chapel Hill N.C., 1977
Arthur S. Link, *Wilson Campaigns for Progressivism and Peace 1916–1917*. 4 vols, Princeton, 1965
Christopher Lloyd, *Lord Cochrane*. London, 1947
E. M. H. Lloyd, *Experiments in State Control at the War Office and the Ministry of Food*. Oxford, 1924
David Lloyd George, *The Truth about the Peace Treaties*. 2 vols, London, 1938
Peter Lowe, *Great Britain and the Origins of the Pacific War*. Oxford, 1977
Edward N. Luttwak, *The Political Uses of Seapower*. Baltimore, 1974
Ralph Haswell Lutz, *Fall of the German Empire*. 2 vols, New York, 1969
Ian MacGibbon, *Blue-Water Rationale, The Naval Defence of New Zealand, 1914–1942*. Government Printer, Wellington, NZ, 1981
Piers Mackesy, *The War for America, 1775–1783*. London, 1964
Isabela de Madariaga, *Britain, Russia and the Armed Neutrality of 1780*. London, 1962
Alfred Thayor Mahan, *The Influence of Sea Power upon History*. Boston, 1895
Sea Power in its Relations to the War of 1812. 2 vols, London, 1905
From Sail to Steam. New York, 1968
Pauline Maier, *Resistance to Revolution*. New York, 1972
W. T. Mallison, Naval War College International Law Studies 1966, *Studies in the Law of Naval Warfare: Submarines in General and Limited Wars*. Washington, 1968

Arthur J. Marder, *The Anatomy of British Sea Power: a history of British Naval Policy in the Pre-Dreadnought Era, 1880–1905*. Hamden, Conn., 1964
From the Dreadnought to Scapa Floe. 5 vols, London, 1961–70
George Martelli, *Italy Against the World*. Newport, R.I., 1978
Kenneth R. McGruther, *The Evolving Soviet Navy*. Newport, R.I., 1978
Michael MccGwire, Ken Booth, and John McDonnell (eds), *Soviet Naval Policy*. New York, 1974
Frank L. McVey, *The Financial History of Great Britain 1914–1918*. New York, 1918
W. N. Medlicott, *The Economic Blockade*. 2 vols, London, 1952
Samuel Pyeatt Menefee, International Maritime Bureau, *A Third Report Into the Incidence of Piracy and Armed Robbery from Merchant Ships*. USA, October 1985
Frank J. Merli, *Great Britain and the Confederate Navy, 1861–1865*, Bloomington, Indiana University Press, 1970
Jean Meyer, *Armement Nantais Dans la deuxième moitié du XVIIIe Siècle*. Paris, 1969
Roger Bigelow Merriman, *The Rise of the Spanish Empire*. New York, 1918–34
Alan S. Milward, *War, Economy and Society*. London, 1978
A. M. Morrissey, *The American Defense of Neutral Rights, 1914–1917*. Cambridge, Mass., 1939
T. H. Vail Motter, *The Persian Corridor and Aid to Russia*. Washington, 1952
Thomas Mun, *England's Treasure by Forraign Trade*. Oxford, 1949 (reprint of 1664 edn)
John F. Naylor, *A Man and an Institution, Sir Maurice Hankey, the Cabinet Secretariat and the Custody of Cabinet Secrecy*. Cambridge, 1984
James Neidpath, *The Singapore Naval Base and the Defence of Britain's Eastern Empire, 1919–1941*. Oxford, 1981
Paul H. Nitze, Leonard Sullivan Jr., and the Atlantic Council Working Group, *Securing the Seas*. Colorado, 1979
D. P. O'Connell, *International Law*. London, 1970
The Influence of Law on Seapower. Manchester, 1975
The International Law of the Sea. Oxford, 1984
M. Oppenheim (ed.), *The Naval Tracts of Sir William Monson*. 5 vols, London, 1892
Mancur Olson, Jr., *The Economics of the Wartime Shortage*. Durham, N.C., 1963
Nils Orvik, *The Decline of Neutrality 1914–1941*. London, 1971
J. H. Owen, *War at Sea Under Queen Anne, 1702–1708*. Cambridge, 1938
F. L. Owsley, *King Cotton Diplomacy*. Chicago, 1969
H. M. Pachter, *Collision Course*. New York, 1963
Peter Padfield, *Donitz, The Last Fuhrer*. London, 1984
R. Pares, *Colonial Blockade and Neutral Rights, 1739–1763*. Oxford, 1938
War and Trade in the West Indies 1739–63. London, 1963
N. G. Parker, *The Army of Flanders and the Spanish Road, 1567–1659*. Cambridge, 1972

C. R. Pennell, '*Piracy and Diplomacy in Seventeenth Century North Africa: The Diary of Thomas Baker, English Consul in Tripoli 1679–1685*. (read in manuscript, 1985)
Lord Eustace Percy, *Maritime Trade in War*. Oxford, 1930
W. Alison Phillips and Arthur H. Reede, *Neutrality*. Vol. II, 'The Napoleonic Period', New York, 1936
Sir Francis Piggott, *The Declaration of Paris 1856*. London, 1919
Gareth Porter, *A Peace Denied*. Bloomington, 1975
Thomas F. Power Jr., *Jules Ferry and the Renaissance of French Imperialism*. New York, 1966
Lawrence E. Pratt, *East of Malta, West of Suez: Britain's Mediterranean Crisis 1936–1939*. Cambridge, 1975
James Pritchard, *Louis XV's Navy 1748–1762, A Study of Organization and Administration*. Kingston and Montreal, 1987
John H. Pryor, *Geography, Technology and War. Studies in the Maritime History of the Mediterranean, 649–1571*. Cambridge, 1988
Philip Pugh, *The Cost of Seapower*. London, 1986
Sir Walter Raleigh, 'Of a war with Spain, and our Protecting the Netherlands', in *Three Discourses of Sir Walter Raleigh*. London, 1702
Armin Rappaport, *The Navy League of the United States*. Detroit, 1962
The British Press and Wilsonian Neutrality. Gloucester, Mass., 1965
Lord George Alyerdice Riddell, *Intimate Diary of the Peace Conference and After 1918–1923*. London, 1933
James C. Riley, *The Seven Years War and the Old Regime in France, The Economic and Financial Toll*. Princeton, 1986
Olav Riste, *The Neutral Ally, Norway's Relations with Belligerent Powers in the First World War*. Oslo and London, 1965
H. Ritchie, *The 'Navicert' System During the World War*. Washington, 1938
Sir Herbert W. Richmond, *Economy and Naval Security*. London, 1931
Imperial Defence and Capture at Sea in War. London, 1932
Sea Power in the Modern World. London, 1934
The Navy as an Instrument of Policy. Cambridge, 1953
Theodore Ropp (ed. Stephen S. Roberts), *The Development of a Modern Navy, French Naval Policy 1871–1904*. Annapolis, Maryland, 1987
E. S. Roscoe, *A History of the English Prize Court*. London, 1924
Studies in the History of the Admiralty and Prize Courts. London, 1932
Stephen W. Roskill, *The War at Sea*. 3 vols, London, 1954–61
Naval Policy Between the Wars. 2 vols, London, 1968
Jeffrey J. Safford, *Wilsonian Maritime Diplomacy 1913–1921*. New Brunswick, USA
J. A. Salter, *Allied Shipping Control. An Experiment in International Administration*. Oxford, 1921
Carlton Savage, *Policy of the United States Toward Maritime Commerce in War*, Vol. I, Washington, 1934
Bernadotte E. Schmitt and Harold C. Vedeler, *The World in the Crucible*. New York, 1984
Donald M. Schurman, *The Education of a Navy*. London, 1965.
Julian S. Corbett, 1854–1922. London, 1981
Robert Livingston Schuyler, *Fall of the Old Colonial System*. London, 1945

James Brown Scott (ed.), *The Declaration of London February 26, 1909, A Collection of Official Papers*. New York, 1919

Louis Martin Sears, *Jefferson and the Embargo*. New York, 1978.

Bernard Semmel, *Liberalism and Naval Strategy, Ideology, Interest, and Sea Power During the Pax Britanica*. Boston, 1986

John M. Sherwig, *Guineas and Gunpowder, British Foreign Aid in the Wars with France 1793–1815*. Cambridge, Mass., 1969

Marion C. Siney, *The Allied Blockade of Germany 1914–1916*. Ann Arbour, 1957

Rear Admiral William Sowden Sims, *The Victory at Sea*. Annapolis, Maryland, 1984 (first printed 1920)

Daniel M. Smith, *Robert Lansing and American Neutrality 1914–1917*. New York, 1972

J. R. Soley, *The Navy in the Civil War*. London, 1898

Harold and Margaret Sprout, *Toward a New Order of Sea Power*. Princeton, 1940

Francis R. Stark, *The Abolition of Privateering and the Declaration of Paris*. New York, 1967 (reprint of 1897 edn)

Lucy S. Sutherland, *A London Merchant, 1695–1774*. Oxford, 1962

Geoffrey Symcox, *The Crisis of French Sea Power 1688–1697*. The Hague, 1974

Craig L. Symonds (ed.), *New Aspects of Naval History, Selected Papers Presented at the Fourth Naval History Symposium, United States Naval Academy, 25–26 October 1979*. Annapolis, Maryland, 1981

David Syrett, *Shipping and the American War, 1775–83. A Study of British Transport Organization*. London, 1970

Jonathan Swift, *Political Tracts 1711–1713* (Herbert Davis, ed.), s.v., 'The Conduct of the Allies', November 1711. Oxford, 1951

H. W. V. Temperley, *A History of the Peace Conference of Paris*. London, 1920

Alberto Tenenti, *Piracy & The Decline of Venice 1580–1615*. [Translated by Janet and Brian Pullan]. London, 1967

Geoffrey Till, *Maritime Strategy and the Nuclear Age*. London, 1984

Seth P. Tillman, *Anglo–American Relations at the Paris Peace Conference of 1919*. Princeton, 1961

Hugh Thomas, *The Spanish Civil War*. New York, 1977

A. Thomazi, *La Conquête de L'Indochine*. Paris, 1934

Christopher Thorne, *Allies of a Kind, The United States, Britain and the war against Japan, 1941–1945*. London, 1978

John Toland, *The Rising Sun*. New York, 1979

Nicholas Tracy, *Navies, Deterrence and American Independence*. Vancouver, 1988

Manila Ransomed, manuscript, 1988

David F. Trask, *Captains & Cabinets, Anglo–American Naval Relations, 1917–1918*. Columbia, Missouri, 1972

R. W. Tucker, *The Laws of War and Neutrality at Sea*. Washington, 1957

Edgar Turlington, *Neutrality*, Vol. III. New York, 1936

United States, *Strategic Bombing Survey*. New York, 1976, vol. IX, 'The War Against Japanese Transportation, 1941–1945 (Pacific Report 55)'

Frank E. Vadiver, *Confederate Blockade Running Through Bermuda 1851–1865, Letters and Cargo Manifests*. Austin, 1947

Chanoine Victor Verlaque, *Histoire du Cardinal de Fleury et de son Administration*. Paris, 1878

M. Vlahos, *The Blue Sword: The Naval War College and the American Mission 1919–1941*. Newport, 1980.

J. M. Wallace-Hadrill, *The Barbarian West*. London, 1952

James A. Williamson, *Hawkins of Plymouth*. London, 1953

C. H. Wilson, *Profit and Power: A Study of England and the Dutch Wars*. London, 1957

S. Woodburn Kirby, *The War Against Japan*, vol. 5. London, 1969

Charles Wright and Charles Ernest Fayle, *History of Lloyds*. London, 1928

Z. A. B. Zeman, *A Diplomatic History of the First World War*. London, 1971

ARTICLES

Unattributed, 'The Nyon Arrangements – Piracy by Treaty?', *British Yearbook of International Law*, 19 (1938), pp. 198–208

David Aldridge, 'Swedish Privateering, 1710–1718 and the Reactions of Great Britain and the United Provinces', in *Commission Internationale d'Histoire Maritime. Course et Piraterie* . . . Paris, *Institut de Recherche et d'Histoire de Textes Editions du Centre National de la Recherche Scientifique*, 1975, pp. 416–40

Olive Anderson, 'Economic Warfare in the Crimean War', *Economic History Review* XIV (1961), pp. 34–47

Daniel A. Baugh, 'Great Britain's "Blue-Water" Policy, 1689–1815', *International History Review*, X (February 1988), Number 1, pp. 33–58

Paul Walden Bamford, 'French Shipping in Northern European Trade, 1660–1789', *The Journal of Modern History*, 26 (1954), pp. 201–219

John S. Bromley, 'The French Privateering War, 1702–13', in *Historical Essays 1600–1750 presented to David Ogg*. [N. E. Bell and Q. L. Ollard, eds], London, 1963, pp. 203–31

'The Jacobite Privateers in the Nine Years War', in *Statesmen, Scholars and Merchants, Essays in Eighteenth-Century History presented to Dame Lucy Sutherland*. [Anne Whiteman, J. S. Bromley, and P. G. M. Dickson, eds]. Oxford, 1973

Alice Clare Carter, 'How to revise treaties without negotiating: common sense, mutual fears and the Anglo–Dutch trade disputes of 1759', in *Studies in Diplomatic History* (eds R. M. Hatton and M. S. Anderson). Hamden, Conn., 1970

Edward P. Cheyney, 'International Law under Queen Elizabeth', *English Historical Review*, 20 (1905), p. 659–72

Carlo Q. Christol and Charles R. Davis, 'Maritime Quarantine: The Naval Interdiction of Offensive Weapons and Associated Materiel to Cuba, 1962', *The American Journal of International Law*, 57 (1963), pp. 525–45

G. N. Clark, 'Neutral Commerce in the War of the Spanish Succession and the Treaty of Utrecht', *British Yearbook of International Law*, 9 (1928), p. 69

Patrick Crowhurst, 'Bayonne Privateering 1744–1763', in *Commission Internationale d'Histoire Maritime. Course et Piraterie* .. Paris, *Institut de Recherche et d'Histoire de Textes Editions du Centre National de la Recherche Scientifique*, 1975, pp. 453–68

François Crouzet, 'Wars, Blockade, and Economic Change in Europe, 1792–1815', *Journal of Economic History*, 24 (1964), pp. 567–88

C. P. Crowhurst, 'The Admiralty and the Convoy System in the Seven Years War', *The Mariners Mirror*, Vol. 57 (1971), pp. 163–73

Ralph Davis, 'English Foreign Trade, 1660–1700', and 'English Foreign Trade, 1700–1774', in *The Growth of English Overseas Trade* (W. E. Minchinton, ed.), London, 1969; and *Economic History Review*, series 2, 6, number 2 (1954), pp. 150–66, and 15 number 2 (1962), pp. 285–303

P. E. Dewey, 'Food Production and Policy in the United Kingdom, 1914–1918', *Transactions of the Royal Historical Society*, series V, 30 (1980), p. 71

Colin Elliott, 'Some Transactions of a Dartmouth Privateer During the French Wars at the End of the Eighteenth Century', in *Studies in British Privateering, Trading Enterprise and Seamen's Welfare, 1775–1900* (Stephen Fisher, ed.) Exeter, 1987

David Evans and Richard Campany, 'Iran–Iraq: Bloody Tomorrows', US Naval Institute *Proceedings*, Jan. 1958, pp. 33–43

Ernest Fayle, 'Shipowning and Marine Insurance', in *The Trade Winds* (C. Northcote Parkinson, ed.), London, 1948

G. G. Fitzmaurice, 'Some Aspects of Modern Contraband Control and the Law of Prize', *British Yearbook of International Law*, 22 (1945), pp. 73–95

C. J. Ford, 'Piracy or Policy: the Crisis in the Channel, 1400–1403', *Royal Historical Society Transactions*, series 5, 29 (1979), pp. 63–78

Norman Friedman, 'World Naval Developments', US Naval Institute *Proceedings*, 114/8/1,026 (August 1988), p. 123

M. G. Fry, 'The imperial war cabinet, the United States, and the freedom of the seas', *Journal of the Royal United Service Institute*, 110 (1965), pp. 353–62

James W. Garner, 'The United States "Neutrality" Law of 1937', *British Yearbook of International Law*, 19 (1938), pp. 44–66

W. F. Gilpin, 'The American Grain Trade to the Spanish Peninsula 1810–14', *American Historical Review*, 28 (1922), pp. 22–44

Richard Glover, 'The French Fleet, 1807–1814; Britain's Problem; and Madison's Opportunity', *The Journal of Modern History*, 33, (1961), pp. 407–22

Norman A. Graeber, 'Japan, Unanswered Challenge, 1931–41', in M. F. Morris and S. L. Myres (eds), *Essays on American Foreign Policy*, Austin, Texas, 1974

Peter Gretton, 'The Nyon Conference – the naval aspects', *English Historical Review*, 90 (1975), pp. 103–12

'The U-boat Campaign in Two World Wars', in *Naval Warfare in the Twentieth Century 1900–1945, Essays in honour of Arthur Marder* (Gerald Jordan, ed.). London, 1977

Paul Haggie, 'The Royal Navy and War Planning in the Fisher Era', *Journal of Contemporary History*, 8, no. 3 (July 1973), pp. 113–31
J. M. Haight, 'Franklin D. Roosevelt and a naval quarantine of Japan', *Pacific Historical Review*, 40 (May 1971), pp. 203–56
C. I. Hamilton, 'Anglo–French Seapower and the Declaration of Paris', *The International History Review*, iv, no. 1 (February 1982), pp. 166–90
C. E. Harvey, 'Politics and Pyrites during the Spanish Civil War', *Economic History Review*, series 2, 31 (1978), pp. 89–104
Holger H. Herwig, 'Prelude to *Weltblitzkrieg*: Germany's Naval Policy Towards the United States of America, 1939–41', *The Journal of Modern History*, 43 (1971), pp. 649–68
'The Failure of German Sea Power, 1914–1945: Mahan, Tirpitz, and Raeder Reconsidered', *International History Review*, Vol. X (February 1988), Number 1, pp. 68–105
J. H. Herzog, 'Influence of the United States Navy in the Embargo of Oil to Japan 1940–1941', *Pacific Historical Review*, 35, pp. 317–28, Aug. 1966
John G. Hibbits, 'Admiral Gorshkov's Writings: Twenty Years of Naval Thought', in Paul J. Murphy (ed.), *Naval Power in Soviet Policy*, Studies in Communist Affairs, Vol. 2, United States Air Force, 1978
A. Pearce Higgins, 'Retaliation in Naval Warfare', *British Yearbook of International Law*, 1927, p. 129
P. S. Holbo, 'Perilous Obscurity: Public Diplomacy and the Press in the Venezuelan Crisis, 1902–1903', *The Historian*, 32 (May 1970), pp. 428–48
J. R. T. Hughes, Review Article, 'Financing the British War Effort', of R. S. Sayers, *Financial Policy, 1939–45*, London, 1956; *Journal of Economic History*, XVIII, pp. 193–9, 1958
Barry D. Hunt, 'Of Bits and Bridles: Sea Power and Arms Control Prior to World War II', paper given to the conference on Naval Arms Limitations and Maritime Security, Halifax N.S., June 1990.
James A. Huston, 'Allied Blockade of Germany 1918–19', *Journal of Central European Affairs*, 10 (1950), pp. 145–66
J. I. Israel, 'A Conflict of Empire: Spain and the Netherlands 1618–1648', *Past and Present*, Number 76 (August 1977), pp. 34–74
A. H. John, 'War and the English Economy, 1700–1763', *The Economic History Review*, 7 (1954–55), pp. 329–44
'The London Assurance Company and the Marine Insurance Market of the Eighteenth Century', *Economica*, 15 (1958), pp. 126–41
J. A. Johnson, 'Parliament and the Protection of Trade 1689–1694', *The Mariners Mirror*, Vol. 57 (1971), pp. 399–413
L. H. Johnson, 'Commerce between Northeastern ports and the Confederacy', *Journal of American History*, 54 (1967), p. 30–42
J. R. Jones, 'The Dutch Navy and National Survival in the Seventeenth Century', *International History Review*, 10, number 1 (February 1988), pp. 18–32
Henry Kamen, 'The Destruction of the Spanish Silver Fleet at Vigo in 1702', *Bulletin of The Institute of Historical Research*, 39 (1966), pp. 165–73
Paul M. Kennedy, 'The development of German Naval Operations Plans against England, 1895–1914', *English Historical Review*, 89 (1974), pp. 48–76

Jacob W. Kipp, 'Russian Naval Reforms and Imperial Expansion, 1856–1863', in *Soviet Armed Forces Review*, 1 (1977), p. 118

Joseph L. Kunz, 'British Prize Cases, 1939–41', *The American Journal of International Law*, 36 (1942), pp. 204–28

Stanley Lebergott, 'Through the Blockade: The Profitability and Extent of Cotton Smuggling, 1861–1865', *Journal of Economic History*, 41 (1981), p. 867–88

Howard S. Levie, 'The Nature and Scope of the Armistice Agreement', *American Journal of International Law*, 50 (1956), pp. 885–6

D. J. Llewelyn Davies, 'Enemy Property and Ultimate Destination During the Anglo–Dutch Wars 1664–7 and 1672–4', *British Yearbook of International Law* 15 (1934), pp. 21–35

James G. Lydon, 'Privateering becomes a Business: New York in Mid-Eighteenth Century', in *Commission Internationale d'Histoire Maritime. Course et Piraterie* . . Paris, *Institut de Recherche et d'Histoire de Textes Editions du Centre National de la Recherche Scientifique*, 1975, pp. 487–510

Wesley L. McDonald, 'The Convoy Mission', US Naval Institute *Proceedings*, 114/5/1033 (May 1988), pp. 36–44

Mike MccGwire, 'The Submarine Threat to Western Shipping', Paper 23, II, 1969

James F. McNulty, 'Blockade: Evolution and Expectation', United States Naval War College International Law Studies 62, *The Use of Force, Human Rights and General International Legal Issues* (Richard B. Lillich and John Norton Moore, eds), Newport, 1980, p. 172.

W. H. Malkin, 'Blockade in Modern Conditions', *British Yearbook of International Law* 3 (1922–23), pp. 87–98

'The Inner History of the Declaration of Paris', *British Yearbook of International Law* 8 (1927), pp. 1–44

Arthur Marsden, 'The Blockade', in F. H. Hinsley, British Foreign Policy under Sir Edward Grey. Cambridge, 1977

Gaston Martin, 'Commercial Relations between Nantes and the American Colonies during the War of Independence', *Journal of Economic and Business History*, 4 (1932), pp. 812–29

W. R. Mayer, 'English Privateering in the War of 1688 to 1697', *The Mariners Mirror*, 67, no. 3 (1981), pp. 259–72

William O. Miller, 'Belligerency and Limited War', United States Naval War College International Law Studies 62, *The Use of Force, Human Rights and General International Legal Issues* (Richard B. Lillich and John Norton Moore, eds), Newport, 1980, p. 164

O. H. Mootham, 'The Doctrine of Continuous Voyage, 1756–1815', *British Yearbook of International Law* 8 (1927), pp. 62–80

Ronald O'Rourke, 'The Tanker War', US Naval Institute *Proceedings*, 114/5/1033 (May 1988), pp. 30–4

E. B. Parsons, 'German–American Crisis of 1902–1903', *The Historian*, 33 (May 1971), pp. 436–52

C. R. Pennell, 'Tripoli in the Late Seventeenth Century: The Economics of Corsairing in a "Sterill Country"', *Libyan Studies*, 16 (1985), pp. 101–12

Marcus Price, 'Ships that Tested the Blockade . . .', *The American Neptune*, 8 (1948), pp. 196–241, 11 (1951), pp. 262–90 and 15 (1956), pp. 97–132

James S. Pritchard, 'The Pattern of French Colonial Shipping to Canada before 1760', *Revue Française d'Histoire d'Outre-Mer*, 63, no. 231 (1976)

P. G. Pugh, 'The Battle of the Atlantic: analysis of its economics', manuscript, 1988

Bryan Ranft, 'Restraints on War at Sea before 1945', in *Restraints on War* (Michael Howard, ed.). Oxford, 1969

'The Protection of British Seaborne Trade and the Development of Systematic Planning for War, 1860–1906', in *Technical Change and British Naval Policy* (Bryan Ranft, ed.). London, 1977

Conyers Read, 'More Light on the London Naval Treaty of 1930', *Proceedings of the American Philosophical Society*, vol. 93 (1949), p. 290

S. W. D. Rowson, 'Italian Prize Law, 1940–1943', *British Yearbook of International Law* 23 (1946), pp. 282–302

'Prize Law During the Second World War', *British Yearbook of International Law* 24 (1947), pp. 160–215

A. N. Ryan, 'The Defence of British Trade with the Baltic, 1808–1813', *English Historical Review*, 74 (1959), p. 443

'Trade with the Enemy in the Scandinavian and Baltic Ports during the Napoleonic War: for and against', *Transactions of the Royal Historical Society*, series V, 12 (1962), p. 123

Patrick Salmon, 'Churchill, the Admiralty and the Narvik Traffic, September–November 1939', *Scandinavian Journal of History*, 4 (1979), pp. 305–26

'British Plans for Economic Warfare against Germany 1937–1939: The Problem of Swedish Iron Ore', *Journal of Contemporary History*, 16 (1981), pp. 53–71

Frank C. Seitz, 'SS Bridgeton: the First Convoy', USNI *Proceedings*, 114/5/1033 (May 1988), pp. 52–7

Marion C. Siney, 'British Negotiations with American Meat Packers, 1915–1917: A Study of Belligerent Trade Controls', *The Journal of Modern History*, 23 (1951), pp. 343–53

Ronald Spector, 'Roosevelt, the Navy and the Venezuelan Controversy: 1902–1903', *The American Neptune*, 32 (Oct. 1972), pp. 257–63

Warren F. Spencer, 'The Mason Memorandum and the Diplomatic Origins of The Declaration of Paris', in Nancy N. Barker and Marvin L. Brown, *Diplomacy in An Age of Nationalism*, The Hague, 1971

David Starkey, 'British Privateering Against the Dutch in the American Revolutionary War, 1780–1783', in *Studies in British Privateering, Trading Enterprise and Seamen's Welfare, 1775–1900* (Stephen Fisher, ed.). Exeter, 1987

O. W. Stephenson, 'The Supply of Gunpower in 1776', *American Historical Review*, XXX (1925), pp. 271–81

C. H. Stockton, 'Would Immunity from Capture, During War, of Non-Offending Private Property Upon the High Seas be in the Interest of Civilization?', *American Journal of International Law*, 1 (1907), pp. 930–43

'The International Naval Conference of London, 1908–1909', *The American Journal of International Law*, 3 (1909), pp. 596–618

Geoffrey Symcox, 'Admiral Mahan, the *Jeune Ecole*, and the *Guerre de*

Course', in *Commission Internationale d'Histoire Maritime. Course et Piraterie . .* Paris, *Institut de Recherche et d'Histoire de Textes Editions du Centre National de la Recherche Scientifique*, 1975, pp. 676–701

Walter R. Thomas, 'Pacific Blockade: A Lost Opportunity of the 1930's?', *United States Naval War College International Law Studies*, (Richard B. Lillich and John Norton Moore eds). Newport, 1980

Nicholas Tracy, 'The Diplomatic Utility of Canada's Naval Forces', ORAE Report No. R60, July 1976, Canada, Department of National Defence

David F. Trask, 'The American Navy in a World at War, 1914–1919', in Kenneth J. Hagan (ed.), *In Peace and War*, pp. 207–8, Westport, Connecticut, 1978.

Peter H. Vigor, 'Soviet Understanding of "Command of the Sea"', in Michael MccGwire, Ken Booth, and John McDonnell (eds), *Soviet Naval Policy*, New York, 1974, pp. 601–22

Michael Vlahos, 'The Stark Report', US Naval Institute *Proceedings*, 114/5/1033 (May 1988), pp. 64–7

Marshal Le Prestre Vauban, 'Mémoire sur la Caprerie', 30 Nov. 1695; in Rochas D'Aiglun, *Vauban. Sa Famille et ses écrits. Ses oisivets et sa correspondance: analyse et extraits*, 2 vols, Paris-Grenoble, 1910

B. A. Wortley, 'Pirata Non Mutat Dominium', *British Yearbook of International Law* 24 (1947), pp. 258–72

Quincy Wright, 'The Cuban Quarantine', *The American Journal of International Law*, 57 (1963), pp. 547–65

TERTIARY SOURCES

Leon Friedman (ed.), *The Law of War*. New York, 1972

Peter Kemp, *The Oxford Companion to Ships and the Sea*. Oxford, 1976

D. Schindler and J. Toman (eds), *The Laws of Armed Conflicts*. Geneva, 1981

Georg Schwarzenburger and E. A. Brown, *A Manual of International Law*. 6th edn, Guildford, 1976

Max Sorensen (ed.), *Manual of Public International Law*. London, 1968

Index

Aachen, 38
Aberdeen, Earl of, 84
Acadia, 64
Non-intervention, 179
Adams, Charles F., 164
Adams, John Quincy, 82
Admiralty *see* navies, British
Africa, 30, 101, 124, 200
agriculture, 97, 170, 197
air, 179, 182, 189–90, 193, 197, 203, 205, 215, 218–19, 222, 225, 229–30
Algeria, 200
Alaska, 99
Alexander I, 72, 79
Alexander II, 87, 89
Alexandria, 177–8
Alexandretta, 61
Alps, 26
Amiens, 146, *see* treaties
amphibious operations, 2
Amsterdam, 46, 49
America, 20, 26, 46, 47, 57, 64, 71, 79–80, 83, 91, 99–100, 140, 143, 186–7 *see* United States
American Journal of International Law, 217
American Revolution, 40, 64, 67, 70, 76, 90
ancient régime, 64
Anderson, Sir John, 196
Anglo–Japanese alliance, 153, 156
Annam, 98–9
Anne I, 38, 56
Antwerp, 46
Arab, 222
Arabian Gulf, 194, 225–30
Araki, General Sadao, 181
arbitration, 100
Archangel, 194
aristocracy, 144
armateurs, *see* privateers
Armistice, 146–7, 153–5, 162
army, 2, 123–4, 134, 138, 143, 144, 145, 170, 188, 193, 200, 220
Asia Minor, 124
Assmann, Vice-Admiral Kurt, 192
Asquith, 25
atomic bomb, 192, 216, 240
Atlantic, 92, 156, 204–5
Aube, Admiral, 95
Austria–Hungary, 62, 69, 138, 144
Australia, 139
Avonmouth, 133

Balfour, Arthur, 162
Ballard, Captain G. A., 123
Baltic, 37–9, 41, 44, 53, 69, 73, 78
Baltimore, 78
Bandar Abbas, 225
banks, 71, 142, 167
bankruptcy, 27, 60, 136
Barbados, 54
Barcelona, 39, 180
Basque republic, 179–80
Bathurst, Lord, 75
battle, 97
battles: Beachy Head (1690), 35; Dogger Bank (1781), 69; Glorious First of June (1793), 74; Jutland (1916), 136, 138; La Hogue (1692), 19, 52; Trafalgar (1805), 72; Toulon (1744), 59; Waterloo (1815), 81; Ypres (1917), 141
battleships, 78, 95, 97, 99, 156
Bavaria, 144
Bayonne, 21
Beira, 222, 243
Belgium, 100, 102, 138, 147, 162
belligerent rights, *see* laws of war
Benelux, 167
Bengal, 198
Benson, Admiral, 154–5
Beresford, Admiral Lord, 96, 103
Bergen, 186

Berlin, 99, 102, 134, 137, 145, 188
Berlin Decree, 72–3
Bermuda, 92
Bethman-Hollweg, 129, 141
Bilbao, 178–9
Black List, 136, 141, 143, 187, 222
black market, 138
Black Sea, 85
Bletchley Park, 194–6, *see* intelligence *and* Enigma
Blenheim, 39
blitzkrieg, 186, 207
blockade, 85, 93–7, 123, 134–5, 137–8, 143, 187–90, 192, 232
  close, 102, 105, 124
  commodities, 143: ball-bearings, 127, 188; beef, 58; bread, 135; bullion, 71; cable, 128; chrome, 188; cinchona, 75; coal, 47, 98; copper, 125, 127; cotton, 75, 80–1, 91, 94, 124, 127, 133–5; explosives, 124; fibre, 187; flour, 78; food, 73–4, 76, 95, 101, 103–4, 125, 126, 130, 131–4, 138, 141, 143, 144, 146, 147–8, 179–81, 187, 196, 215, 236; forage, 82, 126; gold, 80, 129, 146; grain, 34, 36–8, 43, 52, 53, 73–5, 77, 80–1, 96, 130, 139, 140, 147; gunpowder, 25, 40; horses, 37; iron, 125, 134, 179, 181, 187–8; jute, 136; lard, 135; luxuries, 75; mail, 128, 143; meat, 126–7, 135, 147; money, 93, 96, 166–7; naval stores, 17, 34–7, 39, 66, 68–9; oil, 154, 176, 181–2, 187, 188, 190, 196, 221–2, 225, 227 (seeds, 136); pit props, 126; potatoes, 135; rice, 95, 98–9, 135; rubber, 187; rum, 56; silver, 26–7, 44, 61; steel, 182, 204; sugar, 56, 58, 78, 220; tin, 136; tobacco, 56, 66; victuals, 34, 43, 56, 77; wine, 56, 66; wool, 37; wolfram, 188
  commercial, 14, 15, 23, 26, 28, 36, 44, 47, 53, 54, 56, 67, 72–4, 78, 85, 88, 91, 96, 101, 181, 185-end *passim.*, 224
  contraband, 14, 16–17, 30–40, 68, 76, 94, 101–3, 124–7, 130–1, 134, 158, 164, 178, 180, 185–6, 203, 217–18, 220, 224; conditional, 103–4, 126, 186; free list, 103, 124, 125, 133, 224, 226, 240, 242
  distant, 124
  effective, 17, 41–2, 75, 78, 92, 179
  naval, 96
  pacific, 97–100, 176, 215, 217
  running, 92, 94, 101, 104
  self-, 76, 91–2
  see also Britain, government, Ministry of Blockade *and* Ministry of Economic Warfare
  and see bullionism, battleships, black list, bunker control, business, censorship, containment, convoy, cruisers, demonstration, distribution, embargo, entrepôt, escalation, exclusion zone, exports, free trade, granaries, insurance, laws of war, leaks, logistics, *Jeune Ecole*, mercantilism, Navicert, orders in council, panic, privateers, private property, purchasing, quarantine, rationing, relief, roads, ship (container), siege, smuggling, stockpile, submarines, total exclusion zone, *and* transaction books
Boer, 101
bombing, 4
bonds, 23
Bonsal, Philip, 220
Borah, Senator William, 161
Boston, 78, 160
bounty money, 21, 23
Bourbon, 61
Bourgois, Admiral, 95
Braund, William, 58
Brazil, 44

Brest, 39, 74
bribery, 34, 79
Britain, *passim.*, 239–40
government: Admiralty (*see* navies, British); Attorney General, 23; Board of Trade, 56, 75, 86, 127, 153; cabinet, 84, 86, 88, 123, 128, 147, 178, 223 (Secretary, 143, 162); Chancellor of the Exchequer, 162; Chiefs of Staff, 201–2; Committee of Imperial Defence, 96, 101, 102, 105, 123, 133 (sub-committees, 158–9, 161, 162, 176, 185); Commonwealth Secretary, 221; Defence Committee, 187; Director General of Economic Warfare, 166; Industrial Intelligence Centre, 185; High Court of Admiralty, 11, 15, 21, 33–4, 53, 66, 67; Joint Intelligence Committee, 188; Joint Planning Staff, 199; Lord Chancellor, 11, 66; Lord High Admiral, 11, 15–16; Lord President of the Council, 196; Lord Privy Seal, 197; Minister for League of Nations, 177; Ministry of Blockade, 25, 66, 135–6, 139, 185; Ministry of Economic Warfare, 167, 185, 187–8 (Intelligence Division, 185); Ministry of Food, 197; Ministry of Shipping, 197; Ministry of War Transport, 194–5 (Trade Division, 130); Foreign Office, 25, 101, 125–6, 130–2, 135, 136, 146, 161, 185 (Secretary, 161, 164); Privy Council, 11 (Judicial Committee, 132); Shipping Committee, 196–7; Shipping Controller, 139; Treasury, 26, 28, 56, 90, 128–9, 167, 186 (Committee of (1907), 96); War Cabinet, 140, 167, 187, 196–7, 200; War Committee, 134; War Operations Division – Trade Branch, 105, 130
House of Commons, 22, 28, 53, 73, 88, 91, 135, 163, 218 (*see* Horsefall Commission, 88); of Lords, 54, 88, 104 (Judicial Committee, 11)
National Maritime Board, 227
parliament, 16, 45, 61, 63, 78, 84, 95, 104–5: acts: 25 Edward III, 57; Prize (1649), 16; Navigation, 46, 50, 70, 83, 86, 240; Staple (1663), 50; Plantations Duties (1673), 50; *Ordonances de la Marine* (1681 and 1704), 33; Land Tax (1694), 53; 3, 4 Anne C. 14, 57; Cruisers (1708), 21–2, 54; Prize (1756), 16; Privateers (1759), 16, 23, 54, 66; Stamp, 76; Seizure of naval stores (1778), 68; Bank Restricting, 71; Foreign Enlistment, 98
proclamation, 5 August 1914, 127
Royal Commission on Food Supply in time of War, 96–7
British Commonwealth of Nations, 166
'British Navalism', 135
British Petroleum, 221
Brittany, 20–1
Broglie, Comte de, 59, 96
Bryan, William Jennings, 127, 137
budget, 128
bullionism, 25–30, 53
bunker control, 136, 143, 186
Burleigh, Lord, 31
Burma, 200, 203
business, 77, 83, 153, 220

Caesar, Sir Julius, Judge, 11
Cadiz, 27, 28
Calvanists, 44
Canada, 40, 64, 77–8, 89, 99, 166–8, 186, 217–18
government: Minister of National Defence, 217; Prime Minister, 217

Canary Islands, 28
Canton, 176
Cape of Good Hope, 200
capital, 24, 87
capitulation, 147
Cardwell, Viscount, 86
Caribbean, 99
Carleill, Christopher, 27
Carthagena, 56
Casement, Sir Roger, 137
Castile, 44–5
Castro, Fidel, 216
Catalonia, 44–5
Catherine II, 68
Cecil, Lord Robert, 135
censorship, 128, 143
Central Powers, 128, 145
Ceylon, 199
Chagra, 56
Chamberlain, Austen, 96, 161
Chamberlain, Neville, 182
Charles II of England, 48–9, 50
Charles II of Spain, 52
Charles IV, 30
Charles XII, 39
Chesapeake, 77–8
Chicago, 126–7
China, 98, 170, 176, 181–2, 185, 215, 219
christendom, 11, 14
Churchill, Winston, 124, 155, 162, 165, 186, 190, 192, 197, 199, 200–1
Ciano, Count N. G., 180
city corporations, 18
City of London, 123
civilians, 135, 145
Choiseul, Duc de, 39, 62, 64, 70
Clarendon, Lord, 84, 88
Clark, Sir George Sydenham, 101–2, 104
coalition, 128
Cobden, Richard, 91
Cochrane, Lord, 22
Colbert, Jean, 34, 49, 51
Coligny, Admiral, 26
college of commerce, 40
Colomb, J. C. B., 96
colonies, 148
committee of public safety, 91
conferences,
  Argonaut, 202
  Casablanca, 200
  General Disarmament Conference (1932), 164
  Geneva Conference, 160
  Hague Conference, 100–3; *see* treaties
  Imperial Conference (1930), 164
  London Naval Conference (1930), 163, 165
  Paris peace talks (1919), 153, 155–6, 219
  Washington conference, 156–7; *see* treaties, and United States
Constantinople, 24
consul, 92
Consulato del Mare, 13
containment, 89–90, 199–208
continental, 123, 126, 239
Continental Army, 40
Continental System, 70–82
convoy, 35, 37, 52, 66, 68–9, 73, 75, 77, 140–2, 193–4, 197–9, 205, 224–5, 228
Copenhagen, 41, 76, 126–7
corn laws, 83, *see* Britain, Acts, Navigation
cost, 205–7
Counter-Remonstrants, 44
Courbet, Admiral, 99
Croatia, 144
Cromwell, Oliver, 27, 28, 46–8, 177
Crowe, Eyre, 101–2, 126, 133, 154
cruiser, 96, 103–5, 135, 157, 160–1, 163, 182, 186
Cuba, 101, 216–18, 220, 241
customs, 43, 51, 72, 79, 81, 85, 99, 176

damages, 76
Daniels, Josephus, 156
Danzig, 85–6, 148
Dardanelles, 223
death, 144
debt, 71, 98–100
defensively armed, 141
de Gaulle, Charles, 218

demonstration, 175, 224
demurage, 131
Denmark, 34, 35, 40, 67, 68, 73, 75–7, 126, 131, 134, 139
depression, 154
Derby, Lord, 88
Desard, Lord, 123
deserters, 77, 93
destroyers, 157, 179, 180
deterrence, 226
Diefenbaker, John, 217
Dill, Field Marshall, 202
distribution, 141
dollar, 168–9
Donitz, Admiral Carl, 192–3, 196, 198, 203, 205
Don Pacifico, 98
Douhet, Guilio, 203
Dover, 40
Downs, 44
Drake, Sir Francis, 18, 31, 36
Drang nach Osten, 147
Drouyn de Lloys, 84
Ducos, Theodore, 85
Duncombe, William, 40
Dunkirk, 20, 28
Dutch East India Company, 13

East Indies, 14
Eden, Anthony, 176, 180, 182, 201
Eden, William, 70
Egypt, 200, 222, 223, 243
election, 162
Eilat, 222
Elizabeth I, 11, 16, 18, 26–7, 31, 32, 34
Elizabethan, 95
embargo, 39, 43, 78, 81, 91–2, 175, 182, 230
Enemy Branch, *see* Britain, government, Economic Warfare
English Channel, 26, 27, 29–30, 201
Enigma, 194, 196, *see* intelligence
enlistment, 21, 87
Entente, 123, 125–7, 131, 134, 136, 139–43, 146, 153
entrepôt, 92, 126, 131, 169, 226
escalation, 65, 69–70, 81, 104, 162, 216, 225–7, 241
escort, 204, 225
Essex, Earl of, 26–7
Ethiopia, 175–6, 181, 243
Exclusion Zone, 224
Exocet, 225, 229
expeditionary force, 123
exports, 133, 135, 182, 221

factories, 166
Far East, 199
Faw peninsula, 228
Ferry, Jules, 98
feudal dues, 18
finances, 123, 128
Finland, 86
Fisher, Admiral Sir John, 123
fishery, 42, 44, 134, 216
flags, false, 73, 77
flags of truce, 57
Flanders, 13, 23, 26, 28, 29, 37–8, 43–4, 51, 62, 140
flota, 25, 27, 28, 53
Foochow
Foreign Affairs, 181
Formosa, 98–100
fortifications, 38, 42, 156
'Fourteen Points', 153
France, 1–153 *passim.*, 178, 180–1, 185, 187–8, 219, 221, 230, 239
  Decree of Dec. 1799, 72
  Foreign Minister, 219
Franche Conté, 43
Franco, General, 178
Franklin, Benjamin, 82
fraud, 58, 75, 94
free trade, 51, 70, 82–4, 86, 141, 143
freight rates, 54, 93
French Revolution, 64, 70
frigates, 78, 89

galley warfare, 2, 22, 25
Geddes, Sir Auckland, 179
General Council of British Shipping, 226
Genoa, 26, 69
George V, 162
Gentleman's Magazine, 58
Germany, 14, 25, 43, 62, 80, 97, 99, 102, 103, 105, 123–52 *passim.*,

Germany – *cont.*
170, 176–8, 185–213 *passim.*, 231, 239
Gibraltar, 43, 68
Gijon, 178
Gilbert, Sir Humphrey, 27
Giustinian, Marc Antonio, 47, 48
Glasgow, 66
Goa, 25, 217
Gorshkov, Admiral Sergi, 230–1
Sea Power of the State, 230–1
Goths, 30, 32, 38
governors, 57–8, 222
Graham, Sir James, 84
granaries, 96
Grand Banks, 20
Grant, General U.S., 94
Greece, 98, 100, 124, 187
Grey, Sir Edward, Viscount, 103, 124, 133–4, 137, 156–7
Grimaldi, Marquis de, 67
Grotius, Hugo, 13–14
De Jure Belli ac Pacis, 14
Mare Librum, 13
Guadeloupe, 66
guarda costas, 56
Guernica, 179
guerre de course, 52–3, 58–61, 77–8, 89, 96, 103, 129–30, 137, 138–43, 157, 190–213, 225–30
assessment, 139–43, 229
see cruisers, piracy, privateers, ransom, submarines, tonnage
Guidance Notes for Owners with Vessels in the Arabian Gulf, 226
Gulf of Aquaba, 222
Gulf of Hormuz, 228
guns, 38, 40

Hague, 35, 66, 67, *see* conferences
Haiphong (1972), 5, 218–19, 224, 241
Halifax, 186
Hambourg, 33, 34
'Handbook of Economic Warfare', 185
Hankey, Maurice, 105, 123, 134, 143, 162–5
Hanoi, 220
Hansa, 31–2, 44, 72, 79, 81
Harding, Warren, 156
Hardwick, Lord, 23, 66
Harris, James, 68
Hawkins, John, 26–7, 47
Hay, John, 99, 101
Henderson, Arthur, 164
Henry VIII, 25
high seas, 103, *see* navies, German
Hill, Sir Norman, 158–9
Hindenburg, Marshal von, 143
Hisma-Rowak, 179
Hitler, Adolph, 81, 147–8, 169–70, 177–8, 205
Hoare, Sir Samuel, 178
Hobbes, Thomas, 12, 35
Holstein, 79
Holy Roman Emperor, 29–30, 33, 43
Hong Kong, 99–100
Hoover, Herbert, 147, 162–3, 179
Hornbeck, Stanten, 183
Horsefall Commission (1860), 88
Hosier, Admiral, 30, 98
House, Edward M., 142, 153, 155
huguenots, 26
Hume, David, 70
Jealousy of Trade (1752), 70
Hungary, 144

Iberian peninsula, 26, 40, 43, 79, *see* Spain *and* Portugal
Iberian revolt, 78
imports, 196–7, 200
indemnity, 93, 96
India, 25, 64, 199
Indian Ocean, 46, 199, 222
Indies, 26, 28
Indonesia, 25, 170, 181, 183
inflation, 93, 128–9, 134
Ingersoll, Captain, R. E., 181
insurance, 54–5, 58, 60–1, 73, 78, 96, 123, 130, 140, 193, 217, 223
War Risk Association, 226
intelligence, 141, 226, *see* Bletchley Park *and* Enigma
Iran, 222, 224–30, 241
Iraq, 224–30, 241, 244–5

Ireland, 58, 137
Islamic Revolutionary Guards, 228–9
Israel, 222–4
Italy, 43, 72, 80, 99, 126, 128, 134, 156, 176–80, 180, 200–1, 220

Jamaica, 57, 73
James I, 19
Japan, 102, 156, 163–5, 169, 176, 181–3, 187, 190–2, 193, 203, 239–40
Jay, John, 76
Jefferson, Thomas, 76–7
Jellicoe, Admiral Earl John, 140, 144–5, 160
Jenkins, Sir Leoline, 33
Jeune Ecole, 95–7, 103, 157
jobs, 80
Jones, Admiral Hilary P., 159–60
Jordan, 225
Journal Officiel, 98
Just War theory, 12, 15, 208, 240–1
Justinian I, 13

Karachi, 223
Karl I, 144
Kaunda, President, 221
Kelung, 98–9
Kennedy, J. F., 168, 216–18
Kharg Island, 225, 227, 229–30
Kissinger, Henry, 219, 222
Kitchener, Lord, 128
Kiyomizo, 183
Konigsberg, 86
Konstantine, Grand Duke, 89
Korea, 229–30
Kuwait, 217, 226, 228–9

labour, 92, 95
laissez faire, *see* free trade
Lancashire, 92
Land, Admiral, 204
landing craft, 204
Lansing, Robert, 126, 137, 142
Lavan Island, 227
Law Merchant, 11
laws of war, 9–10, 12–16, 23–4, 34, 36, 86, 93, 95, 101, 126–7, 142, 153–73 *passim.*, 207–8, 225, 238, 240
  continuous voyage, 17, 67, 76, 92, 103, 124, 126, 133, 228, 240
  Course of Admiralty, 13, 105, 186
  droits, of the crown and of Admiralty, 16
  'Free Ships make Free Goods', 33, 36, 49, 68, 76, 83, 85
  'Freedom of the Seas', 133, 153, 154
  Letter of Marque, 11, 12, 14, 18, 37, 85
  prize, 11, 13, 15–16, 22, 33–4, 84–5
  reprisal, 9–10, 14, 15, 26, 33, 68, 98, 100, 130, 134, 158, 186, 191, 215
  'Robe', principle of, 33, 36, 69–70
  'Rule of War of 1756', 23, 66, 76, 84
  self-help, 98
  see Law Merchant, Roman Law, *and* statistical evidence; *and see* treaties, Declarations of Paris *and* London, *and* Hague Convention
League of Armed Neutrality, 68–9, 76
League of Augsburg, 33
League of Nations, 14, 153, 155–6, 175–7, 220
  International Blockade Committee, 175
  Union, 175–7
  see Britain, government, Minister for
Leake, Admiral, 39
leaks, 127, 131, 187
Lebanon, 228
Le Duc Tho, 219
Leghorn, 61, 79
'Legionary' submarines, 179
Leith Ross, Sir Frederick, 166
Lend Lease, 166–9, 186, 194, 239
Levant Company, 53
Liberal Party, 103, 123, 127

Liberia, 223
Liberty ships, 204
licenses, 75, 77, 80
Liège, 37
Lincoln, Abraham, 92
Lisbon, 25, 28, 31, 78
Lloyds Coffee House, 73
Lloyds Marine Insurance, 130
Lloyd George, David, 139, 141, 146–7, 154, 156, 163
loans, 129
Locke, John, 12, 23, 35
logistics, 3–4, 31, 37–40, 47, 215, 224, 231
Long, Lord, 154
Louis XIV, 19, 37, 40, 49, 51
Louisiana Purchase, 72
Luddites, 80
Ludendorff, General, 143

MacDonald, Ramsay, 162–4
McKenna, Reginald, 105
McKinnon Wood, 104
Macmillan, Harold, 218
Madeira, 61
Madison, James, 75, 77–8
Madrid, 25, 27, 67
Magens, Nicolas, 50, 67,
  Essay on Insurance (1775), 50, 67
Maginot Line, 189
Majunga, 222
Malagasy Republic, 222
Malekzadeyan, Commodore Mohammed Hoseyn, 225
Malta, 177
Manchester School, 83, 85
Manchuria, 176, 192, 243
Manila, 63
Marcy, William Learned, 85
Maritime Strategy, 1
Marlborough, Duke of, 29, 39, 62–3
Marx, Karl, 92
Marseilles, 60, 81
Maryland, 56
Matamoras, 93
Maurepas, Comte de, 59
Mediterranean, 2, 11, 24, 38–9, 42, 59, 169, 180, 199, 201–3
Medway, 20, 48
Memel, 86
mercantilism, 17, 27, 40–65 *passim.*, 70–2, 74–5, 77–81, 83, 88, 106, 123, 127–9, 136, 143, 153, 157, 165
  utility of, 59–65, 238–9, 242
  see fraud
merchant cruisers, 104
merchant marine, 34, 47, 49–50, 52–4, 58, 68, 87, 90–1, 95, 100–2, 124, 143, 146: dry cargo ships, 200;
  tankers, 225; transports, 199–200
merchants, 28
Merchant Shipping Mission, 194
Mesapotamia, 154
Mexico, 93, 141, 217
middle ages, 18, 240
Middle East, 199
Milan Decrees, 73, 76
Mill, J. S., 88
mills, 92
Milner, Lord, 153
mine, 170
mines, 191, 193, 219–20, 228
minesweepers, 229
missiles, 216
mobility, 38
Molesworth, Robert, 41
monasteries, 26
Monk, General-at-Sea, 46
Monroe, James, 76
Monson, Admiral, 27
Morgenthau, Henry, 168–9
Morocco, 200
Morton, Desmond, 185
Moscow, 219
Mozambique, 221–2
munitions, 92, 128, 133, 168, 186, 226
  and see blockade; contraband
Murmansk, 194
Mussolini, Benito, 177–80, 182
mutiny, 145

Nantes, 67
Naples, 29
Napoleon Bonaparte, 1, 17, 40, 71–4, 76–8, 131, 239

Nassau, 92
nationalism, 144
Nationalist, 178, 179
National Socialist Party, 169, 207
naturalisation, 58, 69
Naval Prize Bill (1911), *see* treaties, Declaration of London
Navicert, 137, 186, 225
navies, 21, 136
  American, 1, 78, 91, 95, 99, 136, 142, 143, 153–6, 181, 190, 219–20, 225, 228–9: Atlantic Fleet, 182; Chief of Naval Operations, 154, 164, 190; Chief of War Plans, 181; General Board, 154, 159; Navy Secretary, 156, 164; Sixth Fleet, 224; War Plans, 181
  Belgian, 229
  British, 22, 69, 73, 90, 124, 146, 155, 177–8, 180, 190, 222, 228–9: Admiralty, 24, 27, 52, 53, 56, 73, 95, 96, 103, 104, 142, 154, 157, 159, 162–4, 179, 182, 198 (International Law Committee, 130) (First Lord, 84, 105, 124, 154, 178) (First Sea Lord, 102, 123, 140, 146) (Naval Intelligence Division, 96, 102 [Director of, 104] [Trade Division, 96, 105]) (Treasurer, 16, 26); officers, 22; Mediterranean Fleet, 177; Navy Board, 47, 68; Victualling Office, 47; War Orders, 105
  Egyptian, 223
  French, 74, 75, 95, 99, 187, 228, 229
  German, 99, 129–30, 145, 155, 182, 231: Cs-in-C, 192, 196; High Seas Fleet, 124, 129; Naval Staff, 203
  Indian, 223
  Iranian, 225–6
  Italian, 179, 182, 229
  Netherlands, 66, 229
  Japanese, 191
  Prussian, 88
  Russian *and* Soviet, 89, 96, 204, 228: C-in-C, 230; Northern Fleet, 224
  Spanish, 180
Navy League, 160
Nelson, 22, 76
Netherlands, 23, 27, 28, 29, 35, 37, 42–9, 51, 55, 63–9, 72, 79, 81, 88, 100, 102, 126, 131, 139, 176–7
  Overseas Trust, 126, 131–3
  Spanish, *see* Flanders
  States General, 45
  war against 1780, 20
'Neutrality' patrols, 207
Newcastle, 47
Newcastle, Duke of, 23
New England, 77–8
New Hebrides, 182
'New Imperialists', 153, 169
newspapers, 99, *see* press
New York Times, 92
Newport, Rhode Island, 20
New York, 20–1, 78, 89, 94, 128, 169
New Zealand, 160
Nicholas II, 102
Nixon, Robert, 218–19
Non-Intervention, 178–9
North Atlantic Treaty Organization, 224, 228
North Sea, 14, 139
Norway, 126, 131, 132, 134, 139, 170, 186
Nova Scotia, 186
Nuremburg, 190, 207
Nyon conference, 180

orders in council, 70, 77, 81
  of 1778, 68
  of 1807, 74
  of 1855, 85
  29 October 1914, 126
  11 March 1915, 131, 133
  20 August 1915, 134
  7 July 1916, 130
Ostend, 29, 42
Ostend Company, 29–30, 51
Ottoman Empire, 98, 100, *see* Turkey

Pacific Ocean, 99–100, 160, 163, 169, 182, 199, 201, 203
pacifism, 175
Palmerston, Lord, 88, 100
Panama, 179
panic, 130, 139, 193, 225
passenger steamers, 137; *see* ships names, *Lusitania*
Paul I, 76
peace movement, 144
Pearl Harbor, 183, 187, 190
pensions, 22
Pepys, Samuel, 52
Pernambuco, 44
Persian Gulf, 194, 226
Philadelphia, 78
Phillip II, 26
Phillip IV, 43
philosophes, 17
Philosophical Radicals, 84
pillage, 22
pipelines, 225–6, 229
piracy, 10, 22, 30, 90, 157, 179, *see guerre de course*
Pitt, William, 19, 23, 66
Plumer, General Sir Herbert, 147
Poland, 32, 34, 62, 89, 147, 217
Pondicherri, 64
pope, 25
Pope-Hennesy, Colonel, 160
population, 74, 81
Porte, 24
Porto Bello, 30, 56, 98
Portugal, 14, 25–6, 28, 31, 38, 44–5, 47, 77, 79, 80, 188, 221 (Foreign Minister, 221)
pound, 80, 128–9
Pratt, Admiral, 164
press, 217
prestige, 142
Preston Brown, General, 160–1
prisoners of war, 57–8
Priuli, Lorenzo, 26
privateers, 9–10, 14, 16–24, 26, 35–6, 39, 52, 53–4, 58, 63, 66–8, 72, 73, 77–8, 84–5, 87–8, 90, 236, 242, *see guerre de course*
private property, 23, 84, 87–8, 98, 103
private war, 82, 101
prize, 16, 53, 104, 242
  court, 14, 23–5, 33, 52, 68–9, 76, 103, 124, 130, 132–3, 185, 216, *see* Britain, government, High Court of Admiralty
  law, *see* laws of war
  money, 16, 17, 22–4, 82, 87–8
  see also Britain, acts, Prize
Protestant, 35
Provence, 60
Prussia, 62, 69, 72, 76, 85, 87–8, 103
'Prussian Militarism', 135, 142
public opinion, 104, 133, 137, 141, 142, 146, 156, 168
purchasing, 141
'Purposeful Force', 100

Quiberon Bay (1759), 39
quarantine, 182, 216

radar, 198
radio, 207
railways, 40, 85, 127, 219, 221
Raleigh, Sir Walter, 26–7
ransom, 54, 66
Rapidan river, 163
rationing, 132, 137, 139, 141, 167
Red Sea, 222
refugees, 179
Reichstag, 143
relief, 80, 138, 147
republican, 147, 178, 179–80
revolt, 91, 95, 130, 145
Reval, 86
Rhineland, 131
Rhodesia, 176, 220–2
Ricardo, David, 83, 129
Ricardo, J. L., 85–6
Riga, 69, 86
Rio de la Hacha, 56
rioting, 73, 130, 138
Rio Tinto, 179
Ripperda, Baron de, 29–30
roads, 220
Robinson, Bishop, 36
Roosevelt, F. D., 168, 181–2, 199, 202, 204
Roosevelt, Theodore, 99, 103

Roman Empire, 13, 30, 32, 38
Roman Law, 11–15, 33, 240
Rome, 79
Rooke, Admiral, 28, 53
Rousseau, Jean Jacques, 82
Social Contract, 82
Rumania, 170, 188
Russell, Admiral, 38
Russell, Earl, 90
Russia, 62, 68–9, 72, 75, 77–8, 81, 83–7, 89, 98, 101, 127, 134, 176, 185, 187–8, 194, 200
see Soviet Union

sailors, 21
St Eustatius, 66, 69
St Lawrence, 39
St Malo, 20
St Petersburg, 68
St Vincent, Lord, 22
Salisbury, Lord, 89, 161
Salisbury, 221–2
Salonica, 124, 140
Salter, Sir Arthur, 194
San Francisco, 89
Santander, 178
Sasol, 221
Saudi Arabia, 244
Savoy, 29, 39
Scandinavia, 131
Scheer, Admiral, 137
Schelt, 45
scholars, modern
economists: Maynard Keynes, 166, 244
historians, 2–3, 95, 106: Robert Greenhalgh Albion, 78; Olive Anderson, 86, 89; Kenneth Andrews, 19; Paul Bamford, 39; C. B. Behrens, 202; A. C. Bell, 124, 126, 132–3, 138, 145; George Beer, 56; John Bromley, 54; Kathleen Burk, 128–9; James Cable, 100, 231; W. H. Carless Davis, 138; Alice Clare Carter, 51; G. N. Clark, 36, 50, 52–3; Carl Marie von Clausewitz, 50, 71, 83, 207, 237; Philip Colomb, 96; Sir Julian Corbett, 104–5, 133, 165 ('Capture of Private Property at Sea', 104, *Some Principles of Maritime Strategy*, 104); François Crouzet, 81; C. P. Crowhurst, 58; Ralph Davis, 47, 49–50, 52, 54, 61, 64; Francis Deak, 32, 34; P. E. Dewey, 141; Martin Doughty, 194; H. Duncan Hall, 169; Geoffrey Ellis, 74; David French, 123; Richard Gardner, 170; J. W. Garner, 25; Freeman Gilpin, 73; C. I. Hamilton, 85, 89; Gerd Hardach, 145, 188, 236; John Hattendorf, 21; John G. Hibbits, 230; F. H. Hinsley, 187–8; Albert Hogan, 100; Michael Howard, 59; Jonathan Trumbull Howe, 223; Jonathan Israel, 42, 44; Philip Jessup, 32, 34; Warren Kimball, 168–9; A. H. John, 63–4; L. H. Johnson, 94; George Kahin, 220; Henry Kamen, 28; Carl Kulsrud, 65; Stanley Lebergott, 94; D. J. Llewelyn Davies, 33; Edward Luttwak, 232; James G. Lydon, 20; Alfred Thayer Mahan, 1–2, 43, 53, 78, 93, 95–7, 101–3, 153, 164, 230, 235, 239, 242 (*Influence of Seapower upon History* (1889), 96–7); Norman Medlicott, 165, 189, 215, 243; Alan S. Milward, 188–9; D. P. O'Connell, 15, 215, 223; Mancur Olson, 73, 141, 189–90, 236; F. L. Owsley, 94; Richard Pares, 19, 61–2; M. R. Pitt, 89, 104; Marcus Price, 94; Philip Pugh, 205–7; James Pritchard, 39; Armin Rappaport, 160; Sir Herbert Richmond, 1–2, 38, 90, 105, 162, 164, 165, 230, 235

scholars, modern – *cont.*
(*Imperial Defence and Capture at Sea in War*, 90, 164; *Sea Power in the Modern World*, 164); James Riley, 60; Stephen Roskill, 147; Carlton Savage, 16; Marion Siney, 104; Harold and Margaret Sprout, 155; David Starkey, 19–21; Lucy Sutherland, 58; Carl Swanson, 19–20, 59–60; Geoffrey Symcox, 53, 97; David Syrett, 40; Alberto Tenenti, 22; Frank E. Vandiver, 94; Peter Vigor, 230; M. Vlahos, 160; J. M. Wallace-Hadrill, 30
lawyers: H. W. Malkin, 133; Sir Francis Piggott, 89; R. W. Tucker, 15; Quincy Wright, 217
Scotland, 124
sea denial, 26, 67
Sea Killer missile, 226, 228
sea power, 1
seasons, 220
Selwen, John, 13
Mare Clausum, 13–14
Seward, William H., 90, 93
Shell Oil, 221
Shimonoseki, 191
ship,
container, 226
construction, 140, 193–5, 198, 204–5
lists, 73
losses, 140, 142, 194, 196–8, 225
names: *Alabama*, 91; *Baron Sternblad*, 133; *Bridgeton*, 229; *General Belgrano*, 224; *Joshan*, 229; *Lusitania*, 136–7, *Panay*, 181; *Powerful*, 96; *Rotterdam*, 133; *Rurik*, 96; *Russia*, 96; *Sabalan*, 229; *Samuel B. Roberts*, 229; *Shahand*, 229; *Stark*, 228; *Terrible*, 96; *Trent*, 93; *Vincennes*, 229; *Wainwright*, 229; *Zamora*, 11, 14, 130, 132
shipowners, 73, 91, 131–2, 241–2
shipping, 124
shipyards, 166
Shumann, Maurice, 219
Siberia, 187
siege, 38
Silkworm Missiles, 228–9
Sims, Admiral, 142
Singapore, 169, 182
sink, 104
Sirri Island, 227
Skagerrak, 37, 105
Skinner, 137
slave, 92, 170
slave trade, 83
Smith, Adam, 70–1, 239
Wealth of Nations (1776), 70
Smith, Ian, 221–2
smuggling, 56, 58, 79–80
Smyrna, 52, 55
socialism, 144
soldiers, 25
Sound, 69
South China Sea, 182
South East Asia, 203
South Yemen, 223
Soviet Strategic thinking, 2, 230–2
Soviet Union, 170, 178, 190, 202, 215–16, 218–20, 222, 224, 228, 230, 241–3, *see* Russia
Spain, 9, 19, 23–8, 29, 34, 44–5, 51, 55, 61, 64, 67, 68, 79, 82, 88, 125, 176, 178–81
armadas, 36: (1588), 18, 26, 28, 31, 36
Cortes, 45
New, 26–7, 57, 61
see wars, *passim.*
Spanish America, *see* America
Speer, Albert, 189
Spring-Rice, Sir Cecil, 137
Stalin, Joseph, 200
Stark, Admiral, 190
statistical evidence, 33, 132
Statutory List, *see* Black List
steam, 90, 95
sterling, 154
Stockholm, 40
stockpile, 48, 56, 60, 95

Straits of Bab-el-Mandeb, 223
Straits of Hormuz, 225
Straits of Tiran, 223
submarines, 105, 129–30, 133–4, 136, 137–44, 146, 157, 179–80, 190–213 *passim.*, 224, 242–3
subsidies, 62, 64, 80–1, 123
Suez, 217, 222
surf, 170
Sweden, 35–6, 44, 68–9, 72, 75, 125–7, 131, 134, 136, 139, 188, 217
Swift, Jonathan, 19, 29, 54
  Conduct of the Allies (1712), 19, 29, 54
Switzerland, 80, 126, 134

Tagus, 32
Takagi, Admiral, 191
tariff, 70, 72, 75, 80–1
TASS, 219
taxation, 52, 77, 81, 86–7, 129, 167
Texas, 93
Thames, 20
thermonuclear, 203, 227
Tirpitz, Admiral, 129, 143
Thomson, George, 221
Tojo, 183, 191
Tokyo, 183
Tonkin, 99
tonnage, 139, 193, 196, 200, 203, 205
torpedo, 95, 231
Torrington, Admiral, 35
Total Exclusion Zone, 224
Total Oil, 221
total war, 84, 86
trade,
  defence, 89–90, 96, 104–5, 142, 191, 207
  patterns, 47–8, 50, 59, 61–4, 77–8, 80, 84, 135, 139, 169
  with the enemy, 56–8, 72, 83, 86, 123, 127, 135
  wartime, 96
  see Britain, government, Board of trade
transaction books, 33
transport, 38, 40, 101; *see* railways
treasure ships, *see* flota, 28, 29–30, 53, 56
treaties, 106
  Munster (1648), 44, 46
  Ryswick, peace (1697), 53
  Dover (1670), 49
  Westminster (1674), 33, 49, 68
  Pact de Famille (1760), 67
  Utrecht (1713), 29, 36, 51, 64
  Anglo–Russian Commercial (1766), 68
  Russo–Danish Convention (1780), 68
  Anglo–Russian Convention (1801), 76
  Peace of Amiens (1802), 71, 72
  Tilsit (1807), 72
  American war trade series, 83, 101
  Russo–American (1854), 85
  Paris (1856), 87
  Declaration of Paris (1856), 9, 14, 24, 82, 87–90, 92, 105, 124, 130, 133, 159, 186, 190, 236, 240, 242
  Hague Convention, 102–3, 130, 137, 190, 207, 216 (Porter convention, 100)
  Declaration of London (1911), 14, 103–5, 124–5, 130, 159, 186, 190
  Japan–US commercial (1911), 182
  Swedish–American (1918), 143
  Versailles (1919), 146–7
  Washington, 156–7
  Four-Power Pacific, 156
  General Arbitration, 161
  Briand–Kellog pact (1928), 14
  London Protocol (1936), 185, 190, 207
  Tripartite Pact, 182
  Russo–German trade (1939–40), 185
Trianon, 80
tribute, 79
Trieste, 79
Truman, Harry, 216
Tryon, Admiral Sir George, 96
Tsingtao, 124
Tucker, Josiah, 70–1
  Cui Bono?, 71
Turgot, 70

Turkey, 72, 153, 188, 225
  see Ottoman Empire
Tuscany, 35

U-boats, *see* submarines and *guerre de course*
Ukraine, 170
Union, *see* United States
Union of South Africa, 221–2
United Arab Emirates, 226
United Nations, 219–20, 222, 226, 229, 244,
  Charter, 14, 215
  Military Staff Committee, 244
  Security Council, 245
United States, 9, 17, 24, 72, 77, 82–4, 87, 88, 90–1, 99, 100–1, 103, 124–end *passim.*, 239–41, 243
  acts of congress: Non-Importation (1807), 77; Embargo (1807), 77; Non-Intercourse (1809), 77; Navy (1916), 136; Vinson (1934, 1938), 165
  Confederate States, 9, 87–8, 90–5
  government: Board of Economic Warfare, 187; Congress, 77, 97, 141, 153, 155, 160, 168–9; Department of State, 16, 134, 137 (Secretary, 222); Joint Chiefs of Staff, 204; Senate, 141, 161: Committee on Foreign Relations, 127; Maritime Commission, 204; Supreme Court, 92, 216; Union, 9, 14, 89–95
  see navy, American, *and* wars, of 1812
United States Strategic Bombing Survey, 191

Vandals, 30
vassal, 79
Vauban, Marshal, 52, 59, 72
  Memoire sur la Caprerie (1695), 52
Venezuela, 99–100
Venice, 22, 26, 35, 46, 54
Verdun, 138
Vergennes, Duc de, 64, 70
Vernon, Admiral, 56
Vichy, 185
Vigo, 28, 53
Vira Cruz, 29
Virginia, 56, 66
Vladivostok, 194
volunteer navy, *see* navy, Prussian

Wager, Admiral, 28, 53
wars
  Spanish–Dutch, 42–6
  Anglo–Dutch, 37: First, 28, 46–8; Second, 33, 46, 48; Third, 48–9
  Anglo–Spanish, 36, 41
  Anglo–French, 50
  Jenkins' Ear (1739), 19–21, 56, 58, 59
  League of Augsburg, 21, 35
  Spanish Succession, 21, 36, 51, 53, 62, 64, 74
  Great Northern, 36, 39
  Seven Years', 19, 21, 23, 39, 58, 60–2, 64, 67, 71, 88, 239
  American Revolutionary, 19–20, 58–9, 63, 175
  Anglo–Dutch (1780), 69
  French Revolutionary, 70
  Napoleonic, 1–2, 17, 50, 70, 88, 123, 127, 129, 131, 153, 164–5, 175, 239
  Quasi-War, 70
  1812, 24, 75, 77–8, 93
  Crimean, 9, 82, 84–6, 92, 101, 123, 239
  American Civil, 9, 14, 40, 87, 89–95, 101, 215, 239
  Franco–Prussian, 40
  Spanish–American, 101
  South African, 101
  Russo–Japanese, 101–2
  World War I, 3, 11, 14, 15, 23–5, 37, 89, 94, 105–6, 123–52, 157, 165, 175, 185–6, 188, 215–16, 236, 240
  Spanish Civil, 178–81
  World War II, 2–3, 15, 22–4, 38, 165, 168, 185–214 *passim.*, 226, 230–1, 236–7, 239, 240

Korean, 215–16, 243
Vietnam, 218–20, 243
Six-Day, 222
Indo–Pakistan, 223
October War, 223–4, 243
Falkland Islands War, 224
Gulf War, 224–30, 241
Kuwait, 244
War Chest, 129
War Zone, 129, 226
Weimar, 146–7
Wellington, General, 77
West India Company, 44
West Indies, 29, 56, 58, 59–60, 77–9, 187
Wemyss, Admiral, 146, 156
William II, 129, 145
William of Orange, 33, 35–8, 49, 50, 63, 65
and Mary, 57
Wilson, Admiral Sir Arthur, 102
Wilson, Harold, 223
Wilson, Woodrow, 133, 136–7, 141–2, 153, 155–6
wireless, 104
Wood, Sir Kingsley, 197

Zambia, 221
Zamora, 11, 14, 130, 132
Zeeland, 21
Zimmerman, Emil, 141
Zumwalt, 231–2